Building

LINUX
CLUSTERS

Building

LINUX
CLUSTERS

DAVID HM SPECTOR

O'REILLY®

Beijing • Cambridge • Farnham • Köln • Paris • Sebastopol • Taipei • Tokyo

Building Linux Clusters

by David HM Spector

Copyright © 2000 O'Reilly & Associates, Inc. All rights reserved.
Printed in the United States of America.

Published by O'Reilly & Associates, Inc., 101 Morris Street, Sebastopol, CA 95472.

Editor: Mark Stone

Production Editor: Sarah Jane Shangraw

Cover Designer: Hanna Dyer

Printing History:

> July 2000:   First Edition.

Library of Congress Cataloging-in-Publication Data

Spector, David (David H. M.)
    Building Linux clusters : scaling Linux for scientific and enterprise applications / David Spector.
        p. cm.
    ISBN 1-56592-625-0
    1. Linux. 2. Operating Systems. 3. Application software—Development. I. Title.

QA76.76.O63 S6647 2000
005.75'65—dc21   99-089455

[M]

TABLE OF CONTENTS

PREFACE

The Need for Speed

It's an old saying that your lifestyle expands to meet your available income. The same can be said of computer processing trends: computing problems always seem to meet or exceed available computing resources. There is always a need for more processing power, more network bandwidth, and greater input/output (I/O) capabilities.

This is a circular problem in information processing. As technology advances, we can do more with our computers, which heightens expectations of what can be done, which in turn pushes the leading edge of technology to create faster computers to push the leading edge of what we can do with our computers. This need for speed has prompted the development of a whole new class of machines: supercomputers. In fact, supercomputer class machines—the construction of which is the topic of this book—influence almost every aspect of modern life.

The effects of these machines can be seen in everything from movies that are replete with spectacular computer generated imagery (CGI), to weather maps on your local newscast that feature a weather system "fly through," to diagnostic imagery from CAT and MRI scanners that let surgeons perform "virtual" surgery on a patient before they ever touch a scalpel. These are a few of the most visible areas, but supercomputers affect your everyday life in many other ways, as well. Did you know that supercomputers affect the price of bread? How about those blue jeans that went on sale downtown at the mall? Supercomputers are used in commodities markets to forecast the price of grain, fuel, and other elements that go into making a loaf of bread and delivering it to the store that ultimately affect its retail price. They're also used to perform "data mining" operations (the search for trends in large amounts of information) to determine when people are likely to buy new jeans, running shoes, or other items and where to cluster these items in a store to make it more likely that you will buy them.*

One of the problems with computer-driven activity is that it requires a lot of computer horsepower. That usually means a commercial supercomputer. Supercomputers are, by their very nature, extremely expensive. After all, they do represent the very cutting edge of technology, and they have traditionally been very costly to develop, maintain, and program. This brings us to an interesting confluence of events that is changing the way people look at high-performance computing and causing a fundamental shift in the economics of these powerful pieces of technology.

The Linux Phenomenon and Beowulf

Back in 1994, a couple of research scientists, Thomas Sterling and Donald Becker, at NASA's Center of Excellence in Space Data and Information Sciences (CESDIS) in Greenbelt, Maryland, embarked on a project to build a parallel computer out of off-the-shelf components. They wanted to make a low-cost, yet efficient, system for processing large space-science data sets. Their first system, a 16-node network of workstations, was constructed out of Intel DX4 processors. It was interconnected by a novel channel bonding method that allowed them to tie together multiple 10Mbit/second Ethernets to balance network performance without the use of then expensive network switching systems. With the addition of message passing software such as the Parallel Virtual Machine (PVM) system, they were able to build a quite effective parallel processing computer on a shoe-string budget. They named the results of their work "Beowulf."

Their experiment in distributed processing was an unmitigated success, principally because of the underlying system software they chose to base their efforts on: Linux.

In 1994, Linux was a little-known Unix clone that ran on Intel processors, with a port being undertaken to the (then Digital, now, Compaq) Alpha processor. Linux offered to the NASA developers unprecedented performance on a range of hardware, with source-code availability at a great price: *free!*

In 1999, as this book is being written, Linux has become a mature and increasingly popular operating system. Although hard numbers are difficult to come by, it is estimated by various industry sources* that there are more than eight million Linux systems currently in use.

Linux is a Unix-compatible Open Source computer operating system that is freely available over the Internet. It runs on almost every kind of computer architecture

---

* There's a classic anecdote about data mining that recounts that a certain U.S. retailer discovered that when men go shopping, if they buy beer, they are also more likely to buy diapers. When this retailer placed the beer next to the diapers, the sales of both increased by several hundred percent. This little tidbit could have been discovered only by analyzing the buying habits of hundreds of thousands of men over a very long time; discovering these kinds of trends is a classical case of a job for a supercomputer.

* The Gartner Group, a computer industry research firm, and Linux.org, a Linux advocacy group, are two such groups. They have differing numbers (7.5 million for Gartner, and 10+ million in the Linux.org estimate), but general consensus in the Linux community is that there are well over seven million Linux users in the world, and growing by tens of thousands of users per month.

available (including Intel, PowerPC, Sun Sparc, StrongARM, and Alpha), and supports hundreds of peripherals from gigabit network cards to data point-of-sale terminals along with thousands of application packages ranging from music composition and word processing to nuclear and chemical engineering and semiconductor design. With all of these features, it is increasingly popular in the high-performance computing community, and researchers are using it as the starting point for all sorts of interesting areas of research.

A Few Words About Linux

Linux is at the vanguard of something called *Open Source* software. Open Source software is software that is often given away with a license that guarantees that you can get the original source code should you want it (in most cases the executable binary program comes packaged with the source code). The whole issue of Open Source Software is the topic of another O'Reilly book entitled *Open Sources*, written by Chris DiBona and Sam Ockman, which is an excellent read and gives many insights into the motivations behind this software movement and how it works.

Linux is the kernel portion of an operating system that was started by a Finnish college student named Linus Torvalds. The whole Linux operating system is the kernel plus a large number of tools and applications that make up a complete Unix-compatible system. Linux is a commercial quality operating system that has been collaboratively developed by a cast of thousands of programmers who have dedicated their time and talent to create software that is freely available for anyone to download via the Internet.

If you are only minimally familiar with Linux, you might have the impression that there is "one Linux" and everyone uses it. Nothing could be further from the truth—in fact, one of the most important strengths of Linux is that in its openness, diversity has bloomed. There are, in fact, many variants (called "distributions") of Linux. As of this writing, there are over a dozen "flavors" of Linux available either as commercially packaged distributions or to download for free over the Internet.

For the purposes of this book, I will be using a particular version of Linux called "*Red Hat Linux*," which is published by Red Hat Software of Raleigh, North Carolina.

The choice of Linux distributions is something of a "religious" issue among many Linux devotees. I have chosen Red Hat Linux as the basis for the architecture and examples in this book because it is the one I use in my own work. It is readily available in most large national computer stores in the United States as well as on thousands of Internet sites (a list of these sites can be found in Appendix A, *Resources*). I am quite sure that everything I will recommend in terms of configurations, tools, and packages will be available on almost every available Linux distribution. The only possible exceptions might come into play where there are packages that are heavily dependent upon some hardware feature that exists on Intel platforms that doesn't exist on another architecture (or vice versa), or if there is some package that cannot be compiled on a 64-bit platform such as the Compaq *Alpha* or the Sun *UltraSPARC* chips. Such variances are, fortunately, quite rare.

Intended Audience

This book is designed to be a "how to" for those interested in designing, building, and programming a Beowulf Class supercomputer, or *Parallel Linux Cluster* as I will refer to these kinds of systems for the remainder of the book. It is not meant to be an academic book on the deep, computer-science view of supercomputing and code completeness. This work is also not meant to be the "end-all" on the topic of low-cost high-performance computer systems, but to provide a solid starting point and avenues for deeper exploration. In the bibliography at the end of this book, I will present a list of resources that I hope will give you a large number of avenues for further exploration on the topic of Linux clusters in particular and high-performance systems and programming in general.

Prerequisites

Since building and programming supercomputer-class systems is a complex topic and this is a hands-on book, I expect you to have some previous experience with several areas that will help you to be successful using this book. If any of the following tools and concepts are unfamiliar to you, the bibliography at the back of the book lists several excellent suggestions for further reading that will help you get up to speed.

In general, you should have some experience with Unix-like operating systems (such as Linux) as well as a working understanding of TCP/IP networking. Experience installing Linux and configuring a network is helpful but not necessary, as is exposure to the concepts of network routing.

From the software perspective, you should be comfortable with the following:

- Using an editor such as vi or Emacs.

- Using Shell programming (the Bourne, Bash, and C shell scripts are used throughout the book).

- Running utilities and tools such as grep, awk, and perl.

- Starting up and shutting down systems.

- Compiling programs with C and/or FORTRAN compilers (such as GCC or F77).

- Having a basic level of programming ability in C or FORTRAN. This will be very helpful in actually using a Parallel Linux Cluster and understanding the example applications in Part 2 of the book.

From a hardware point of view, a working knowledge of how modern Intel-based workstations are put together will be helpful in sections about designing your own compute nodes, but I will have enough introductory information to make everything I am demonstrating clear and unambiguous. All of the concepts I will be illustrating will be applicable to other architectures such as the Sun Microsystems Sparc family or the Compaq Alpha family, so don't be alarmed at mention of specific hardware characteristics or features of these systems.

Structure of This Book

This book is divided into an introduction, three major parts, several appendixes, a bibliography, and a glossary:

This *Preface* has discussed some of the history behind the development of high-performance computers and supercomputers in general and clustered systems in particular, with attention paid to the kinds of application areas that are amenable to these systems.

Part I, *Cluster Design, Development, and Management*
>   This section of the book focuses on the design, development, and management of Linux clusters. It is of interest to readers who really want to get their hands dirty in the whole experience of rolling their own Parallel Linux Cluster, from the initial conception all the way through the deployment of a system that can be put into a data center and run like any other "production" system. Part I contains the following chapters:

Chapter 1, *Introduction*
>   This chapter presents an overview of the topic of the high-performance computer: where it came from, what led up to the development of Linux clusters, and where all of this technology may be leading.

Chapter 2, *Basic Concepts*
>   This chapter gives you a short history of supercomputing so that we can have a common understanding of how these machines evolved and where they're going. This is followed by an overview of the basic concepts behind clustered systems and what separates these systems from both regular desktop systems and commercial supercomputers. It includes examples of the kinds of systems that are commonly used at the time of the writing of this book, the software that supports cluster, and the trends to look for into the future.

Chapter 3, *Designing Clusters*
>   This chapter presents guidelines for designing clustered systems, including topologies, heterogeneous versus homogeneous clusters, network selection, software and hardware routing, software selection, and disk/software layout.

Chapter 4, *Building Clusters*

Once you have decided on an overall design for your Parallel Linux Cluster, this chapter will help you decide how to put it together and will offer some suggestions on the construction of your system that will help you build a system that is both fast and maintainable.

Chapter 5, *Software Installation and Configuration*

Installing software on a cluster can be quite an involved process. This chapter will present strategies for dealing with the installation of Linux itself, along with the other software required to make your cluster work, that will speed the installation process if your cluster contains 5 nodes or 512 nodes.

Chapter 6, *Managing Clusters*

After you put together the initial hardware and software, there is still a long way to go until you have a really top-flight system. The hardest part of any large system is making sure that you can manage its operation. This chapter will cover the selection, installation, and use of a number of job scheduling/queueing packages and job accounting systems as well as other software that can help you keep tabs on how your cluster is being used and how well it is performing.

Part II, *Cluster Programming and Applications*

Focuses on the programming environment on a Linux cluster. This part is aimed at readers who have just built or have access to a Linux cluster and want to start harnessing its power. The chapters contained herein will cover a variety of programming areas such as the selection of programming language for cluster programming, publicly available programming libraries, and tools that are specifically oriented to clusters. They will also show some complete but non-trivial examples of complete applications that can be used as the basis for larger systems. Part II's chapters are as follows:

Chapter 7, *Tools and Libraries for Parallel Programming*

This chapter covers a number of publicly available libraries that are designed specifically to aid the process of developing clustered applications as well as debugging tools and system-level extensions that can enhance parallel clusters.

Chapter 8, *Programming in a Parallel Environment*

This chapter explains the concepts of programming for clustered systems and how this differs from traditional single-CPU environments with emphasis placed on how to look for innate parallelism in problems that can be exploited with a cluster. Additionally, if the Parallel Linux Cluster you have designed (or have access to) is constructed out of dissimilar machines (such as a mixture of Intel boxes, Alphas, and Sparc machines), this chapter will suggest ways to make your development a little easier by writing your application and its supporting utility files to be less environment-specific.

Chapter 9, *Application Examples*

> This last chapter presents several real-world applications where you will be able to see the power of clusters first-hand. These applications are freely usable under the GNU Public License (GPL) and can be used as starting points for your own applications.

Part III, *Appendixes*

> This section contains additional resources on clusters and parallel computing.

Appendix A, *Resources*

> This appendix will present some of the most popular resources for those interested in clustered programming.

Appendix B, *Message Passing APIs*

> This appendix will present a quick reference to the two most popular message passing APIs, the Message Passing Interface (MPI) and the Parallel Virtual Machine (PVM).

Appendix C, *Installation Scripts*

> This appendix presents the internals of the installation scripts that drive the bootstrap process.

Appendix D, *The Cluster Administration Database*

> This appendix presents the design and internals of the cluster administration database.

Bibliography

> The bibliography is broken up by areas of experience and interest (in case you are interested in some of the prerequisites mentioned earlier) and covers a wide range of topics.

Glossary

> Unusual technical terms or those that have special meaning in the context of parallel and cluster programming will be fully defined here.

Conventions Used in This Book

The following typographical conventions are used in this book:

Italics

> Introduces news terms and indicates URLs, email addresses, filenames, commands, command-line options, file extensions, directory or folder names, and pathnames.

Constant width

> Indicates code examples, command-line computer output, and IP addresses.

Constant width bold

> Indicates input in examples that users should type literally.

Bold
> Indicates device names, hostnames, usernames, and passwords.

ALL CAPS
> Indicates keyboard commands, such as ENTER and RETURN.

How to Contact O'Reilly

I've done my best to make sure that what I've written in this book is correct, clear, and well documented. If you find a problem or have a suggestion about how to make the book better, please let me know by contacting the publisher:

> O'Reilly & Associates, Inc.
> 101 Morris St.
> Sebastapol, CA 95472
> 800-998-9938 (in the U.S. or Canada)
> 707-829-0515 (international/local)
> 707-829-0104 (fax)

You can also send messages electronically. To be put on a mailing list or request a catalog, send email to:

> *nuts@oreilly.com*

To ask technical questions, or comment on the book, send email to O'Reilly technical support:

> *bookquestions@oreilly.com*

You can also send email to me, the author:

> *spector@zeitgeist.com*

Acknowledgments

The poet John Donne said "No man is an island entire of itself," and so it is with each of us. I have been blessed by parents who taught me at a very early age that learning new things is something that you do every day, and the more that you learn, the more freedom you have to do anything you set your mind to. To my mother, Astrid, and my father (who would have been fascinated by this topic), Sy, thank you for instilling in me the passion to learn continuously and to live in the moment as often as possible.

Everyone has mentors who helped them learn their craft. For me some of the most important have been: my friend Steven J. Wandell, who died much, much too young in 1979 at age 23 and taught me that life, unlike Macro-36, my first programming language, is not a skip/noskip proposition; my first real boss at New York University's

Courant Institute/Academic Computing Facility, Edi Fransceschini; and Bill Russell, Steve Tihor, and Ed Friedman who spent countless hours pouring knowledge and experience into my head, as did Richard Reich, another Courant veteran. I would also like to thank Joe Clugston (for whom I worked), Steve Degler, Steve Jones, Chuck Yerkes, and Valerie Acton all of whom worked for me at JP Morgan in the early to mid-1990s. We created a lot of very cool technology with some very fast machines and changed the face of computing on Wall Street.

My current business partner, Eric Schnoor, has been an inspiration in his perseverance that there is a living to be made developing these kinds of systems and the services that make them work.

My wife, Michelle Smith, made this book possible with neverending amounts of support and understanding of the long hours required when you're both writing a book and running several consulting businesses. And, even though she's in the computer business too, she puts up with way more than her fair share of computer stuff permeating the house (are we up to 25 systems yet?) and endless computer discussions in her off-duty time.

On the publishing end of things, a special tip of the hat to my editor Mark Stone. He's taken quite a chance on this work, both on an esoteric topic using an up-and-coming operating system and on a first-time author as well. Mark's right hand on this project, Katie Gardner, has been invaluable to me in helping me sort out everything from FrameMaker to graphics file formats.

The CD-ROM that accompanies this book comes with hundreds of megabytes of software that could not possibly be the work of a single author. The CD-ROM makes use of many Open Source and publicly distributable software packages that allow Linux clusters to work.

I would also like to acknowledge the work of the talented people who helped make my book possible. Unfortunately, it is not possible to list everyone who has worked on software that is used by Linux or the clustering extensions and tools provided here, but these people and groups present some of the most critical or most extensively used packages included on the CD-ROM that accompanies this book. Many thanks to:

- Linux Torvalds and the kernel team that keeps Linux evolving.

- Red Hat Software for creating a well-structured and easy-to-customize Linux distribution.

- Chris Cason and the POVRAY Team for allowing me to include the sources for their extraordinary package, the Persistence of Visions Ray Tracing package.

- Stuart Herbert, an independent consultant and maintainer of the Generic Network Queuing System, GNQS.

- Werner G. Krebs, primary author of GNU Queue.

- The NIST parallel programming group including: Eric Baland, Charles Clark, Judith Devaney, James Dray, Mark Edwards, Delphine Goujon, Cyril Hansen, Howard Hung, John Koontz, Robert Lipman, Minwen Lo, Ryan McCormack, Martial Michel, William Mitchell, Katherine Pagoaga, Jasper Peeters, Gale Richter, Thibaut Rouffineau, Justin Turner, and Koen Vrielink who created the PADE development environment and associated tools.

- The PostreSQL development team.

PART I

CLUSTER DESIGN, DEVELOPMENT, AND MANAGEMENT

This half of the book is focused on the design, development, and management of Linux clusters. This part is of interest to readers who really want to get their hands dirty in the whole experience of rolling their own parallel Linux cluster, from the initial conception all the way through the deployment of a system that can be put into a data center and run like any other "production" system.

CHAPTER ONE

INTRODUCTION

This book is about how to take off-the-shelf computers and components, like Intel-style personal computers, and turn them *en masse* into a high-performance computing engine.

This book will present a kind of digital alchemy that will allow you to spend a relatively small amount of money on a set of computers, some networking hardware such as network interface cards, a hub, and cables. And then, using a special copy of Linux operating system that may be found on the CD-ROM that accompanies this book, you can get the kind of performance that was previously reserved for big companies with multi-million dollar budgets. In other words, by the time you are done with this book you will be able to build your own personal supercomputer. Whether you're interested in animation or stock market analysis, or you need a system for accounting, resource controls, and billing, you'll have a computing tool suitable for these tasks.

I have tried to make this book as "hands-on" as possible, so that once you have made such a machine (or have access to one), you can manage and program it and expand it as your computing needs grow.

Conversely, I have tried hard not to make a book about the theory of computation, or a discussion of the best algorithms for matrix transformation; there are many good books available on such topics (some particularly good ones are listed in the , *Bibliography*). In fact, I will try to steer purposefully away from the more esoteric aspects of computer theory and keep things on a practical implementor's level. My principal goal is to help you understand enough about the theory of high-performance computing that you will have some ideas on how you might be able to use the kinds of machines I will present to help solve your business, research, or even hobby problems more effectively.

What Makes a Supercomputer "Super?"

Before we get into exactly how we go about turning silicon into gold, let's explore just how we got here. Where did the concept of supercomputing come from? What does the term mean, apart from the image of large boxes with lots of spinning tape drives and blinking lights? And, where might all of this be leading?

Supercomputers are defined as the fastest, most powerful computers in terms of CPU power and I/O capabilities.

Since computer technology is continually evolving, this is always a moving target. This year's "supercomputer" may well be next year's entry-level personal computer. In fact, today's commonly available personal computers deliver performance that easily bests the supercomputers that were available on the market in the 1980s.

"Supercomputing" as a specific genre of computer science has only been around since the mid-1970s when a now legendary engineer named Seymour Cray took a bunch of readily available computer chips and turned them into a commercial computer whose performance had never been seen before.

Before Cray started making his computers out of what amounted to off-the-shelf parts, the design and manufacture of high-performance computing systems was something that was usually done as a "one-off" venture by big companies like IBM, Control Data Corporation (CDC), and Univac in order to meet the needs of a special customer such as the U.S. Government or an oil company. It wasn't a big business with tens of thousands of customers. The computers of the day were large, often taking up thousands of square feet. They were expensive to run because they needed special power systems and many tons of air conditioning to keep them from overheating. And there just weren't that many applications in the mainstream of business information systems that required such high performance systems. The application of these really big machines was limited to strictly numerical applications such as analysis of oil field data, the design of nuclear weapons, and code breaking.

Seymour Cray was an "engineer's engineer." He would design a new machine from the ground up if he thought there was a way to optimize its performance. One of the most interesting pieces of industry lore about Cray was that he was able to take a load of factory-second transistors—parts that tested out below their specified design requirements—and capitalize on their quirky performance to build an enhanced logic circuit for the CDC-1600 series that gave the machine a performance edge over competing machines.

CDC was the master of high-performance computing for all of the 1960s and early 1970s. Their machines became the standard for any application that required serious number crunching. Even as CDC dominated the market for these machines, its management became complacent and more and more reluctant to take new risks on new systems. Risk aversion was not something that a creative mind like Cray's could tolerate, so in 1974 Cray left CDC to start a new company, Cray Research Corporation, whose goal was to design and sell only one kind of computer: supercomputers.

Seymour Cray envisioned a new world of computing where computers were more than simply machines that crunched numbers or moved records around in databases. In Cray's world, computers were instruments where simulation could replace direct manipulation, a world where designers could make models of real-world objects and then test them, change them, and test them some more, before ever having to commit to building a real-world object. The idea was that the digital models were a lot more cost-effective than the real thing, and a lot easier to change if you had discovered some fatal flaw in your design.

Seymour Cray, of course, didn't invent simulation—for as long as computers have been around people have been using them to simulate one thing or another. What Seymour Cray brought to the table was the brilliance of a computer designer who could design machines that were powerful enough to make simulation as easy as doing any other kind of computing task. Though the concept of simulation may seem obvious now, what Cray was trying to do was more science fiction than science fact in the mid-1970s.

Cray's machines were ground-breaking because of their speed and his way of capturing the imagination of people who needed to be able to visualize things that would be invisible without the power available in a supercomputer.

Pushing the State of the Art

From the 1950s though the 1970s the discipline of computer design changed little. The big companies of the time, IBM, Control Data, Data General, and Digital Equipment Corporation, all had various models that were targeted at market niches, such as business computing, scientific computing, and databases, but their designs were usually similar (for a given line of machines at a given company). They were interested in selling large numbers of machines to the lowest common denominator of business computer user. Digital, for example, had more than twenty different models of its PDP-11 line of minicomputers, each one basically the same as all of the others, with small differences in one model to meet the needs of people using the machine for lab equipment, and another set of features for those using the machine for a business inventory tracking system. IBM did the same thing, but their machines were usually physically much larger and had much larger price tags. Control Data made some of the biggest and most powerful machines in the world, the kind of machines that were, for their time, supercomputers in their own right, and these were often sold to oil companies and mysterious places like the US National Security Agency and the CIA. All vendors had one thing in common: they all moved very slowly when introducing new technology.

In the early 1970s, a small semiconductor company called Intel shook things up by developing something they called a "microprocessor." Intel tied all of the components that we recognize in a computer (the Arithmetic-Logic Unit, the memory controller, and the I/O controller) into a tiny package smaller than the diameter of a dime. Until then, all computers were "writ large." They looked a lot like the archetype of computers you would see in 1950s/1960s science fiction movies—they were really big boxes with lots of blinking lights and spinning tape drives. In a word, they were huge.

Before the invention of the microprocessor, and all of the specialized integrated circuits that followed, computers were designed from the ground up with what are known as "discrete components." Modern computers are made up of collections of what are called "integrated circuits" (ICs), which is just a fancy way of saying there's a whole lot of functionality packed into a single chip. Discrete component technology is exactly the opposite. It's a lot of functionality built up from a large number of individual components such as transistors. So, where the Intel 4004 microprocessor had about 5,000 transistors that made up all of the circuitry required for a CPU, memory controller, and I/O, a mainframe or minicomputer would have the same basic functionality spread across three refrigerator-sized objects.

Although revolutionary, Intel's new microprocessor wasn't about to displace its larger cousins. It had limited capabilities and couldn't compete with even the smallest minicomputers of its day. Industry legend has it that the "4004" (the designation of the first microprocessor) was actually originally developed as a traffic light controller. Nonetheless, it did start a trend of miniaturization and specialization of functionality that would lead to everything from video games and VCRs to global positioning systems and cellular phones.

Fortunately for companies like IBM and Digital, the little microprocessor pioneered by Intel was a toy by comparison to their "big iron." There was still a lot of computational performance to be had by making very large boxes with very large circuit boards populated with individual transistors. With the state of chip fabrication in the early 1970s, it wasn't possible to duplicate the kinds of I/O and memory systems that could be made with those discrete transistors. But this was not an advantage that would last for long.

In the late 1970s, Seymour Cray started his company, Cray Research, with the intention of taking all the innovations in semiconductors to make something so new that it would change the world. His first computer, the Cray I, was a blend of the architectures he developed while he was an engineer at Control Data and the new technology of integrated circuits. Cray realized that with the miniaturization possible with ICs he could make a much smaller machine that was blazingly fast. The Cray I was so much faster than anything ever built that it took the next fastest machine around (then, a CDC 6600) to feed it data in order to keep the Cray busy one hundred percent of the time.

Companies that bought Crays immediately found interesting and novel uses for them. Oil companies could actually make 3-D models of oil fields based on sounding data that was previously looked at as just a pile of numbers. They could look at the models as though they were cross-sections of the earth in order to gain an understanding of the geology of the area they were looking at.

Medical researchers used Cray supercomputers to make 3-D images out of x-rays and to model new drugs for the treatment of diseases. Architects designed and tested new planes without ever using a wind-tunnel.

Perhaps most importantly, with the speed of supercomputers, computer circuit designers could simulate new, faster computers in real-time. So, instead of the hit-and-miss method of drawing a circuit on paper, making a mock-up out of discrete components, and then, if you were really lucky, making a first cut at the actual chip, semiconductor makers could go from design to simulation to manufacture in extremely short time frames. Where it once took more than a year for the design/production process, new chips could be out on the market and in the hands of system manufacturers in a matter of months.

Once Cray had established that there was a market for ultra-fast computers to meet a wide variety of business and research problems, all sorts of companies got into the business. CDC, IBM, and a whole host of startups wanted to help exploit the new trend in simulation and visualization. In the 1980s, there were more than twenty companies making various kinds of supercomputer-class machines, including Cray Research, its own spin-off, Cray Computer, IBM, Thinking Machines, Kendall Square Research, Dataflow, Ridge Systems, and others. To meet the needs of this marketplace, supporting businesses sprang up to develop high-performance adjunct systems, such as disk arrays that could hold trillions of bytes of data, and high-speed networking systems to ensure that these really powerful machines could be supplied with data and kept busy.

At the same time, new, faster microprocessor chips that brought higher and higher computer performance directly to the desktop were being developed. Led by Intel, that small semiconductor manufacturer that developed the first microprocessor in the early 1970s, new generations of microprocessors were gaining the features of their mainframe cousins. Workstation companies like Sun Microsystems brought faster and faster storage systems to the market, and all of this started to erode the distinction between "little computers" and mainframes like the supercomputer. And, by 1995 all of the companies that sprang up during the supercomputer gold-rush were either out of business, or absorbed into larger companies such as IBM and Sun Microsystems.

The Trickle-Down Effect

As the computer industry entered the 1990s, engineering workstations became as fast as the mainframe computers of just a decade earlier. At the same time, personal computers became more powerful, too. Prices also dropped from over $25,000 for a high-end engineering workstation, to under $2,500 for a personal computer with similar computing capabilities. The supercomputer business had practically optimized itself out of existence.

The consolidation of the supercomputer market and the performance increases of workstations and PCs didn't spell the demise of the supercomputer. Supercomputers are still around, made by IBM, Silicon Graphics, and Sun. However, with the advent of powerful personal computers and scalable workstations that can have multiple CPUs, supercomputers have turned into extremely exclusive devices that are available only to those groups with very large budgets.

If we go back to the definition of a supercomputer—the fastest computer it is possible to build at a given moment in time—we find that as workstation and consumer computers become faster and faster, supercomputers by their very definition must be the most expensive machines that can be built. This is because they rely on the most cutting-edge technologies available. The research and development required to keep a computer within the definition of "supercomputer" takes the resources of an extremely well-funded company. The cost of keeping pace with such developments will keep commercial supercomputers out of reach of most budgets for the foreseeable future.

So, if you are a researcher with a cool project idea or a business that needs supercomputer processing power to design your next great product, you either beg for time on someone else's supercomputer or run your work on slower machines. This often means you wait weeks or even months to see results from your work.

Throughout the 1980s, researchers at a number of universities tried to harness the power of engineering workstations to bridge the gap between the power needed for advanced simulation and the budget needed for an actual supercomputer. The results came in the form of innovative operating systems like Spring, Chorus, and Amoeba. These systems deployed innovations like message passing and task sharing that would lead directly to the development of the kinds of clusters described in this book. Only two things kept these powerful developments from taking off: software licensing and the cost of hardware. Most of these extensions were made to commercial versions of the Unix operating system—which would be expensive to license, and the workstations from companies like Sun Microsystems, Apollo, Digital, and others were still extremely expensive—in the tens of thousands of dollars per machine.

Fortunately, in the mid-1990s, something interesting happened: the performance of personal computers started to match the performance of high-end workstations, and the cost of computer networking equipment plummeted. The availability of inexpensive hardware and networking was met by the development of a free operating system written by a 21-year-old college student from Helsinki, Finland by the name of Linus Torvalds. Linus' operating system, which he dubbed "Linux," was a functional clone of the Unix operating system developed by AT&T's Bell Labs, which is the staple of large computing installations all over the world. Because of Linux's compatibility with Unix, and the fact that it could be made to run on powerful, inexpensive off-the-shelf hardware, scientists latched onto it as a way to satisfy their need for computing power without having to buy expensive engineering machines or supercomputers.

In 1994, NASA researcher Donald Becker developed a technique that made this book possible. He and his team needed a way to get supercomputer performance but didn't have the budget to buy one, so he invented a way to hook up off-the-shelf personal computers with special software to create a system that could be scaled up to deliver supercomputer class performance.

Their "Beowulf" system has become a popular tool for researchers all over the world who need extreme amounts of computing power to model subatomic particles, as well as designers of Internet "search engines" that allow you to find out where something that interests you can be found on the Internet. The majority of the chapters in this book focus on how to build Beowulf-style supercomputer clusters, what I call "parallel Linux clusters," and how you might use the power inherent in such machines.

Now, clustering isn't exactly a new idea. Large computer companies like Digital Equipment Corporation (a division of Compaq) have made commercial clustering products for years. DEC's VAXClusters allowed system managers to design large-scale systems that allowed sharing of processors, tape drives, and disk arrays, IBM has various forms of clusters for their higher-end AIX systems, and Sun's flagship product, the Enterprise 10000, is a clustered system that can have up to 64 processors in a single box.

The watershed event created by NASA was the creation of clusters out of truly commodity systems. With Beowulf, clusters can even be make up of old cast-off systems such as old Intel 486 class systems that are certainly no longer state of the art, but can be used to add cheap computing power to a cluster.

The fact that it is possible for anyone with a little time and some inspiration to create his or her very own supercomputer lends itself to some interesting possibilites. To steal a line from William Gibson's cyberpunk classic, *Neuromancer*, as with any new tool, product, or capability, "The net finds its own uses for things..."

Science Fiction Becomes Science Fact

One of the wonderful things about science fiction is the way it inspires people to use what they read to invent the future. From H.G. Wells' *The Shape of Things to Come* and Isaac Asimov's *Foundation* novels, to Verner Vinge's *True Names* and Neal Stephenson's *The Diamond Age*, the worlds postulated by these and other authors have been the basis for technological creations from interstellar probes to cellular phones and much more.

One of the powerful things about computer science is that anyone with a computer, a compiler, and a good idea can change the world. Programmers and engineers are among the few classes of people in the world whose work actually can affect everyone else with one well-timed and well-implemented idea.

As the use of computers in our everyday lives becomes more and more common, that well-placed idea can change the way we think almost overnight and can set our expectations about how the world might be. Computer programmers can invent whole new worlds in the form of video games and "interactive fiction" (like the game *Myst* that sold millions of copies with its impressive scenery and intricate puzzles) or infor-mation tools such as Netscape that become so popular that they seem to be every-where all at once.

The growth of information technologies and the Internet has had just such an effect on the public at large. High-performance computers and systems such as parallel Linux clusters in particular can have the same effect on the people who *make* the informa-tion tools and environments that capture the imagination of the rest of the world.

What Can Clusters Be Used For?

Not too long ago, good programmers optimized their programs for speed because computer power was a valuable commodity. There was a limited amount of horse-power available in each computer, and not a lot of ways to connect them together to allow groups of computers to accomplish a task cooperatively.

Clusters allow anyone to build a scalable computing system that can be used for tasks as diverse as a system to perform *data mining* (a technique for discovering trends in seemingly unrelated collections of information) and a system for processing signals from outer space in the search for extraterrestrial life.

The point is that high-performance computing starts with speed, and becomes some-thing more. Clusters give developers the ability to apply parallel processing to prob-lems that were unsolvable before because time-slicing—the way computer time is allo-cated on most computer systems—only gets you so far.

General High-Performance Computing

Clusters can be used as general-purpose, high-performance computing platforms. They can perform all of the usual mathematical tasks that you would expect from a super-computer. In fact, because of the standard libraries (called "message passing inter-faces") that are used on all commercial supercomputers, porting applications to a par-allel Linux cluster is pretty easy.

Parallel Linux clusters can offer some advantages over a commercial supercomputer that go beyond simple price comparisons. Unlike a commercial supercomputer, a clus-ter can be made more powerful "on the fly" to increase its performance by adding new nodes. Upgrading a Linux cluster is as easy as buying whatever the "latest, great-est" off-the-shelf system is and adding it into the cluster; the cluster can be upgraded as a whole, if the budget allows, or in a slower fashion.

Bulk Disk Servers

When you hear the term "supercomputer," the first thing that often comes to mind is a machine that is exceptionally good at number crunching, not a file server. Usually, supercomputers are not used as really fast file servers. In fact the opposite is true—really fast file servers are often required to be able to keep supercomputers adequately busy.

With a parallel Linux cluster, however, it is possible to construct a file server that is faster than most commercial high-performance, dedicated file servers. That can be done with a Linux cluster because of the multiple systems and multiple network connections inherent in these clusters

Such a server is useful for applications like database systems where major bottlenecks in performance occur when data cannot be moved from disk to memory effectively or web applications where transaction speed is critical to the success of an application.

One of the software systems that comes on the CD-ROM with this book will allow you to implement just such an advanced file server.

High-Performance Web Servers

Another excellent use for Linux clusters is the creation of high availability web servers and other mission critical high-availability systems.

By their very nature, Linux clusters lend themselves to the creation of redundant systems. Linux clusters can be designed so that they are all running duplicate copies of a particular application, and have monitoring systems that detect the failure of a member of the cluster and fill in for the inoperative machine. The same kinds of software can also be used to distribute the load (requests) across such a server to ensure that the requests are serviced in a timely fashion and that no one machine is too heavily loaded.

Flight Simulators

Linux clusters are extremely good vehicles for the design and implementation of systems such as flight simulator systems. Simulating a plane is a pretty complicated process, so there's a lot going on in such systems. There's the physics of flight itself, the instruments that must respond to and display information to the pilot, the environment in which the plane itself is flying, and so on. All of these processes are ripe ground for the world of clusters, where each system or group of systems can be run on a separate cluster node.

In fact, companies such as Boeing and Aerobus Industries use clusters to make their flight simulators, both for planes that they currently manufacture and those that are just experimental concepts for possible future planes. In effect, they create "concept planes" and fly them in virtual skies. It's a lot less expensive to design, fly, and potentially crash a plane in the simulator than in the real world. And, it saves wear and tear on the test pilots. Car manufacturers also make extensive use of simulators for the same reasons.

A number of online services allow users to participate in virtual flights with other online users. Linux clusters can also make a great environment for simulators of the entertainment variety and could offer unparalleled realism to the flight simulation experience, or allow a user to fly more advanced planes.

Virtual Worlds

One of my personal interests is in the simulation of virtual environments. One of the areas in which I use my own personal clusters is in the development of online worlds known as MUDs or Multi-User Domains. MUDs are places akin to chat-rooms on the Internet, but with a twist: there's scenery and objects (such as robots, or other non-human characters) that exist in these virtual spaces, and when all the people leave, the places continue to exist in the virtual environment. People can log in to these virtual spaces and explore them, interacting with both the human and non-human (programmatic) entities that live there. In effect, they're virtual communities that grow and evolve over time.

Linux clusters allow me to develop these concepts so that they extend beyond the domain of a single machine and have even larger capabilities. Some nodes on my cluster act as computer engines for virtual robots performing tasks for users of my MUD, others compute the "weather" and provide other services that make my virtual world(s) more interesting.

ALife

A very interesting use for clusters is their use in the expanding field of Artificial Life or "ALife." Artificial Life isn't about creating bugs in a test-tube, rather it is the exploration of how natural-seeming behaviors can be simulated in a computer program. Such analysis can help us better understand the behaviors of living things in the real world.

With a cluster, you can use one cluster node per organism being simulated, and other cluster nodes to simulate parts of the organism's environment. The ability to dedicate such resources allows researchers to create more detailed simulations since there are more resources overall, and more detail (called *granularity*) can be written into each simulation.

AI and Agents

One of my other personal interests is the application of clusters to the problems of Artificial Intelligence, or AI, and the subdomain of developing intelligent agents to perform useful tasks on my behalf.

With clusters, it's possible to dedicate a lot of computing power to the tasks of information and concept analysis on one set of nodes and then have other programs using everything from neural-networks to classification systems to carry out specific tasks on other nodes.

One of the areas that I am using my cluster for is the application of such intelligent agents in virtual environments (as in the MUDs described earlier). My virtual environments are inhabited by intelligent agents that read my email and determine which of the thousands of pieces of email I receive each day need my immediate attention. The agent(s) also figure out which messages can be safely ignored and which others will be summarized into a personal daily newspaper that is presented to me when I log on to my computer in the morning.

Again, the inherent parallelism in a cluster allows me to break up tasks and spread the computational load across a number of machines so that I am not bound to a single machine that can become so overloaded that nothing is ever accomplished.

What's Next?

Obviously, this chapter presents just a small taste of things that can be done with parallel Linux clusters. Supercomputers and clusters are very powerful tools. As with all developments in information technology, the applications that will be eventually found for clusters are likely to surprise everyone. In 1974, no one could predict the effect that the Cray I would have on the development of physics, biology, chemistry, and microelectronics. The availability of such high-performance systems outside the traditional data centers where supercomputers are usually found will probably have a profound effect on all of our lives.

In the business world, there are untold numbers of businesses that could benefit from performance of a supercomputing cluster to find new markets using these systems for data mining. Other businesses will most certainly use these systems to design their next product and get it out the door a year ahead of their competitors.

I expect that the most surprising effect of clusters will come from some enterprising young person who has some extra machines and a good idea, and who will invent that next great advance in information tools. Perhaps paperback-sized appliances that use artificially intelligent agents will act as your personal *majordomo* and mind your affairs while you're walking down the street.

"The net finds its own uses for things"…only time will tell.

CHAPTER TWO

BASIC CONCEPTS

This chapter deals with some of the fundamental issues behind clustered computing, including answering the basic question: Why Clusters? We will also cover some basic concepts involved in parallel computing, program optimization, and some basic network technology. This background will enable us to work from a common vocabulary when we move on to the actual design, installation, and configuration of clusters.

If you are familiar with clusters, parallel programming, and networking terminology, you might wish to skip ahead to Chapter 3, *Designing Clusters*.

Why Clusters?

Why bother with the hassle of designing and building clusters when there are perfectly good commercial supercomputers available on the market? The short answer is: money. Do you have several million dollars you'd like to tie up?

Clustered systems were first explored by Don Becker and his colleagues at NASA because budgetary restrictions precluded them from access to the kind of commercial supercomputer they needed to perform complex analysis of the very large space data sets that NASA missions tend to generate. They found a way to get the computational performance they needed without committing millions of dollars they didn't have. They named their creation "Beowulf" after the mythic hero of tenth century English lore.

Clusters are surprisingly powerful. There is a semi-annual listing put together by the University of Manhiem in Germany that describes the top 500 supercomputers in the world*. Until 1997, almost all of the systems listed were commercial supercomputer systems from well-known manufacturers such as Cray, Silicon Graphics, and IBM. In

---

* The *Top 500 Supercomputer List* comes out several times per year and may be viewed at *http://www.top500.org*.

1998, something extraordinary started to appear on this list: Linux-based parallel clusters. Two of the systems near the top of the list—number 97, called "CPlant" developed by Sandia National Labs, and number 113, called "Avalon" developed by Los Alamos National Labs—are Linux-based Beowulf clusters.

The supercomputer has also come to play a larger role in business applications. In areas from data mining to fault tolerant performance, clustering technology has become increasingly important.

Commercial products have their place, and there are perfectly good reasons to buy a commercially produced supercomputer. If it is within your budget and your applications can keep the machine busy all the time, you will also need to have a data center to keep it in. Then there's the budget to keep up with the maintenance and upgrades that will be required to keep your investment up to par. However, many who have a need to harness supercomputing power don't buy supercomputers because they can't afford them.

And then there is the upgrade problem.

By the time your machine is delivered, it is often out-of-date and a newer model will have taken its place. If you would like to upgrade your machine, the manufacturer gives you limited options, short of buying "next year's model."

Clusters, on the other hand, are a cheap and easy way to take off-the-shelf components and combine them into a single supercomputer. In some areas of research clusters are actually faster than a commercial supercomputer. Clusters also have the distinct advantage in that they are very simple to build using components available from hundreds, if not thousands, of sources.

You don't even have to use new equipment to build a cluster. One of the most interesting stories in the Internet community of cluster developers is that of the "stone supercomputer," that was built by a group at Oak Ridge National Labs. Oak Ridge built a Beowulf cluster, and rather than spend any money on the hardware at all, they solicited donations from other groups in their organization. So, for no investment other than their own time, they built a several-dozen node system out of discarded 486 machines, slow Pentiums, and other systems. It may not have been pretty, or have had the latest, greatest processor, but it got the job done.

Once you understand the basics, clusters are simple to build. Unlike commercial products, they are independent of a single vendor or single source for equipment. The most economical aspect of parallel clusters is that they can be built from commodity hardware.

"Commodity hardware" includes two distinct kinds of computers. First, there is commercial, off-the-shelf systems from any well-known desktop or server PC manufacturer such as Dell, Compaq, or Micron. If you want to build a cluster for your business and you have little experience building things from kits, I would suggest that you buy systems for your cluster from a manufacturer you already know or with whom you have a relationship.

The second meaning of "commodity hardware" is that you can, literally, buy hardware as a commodity. This means buying motherboards, cases, memory, disk drives, and so on in bulk, and then using these components to build the individual systems that will become the elements of your cluster.

Building systems from scratch is not for everyone, but if you take the plunge, you can build a completely customized cluster that is tuned specifically for your applications and can be upgraded and enhanced more cost effectively than a cluster made from off-the-shelf commercial systems.

If you are willing to put it all together yourself, you can save 50–70 percent of the cost of an off-the-shelf system, but this requires a more in-depth understanding of all of the various subsystems that make up high-end systems, and a willingness to roll up your sleeves and build computers from the system board up.

Whichever way you choose to start your cluster, either with commercial systems or with ones your build yourself, you can always upgrade your cluster to increase its performance. You can do it either as a whole, or a node at a time by simply adding more systems or upgrading components.

Clustering Concepts

Clusters are in fact quite simple. They're a bunch of computers tied together with a network working on some large problem that has been broken down into smaller pieces. There are a number of different strategies you can use to tie them together. There are also a number of different software packages that can be used to make the software side of things work. But first, let's define the major concepts and themes that you will encounter as you explore and build these systems.

The Big Picture: Parallelism

The name of the game in high-performance computing is parallelism.* Parallelism is the quality that allows something to be done in parts that work independently rather than a task that has so many interlocking dependencies that it cannot be further broken down. Parallelism operates at two levels: hardware parallelism and software (algorithmic) parallelism.

---

* Parallelism and the performance analysis of software is such a complex topic, I can't hope to cover it completely here. In fact, it's so deep that you could write a whole book on the topic. Fortunately, two people already did. Kevin Dowd and Charles Severance are the authors of O'Reilly's *High Performance Computing*. This book is a "must have" reference work for anyone truly wishing to explore high-performance programming. More information on this book can be found in Appendix A, *Resources*.

Hardware Parallelism

On one level, hardware parallelism deals with the CPU of an individual system and how you can squeeze performance out of sub-components of the CPU (including caches, pipelines, and multiple execution units) that can speed up your code. At another level, there is the parallelism that is gained by having multiple systems working on a computational problem in a distributed fashion. These systems are known as either "fine grained" for parallelism inside the CPU or having to do with multiple CPUs in the same system, or "coarse grained" for parallelism of a collection of separate systems acting in concert.

CPU-level parallelism

A computer's Central Processing Unit (CPU) is commonly pictured as a device that operates on (or executes) one instruction after another in a straight line, always completing one step or instruction before a new one is started, as shown in Figure 2-1. For example, a single instruction might load a value from memory location 12345 and store it in a CPU register.

This serial execution continues until the CPU is forced for some reason to follow the code as it branches someplace else (as in a subroutine call) to start executing another set of instructions.

In older machines, like the DEC VAX, the Intel 8088, and the Motorola 68000, this is exactly what happens; the flow of instructions is very deterministic and predictable. At any given moment, there is exactly one instruction being executed by the CPU.

Newer CPU architectures, such as the Sun UltraSPARC, the DEC/Compaq Alpha, and even the Pentium II/III, have an inherent ability to do more than one thing at once. The logic on the CPU chip divides the CPU into *multiple execution units.*

An execution unit is the part of a computer's circuitry that actually does the work we associate with the "compute" in the word "computer." It moves data from memory into the internal storage of the processor (called the registers) and then performs the operations that the particular instruction calls for (ADD, SUBTRACT, MULTIPLY, etc.). Then it sets flags to indicate the result of the instruction and moves results for the register back to memory, and so on.

Systems that have multiple execution units allow the CPU to attempt to process more than one instruction at a time. I use the word "attempt" deliberately because part of the process of executing multiple instructions includes keeping track of the instructions that are being executed, the results of the operations in terms of registers that may have been modified, condition codes that are set, and branch instructions that are to be called. If, for some reason, the execution of an instruction would cause the CPU to have to stop what it's doing and branch to some other place in the program, it's quite possible that all of the other instructions being worked on in other parts of the CPU would be invalidated and discarded.

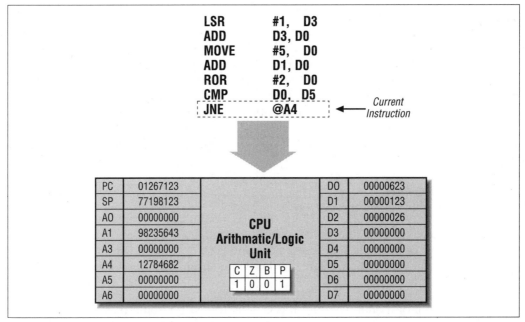

Figure 2-1. Instructions stream on a CISC machine

Although it seems like a waste of work, most computer programs are very linear entities. Well-written programs (or, more to the point, well-optimized code from a high-quality compiler) will arrange binary executable code so that it spends as little time branching as possible. This allows the CPU to work more efficiently; preprocessing the instructions that might not be executed is more efficient than leaving CPU resources idle.

Two additional hardware features of modern CPUs support multiple execution units: the cache. The pipeline is a small area of memory inside the CPU where instructions that are next in-line to be executed are stored. The pipeline gives the CPU a chance to get ready to execute the instructions. This is done by analyzing (or decoding) the instructions and getting (or fetching) any additional information the CPU will need to actually operate on the data for these instructions.

Instruction pipelines help keep work flowing to a CPU and, for optimized code, will keep the CPU busy as long as the code doesn't have to jump too far away to execute something that isn't stored in the cache.

The cache is a much larger area of memory, often several megabytes, where large portions of programs are stored in anticipation of eventual execution by the CPU. Cache memory is orders of magnitude faster in terms of access time than the system's main memory, so getting instructions out of the cache and putting them in the instruction pipeline is only slightly slower than accessing data that is actually inside the CPU in registers.

Taken together, the cache, the pipeline, and the CPU itself act like a coordinated assembly line for instruction execution.

Such parallelism allows impressive increases in CPU performance. It also requires a lot of intelligence on the part of the compiler to arrange the executable code in such a way that the CPU has a good chance of being able to execute multiple instructions simultaneously.

It's not important that you understand all about the theory behind this level of CPU parallelism, but for the purpose of building and operating a cluster, you should understand that well-optimized code, along with an efficient CPU, can help speed up your applications.

System-level parallelism

At a higher level, system-level parallelism is the crux of what clustered computing is all about. It is the parallelism of multiple nodes coordinating to work on a problem *in parallel* that gives the cluster its power.

There are other levels at which even more parallelism can be introduced into this system. For example, if you decide that each node in your cluster will be a multi-CPU system (called a *symmetric multiprocessor*) you will be introducing a fundamental degree of parallel processing at the node level. Having more than one network interface on each node introduces communication channels that may be used in parallel to communicate with other nodes in your cluster. Finally, if you use multiple disk drive controllers in each node, you create parallel data paths that can be used to increase the performance of the I/O subsystem.

Each decision you make will have an effect on the hardware level of parallelism on your cluster. As you design your cluster, you will make various decisions about how many nodes you will configure the system with, how many CPUs per node, and how many network connections and disk drives or controllers will be connected to each node.

All of these areas of hardware parallelism can be used to great advantage in the solution of your problems on a cluster, but only if your problem is amenable to them.

Memory systems

Memory is, next to the CPU, where all the action takes place in a cluster or any computer. Having too little of it means that the computer's operating system will take up most of the space, leaving very little room for your program, causing your program to endlessly thrash around trying to find enough resources to run. Having too much of it means...well, you can never have too much memory in a computer.

There are two kinds of memory we are concerned about: cache memory and main memory.

Cache memory. Cache memory is a specialized kind of memory that is almost an extension of the register set of the CPU. Cache memory is designed to be very fast (access times are on the order of nanoseconds). Chunks of a running program are stored in the cache so the CPU can access it immediately without waiting for access to the main system memory, which can be several orders of magnitude slower than the cache. As pieces of the program (and data) are retrieved for eventual execution by the CPU, more code/data is pulled in from main memory or from disk to replace it.

The major role of the cache is to help keep the CPU's instruction pipeline full; again, this is to keep the CPU from having to go to the slower main memory system to fetch more instructions to execute.

Main memory. This is where your programs are stored after they are read in from some semi-permanent form of storage such as hard disk or tape. The memory system of most machines is governed by three major factors: the memory access speed, the number of memory wait states, and the system bus speed.

Even though the CPU is the focus of the computer's computational activity, there are a lot of other things going on. Not surprisingly, each of them, ultimately, has an effect on the performance of your system and, by extension, your cluster.

The *memory access speed* is the amount of time it takes for a memory chip to recover after a read or a write. Even though action can seem instantaneous on a computer, there is a lot of "waiting" going on. In a memory chip, when something is read from or written to memory, time must pass before that location can be written to or read from again. This is because the way most common forms of computer memory are designed, it takes time both for a memory cell to be refreshed with a new value once it has been written to, and for the memory cell to be refreshed if it has been read from. Depending upon the density of the chips, and a number of other factors, this speed can be as fast as forty nanoseconds, or as slow as one hundred nanoseconds (100ns). One hundred nanoseconds seems like a short amount of time, but if the CPU has to wait that 100ns for a frequently accessed memory location, it can really slow things down. The time required to refresh a memory location is also known as the *refresh rate*.

Wait states are delays forced upon a CPU in order to better synchronize itself with a memory system. Systemboard designers put delays into the hardware to ensure that the CPU won't falsely sense a hardware failure when it attempts to get a value from memory and that memory location is still in the middle of a refresh cycle. Wait states are a necessity in many systems because of the great disparity in speed between the CPU and main memory; this is also why cache memory exists, to help add a mediation layer between worlds of slow main memory and the much faster world of the CPU.

The *system bus speed* is a measure of how fast information can be moved between the CPU and peripherals, such as a display controller or a disk controller. Most high-end x86 style machines support a 66MHz bus speed. Newer models support 100MHz. The difference is in how much time the CPU spends waiting for its peripherals to complete commands given to them and how fast those peripherals can send process information sent to them over the system bus. The faster the bus speed, the busier the CPU can be when it's accessing peripheral devices. A peripheral might complete an action requested by the CPU and itself be waiting to finish up a request, and find itself at the mercy of a system bus that is slower than its own ability to process information.

Some systems use specialized memory systems to allow any CPU in the system to have fast unhindered access to any range of memory. These are called *crossbar switches*.

A crossbar switch is a device that is designed like a grid of streets whose traffic flow is controlled by traffic lights, as shown in Figure 2-2. The role of a crossbar switch is to arbitrate access to the resources connected to it. In the example of a fast computer system, crossbar switches are used to provide uniform access between CPUs and memory systems where none of the CPUs have to explicitly manage the memory systems.

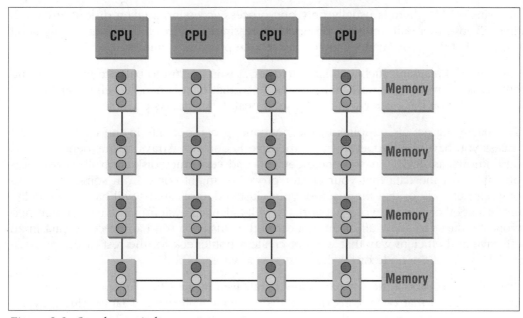

Figure 2-2. Crossbar switch

In short, a crossbar switch acts like a traffic cop in a large city whose job is to ensure that a given driver can get his car from point A to point B without encountering any red lights or stop signs. A crossbar switch performs this function for CPUs and memory. It allows a CPU to access memory systems without being concerned that there may be other CPUs nearby that are also accessing other areas of memory. All of this happens "behind the back" of the CPU that just accesses the memory area it is interested in as though it were the only CPU in the system.

Not having any of the CPUs manage memory access from the other CPUs is a big win. Such memory management is very complex to program and generates a lot of overhead in the operating system. That's the "good news."

The "bad news" is that crossbar switches are expensive to design and build. Also, there's a practical limit to how large you can make a crossbar switch before the internal logic of the switch itself becomes a source of communications overhead between the CPUs and memory systems connected to it.

Input and output

A final aspect of hardware parallelism is input and output, or simply "I/O." Unlike a single processor being used by a single person, parallel clusters need their data input and output to be as fast as possible, otherwise the CPU can get tied up waiting for data to be read or written.

In a single CPU, there is usually only one process accessing a given disk at any given time. Even if there are multiple programs accessing a device, the wait is usually short enough that the performance impact on any one program is minimal.

On a parallel machine such as a Linux cluster, it is important to balance input and output across as many channels as are available so that data is handled efficiently and all of the nodes on the cluster work as close to peak efficiency as possible.

This balancing act also applies to the networking components in the cluster as well. Unless you have the budget to buy expensive Redundant Arrays of Inexpensive Disks (also known as "RAID" mass storage devices) and very fancy disk controller cards, it is probable that the data that your cluster processes might come from some other host on your network, or that the result of your clustered applications will have to be delivered to another host on your network. A well-balanced system will have enough network interfaces to allow all of the nodes on the cluster to send and receive data in an effective and efficient way that will not create a bottleneck for the rest of the processing elements of the node or for the cluster as a whole.

I've talked a bit about the CPU and how parallelism in the CPU can speed up processing, and hinted that collections of systems are what will make a Linux cluster work. But what else is there to parallel processing on such a system? A CPU without a supporting infrastructure is pretty useless, so I'll talk a bit about the peripherals and software that allow everything to work together.

Software Parallelism

This brings us to the really hard part of problem solving with a cluster (or, in fact, a commercial supercomputer): software parallelism. Software parallelism is the ability to find well-defined areas in a problem you want to solve that can be broken down into self-contained parts. These parts are the program elements that can be distributed and give you the big speedup that you want to get out of a high-performance computing system.

Before you can run a program on a parallel cluster, you have to ensure that the problems you're trying to solve are amenable to being done in a parallel fashion. Unfortunately, parallel computing is not as simple as just writing a program and saying "make." In fact, some classes of programs just cannot be run on a parallel computer.

Many classes of problems can be analyzed to find the inherent parallelism within them. Some of the more obvious problem domains include weather modeling, stock and options modeling, rendering of computer generated imagery, and various kinds of simulations.

I say these are "obvious" because they are the kinds of problems that contain "sub-problems" within them. For example, weather modeling involves solving problems relating to the heating and cooling of the atmosphere, the absorbing of sunlight by clouds and cities, as well as the movement of pressure fronts.

Financial modeling is a complicated system that, like weather modeling, requires a large number of sub-problems to be solved in order to gain an understanding of a larger picture of some element of finance. There are currency fluctuations, the availability of basic materials, and even the "value" of public sentiment.

Almost any problem that is composed of smaller sub-problems that can be quantified can be broken down into smaller problems and run on a node (or nodes) on a cluster.

The key to finding parallelism is finding the dependencies in a problem and isolating them. For example, in a program that processes data in some sort of loop, it makes little sense to have the process that reads the data from wherever it is coming from, read that data from inside the body of the loop. A simple example of this can be seen in the following code fragment:

```
int i,j;
for (i = 1; i <=10000; i++) {
    read_data(someDevice, &i);
    process_data(i);
}
```

This fragment of code processes data, one piece at a time, reading then processing it until it has completed 10,000 iterations.

Even though this example is only four lines long, it is ripe for optimization. If all the data were already read into the system, the **process_data()** routine could be rewritten to process all of the data at once. As presented in this example, it is executed 10,000 times. While this might seem like a trivial example, the overhead involved in calling and executing this loop and calling the enclosed subroutines is actually *quite* substantial. Registers have to be saved, data is copied, operated on, and copied somewhere else, and so on. Potentially, at each call of the `read_data()` and `process_data()` routines, the CPU also has to pull in a program from main memory, as opposed to operating on data and instructions in the CPU cache. The major point here is that finding parallelism and places for optimization in most software is quite easy if you look at your application carefully and look for ways to optimize operations.

There are a lot of software tools and paradigms at the disposal of programmers looming to increase the performance of their applications. We will examine software profiling tools later when we get to Chapter 8, *Programming in a Parallel Environment*. As a basic concept of clustered computing, you should walk away with the idea that well-defined problems and well-written code is where the performance benefits of a cluster (or a traditional supercomputer) come from.

Underlying concepts

In the previous example, we looked at a small code fragment that, with appropriate refinement, could be made more efficient and even allow some of its work to be done in parallel. Before we try to optimize that fragment to take advantage of the parallelism we know is there, there are some underlying concepts that will help you to take advantage of it when you find it.

Granularity

Granularity is the amount of work that can be done at a given scale of computation between times that some level of synchronization must occur.

For example, in a pipelined CPU, while an instruction is being executed, another can be in the process of being decoded while a third is being fetched. On an SMP machine, you can divide a loop among processors, syncing up only at boundary points in the loop. Or, on a cluster of workstations, an image processing application can split the work of rendering a frame among sixteen workstations, each of which works on its own local piece of the frame, and the pieces are recombined at the end of the process.

Dependencies

Dependencies are the points where one piece of code depends upon the results of some other action. Dependencies have two forms: data dependencies and control dependencies.

Data dependencies

A data dependency exists where some operation cannot proceed until data becomes available as a result of some other operation. For example, in the code fragment:

```
i = b+2*sqrt(a)
j = 24 * i;
```

the computation involving `j` cannot continue unless `i` is available. This is a fairly obvious dependency, and isn't an issue for non-parallel code. But for a parallel application, this kind of dependency creates a need to localize bits of code like this so they can be executed serially, not executed in parallel, which would result in incorrect results (or at least cause one parallel task to have to wait for the other).

Control dependencies

Control dependencies are even more common. These are dependencies that relate to one thread of control being tied to another. For example, the code fragment:

```
if (needToLoop == 1) {
    for (i = 1; i <= maxVal; i++) {
            /* do something... */
        }
}
```

has a direct dependency between the test in the "if" statement, and whether or not the loop is ever executed.

There are also problems that are not as easily made parallel. Some kinds of database queries and problems that have large dependencies on real-time user input are hard to run on clusters. These are often issues that can be handled by a parallelizing compiler. You can help the compiler out by crafting your code so that there are as few data and control dependencies as possible.

Optimization Versus Parallelism

Many people merge the concepts of parallelism and optimization and mistakenly think that they are interchangeable. So, what is optimization?

Optimization is the art of writing or generating (if from a compiler) code that has as few wasted instructions and that branches as little as possible. The longer a program can run without stopping to go "someplace else" (which entails saving variables, registers, etc.) or wasting time executing instructions that are not part of whatever problem is being solved, the faster that code will be.

Compilers optimize your code by using all sorts of analysis to find tricks to reduce the complexity of the machine code that is generated as the output of the compiler. This reduction in complexity can be simple things like reducing a common subroutine that is called 10,000 times to some code that is inserted inline 10,000 times rather than being branched to. For small, common subroutines, this process is often more efficient than the overhead involved in calling a subroutine.

Another compiler trick is to arrange the machine code so that commonly called subroutines are stored near each other when a program gets loaded. This speeds up programs by allowing a subroutine call to branch to something that is often already in memory, and not to something that has to be read in from a slower system such as a hard disk drive.

Optimizing compilers can also try to reduce mathematical expressions to efficient forms that keep operands in CPU registers rather than load them from memory.

This is just the tip of the iceberg in optimization. There are several dozen wonderful books and countless PhD theses written every year on this topic. For most applications, it's not important that you are an expert in these concepts, rather simply that you know of their existence.

Parallelism involves finding the sub-units of work in a given problem and executing a program on hardware that can support farming out work and joining results. Optimization plays an equally important role in single processors as it does in parallel processors—the goal in both cases is to make programs more effective by making them execute more efficiently.

In the context of parallel processing, optimization and parallelism are two sides of the same coin: finding the sub-units of work in a piece of code, and then making those bits of code as efficient as possible.

Multiprocessor Software Concepts

Clusters are fundamentally all about multiprocessing of various flavors, either inside the same system or as collections of systems. There are a number of different concepts relating to how processing is done on such a system that you should be aware of.

Multiprocessing

Mutiprocessing is the idea that the control program of a computer, what we usually call the "operating system," can support (load/unload/schedule) multiple, *independent*, simultaneous threads of control. If the operating system can support multiple threads of control, support each thread of control, or process in an independent fashion, we can describe that operating system as supporting multiprocessing.

You'll notice in the definition above that I give special emphasis to the word *independent*. In order to support multiple processes, an operating system must give the user program the illusion that it's running on its own computer, complete with its own registers, stack, data space, and so on. Additionally, this space must be free from interference from other programs running on the same system. Operating systems that do not enforce process spaces that are protected from one another are not truly multiprocessing systems because any badly behaved program can crash the whole system.

Threaded programming

Once you have an operating system that can support independent processes, the next logical step is to allow something called *user space parallelism*. User space parallelism is more commonly referred to as *threading*. The operating system provides the abstraction of a process that gives users their own view of an entire computer. Threading gives yet another layer of process abstraction, but this time solely in the user's space. Threading is a way of writing programs that have a controlling portion and subordinate, or child, threads of control that share resources.

Threads are often called "lightweight processes" because they usually don't have all of the protections that a regular operating system process has, such as complete memory partition from other threads running in the same process. They are usually also forced to live within the bounds of runtime scheduled for their parent process. Child threads belonging to a process also live in the stack space of their parents. This is efficient because a whole system-level process doesn't have to be created, and the process stack is a memory that's pre-allocated to a process so creating threads is not expensive in terms of memory allocation.

Additionally, since threads are not truly standalone processes, they must cooperate with each other in order to get their work done. This means that threads call special routines to yield control back to their controlling process, and that they must take out locks (called *semaphores*) to ensure access to shared resources such as variables.

Synchronization

Synchronization is the process of putting disparate processes back in step. For example, a weather simulation, where there may be 1,000 processes, each computing a different aspect of local weather phenomenon. At some point, results of these calculations must be brought together to allow a larger result to be created. Synchronization is the process that takes place when merging the results of some process must occur.

Now that you've gotten some of the operating system and parallel processing jargon and concepts down, we can move on to the really interesting stuff: how all of these concepts are used to make high-performance parallel processors.

Parallel Processing Schemes

The area of parallel processing has been an active area of research for many years. There have been a number of different approaches to creating effective parallel computers, and all of them (including parallel Linux clusters) have different levels of effectiveness for different kinds of problems. Some of the best known methods are:

- Symmetric Multiprocessor (SMP)

- Non-Uniform Memory Access (NUMA)

- Uniform Memory Access (UMA)

- Single Instruction Multiple Data (SIMD)

- Multiple Instruction Multiple Data (MIMD); Linux clusters are an instance of this method

Some of these names may be familiar if you have studied computer science. They represent the most common names given to different kinds of parallel computing systems.* Some of these architectures are subsets of other kinds; which ones are subsets will become clear as we examine each one.

SMP machines

Symmetric Multi-Processor machines have more than one CPU, and each CPU has access to the memory system and all of the attached devices and peripherals on the machine. These systems usually have a "master" CPU at boot time, and then the operating system starts up the second (and higher) CPU(s) and manages access to the resources that are shared between all of the processors.

SMP machines allow programmers to write both multiprocessing and multithreaded applications.

When they first appeared in the 1980s, commercially available SMP machines (as opposed to experimental machines built in government labs or at universities) were very expensive. This was primarily because all of the other components that had to be put into a system to support multiple CPUs themselves were quite expensive. For most of the 1980s, things like memory, disk drives, and other supporting hardware were quite expensive and not yet commodity items. With the steep price drops and commoditization of computer systems, SMP machines now have become very popular and affordable.

Most SMPs available in the consumer marketplace have the capability to have two CPUs in a system, although at the time of this writing some four and eight CPU systems are starting to show up.

For commercial use, manufacturers like Sun Microsystems sell SMP systems that can have dozens of processors. As you add more processors to the SMP systems and add hardware such as crossbar switches to make the memory access orthongonal, these parallel processors become something called Massively Parallel Processors or "MPPs."

The following machines are special varieties of SMP machines that have made a leap from small-scale parallel processing to large-scale parallel processing.

NUMA machines

Non-Uniform Memory Access machines are very much like UMA machines in that every processor has unrestricted access to memory; however, unlike UMA machines, not all parts of the NUMA memory system have the same performance profile. Usually this is because NUMA machines have local fast memory on a per-CPU basis, and then a large, slower shared memory system.

---

* The common nomenclature of computer science is to call a computer of a particular type an "*x* machine" where *x* is a particular style of computer. For example, a Symmetric Multiprocessor is called an "SMP machine." Occasionally I will use the architecture's full name, and occasionally I will use the former designations for the sake of brevity as I discuss these various kinds of parallel computers.

UMA machines

Uniform Memory Access machines are those machines where each processor has equal priority access to the main memory of the machine without arbitration from a master processor. This is usually accomplished by means of a crossbar switch.

SIMD machines

Single Instruction Multiple Data machines are unique. They are a class of machine that contains many processors (usually hundreds or thousands) where the same program, down to the instruction, is executed on each of the processors. Each processor is working on a unique piece of data. SIMD machines usually require very specialized memory and bus architecture in order to be effective. One of the most famous SIMD machines was the "Connection Machine" made by Thinking Machines Corp.

MIMD machines

Last, but not least, are Multiple Instruction Multiple Data machines. As the name implies, these machines operate with multiple instruction streams and multiple data streams. In essence, parallel computers of this type are individual machines that by some mechanism, usually some set of software libraries, cooperate to solve a computational problem.

Linux clusters are, by definition, MIMD machines.

Networking Concepts

Linux clusters are simply collections of computers that are connected to networks that take advantage of special software systems to agglomerate the power of individual machines to create computing capabilities like those of traditional supercomputers. Networking systems allow computers to be connected together in systems that allow individual participants to communicate either individually computer to computer, or in large groups where one computer broadcasts some piece of information to others. In order to build these systems, a basic understanding of how networking systems are constructed is necessary.

Networking technologies consist of four basic components and concepts:

Network protocols

Protocols are a set of standards that describe a common information format that computers use when communicating across a network. A network protocol is analogous to the way information is sent from one place to another via the postal system. A network protocol specifies how information must be packaged and how it is labelled in order to be delivered from one computer to another, in much the same way that a letter is put into an envelope and then addressed with a destination address and a return address for delivery by the postal service.

Network interfaces

The network interface is a hardware device that takes the information packaged by a network protocol and puts it into a format that can be transmitted over some physical medium like Ethernet, a fiber-optical cable, or even through the air using radio waves.

Transmission medium

The transmission medium is the mechanism through which the information bundled together by the networking protocol and transmitted by the network interface is delivered from one computer to another. This can be something as simple as a twisted pair of wires (as in the ubiquitous 10BaseT networking standard) or as esoteric as a wireless network system that uses radio waves to move data from place to place. For physical media such as wires and fiber-optical cables, the data received from and sent to network interfaces is in the form of on and off pulses that are either volutes on a wire, or pulses of light. For radio-based networks, the ones and zeros are translated into modulated radiowaves on a given set of frequencies.

Bandwidth

Bandwidth is the amount of information that can be transmitted over a given transmission medium over a given amount of time. It is usually expressed in some form of "bits per second." Depending upon what medium is being used, bandwidth can range from hundreds of bits per second, which is agonizingly slow (fortunately, this is a rarity these days), to trillions of bits per second. Most networks in use in the late 1990s are from 10 to 100 Mbits/second for home and office networks to many gigabits per second for long-haul commercial voice and data networks.

For the sake of simplicity, we will stick to the most commonly used kind of networking system, Ethernet. Ethernet is a network technology that was developed at Stanford University in the 1970s that uses a very simple strategy to deliver information from one computer to another. Ethernet specifies a set of message formats (called *packets*) for information that is transmitted over the network that starts out with some address information, the data that is to be sent, and then some trailing information that can be used to determine if the packet has been damaged in transit. The most common available bandwidths for Ethernet networks are 10Mbits/second and 100 Mbits/second.

A Simple Network

A good way to explore the networking components actually at work is to look at the simplest cluster you can make, which is simply a network with some machines connected to it, such as the four-node network shown in Figure 2-3.

Each computer that participates in the network has a network interface, usually some kind of an expansion card designed for that system that supports a particular network medium.

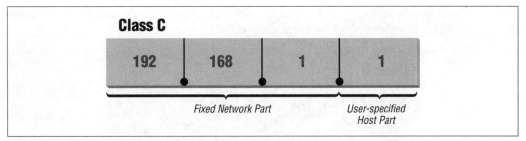

Figure 2-3. A simple four-node network

The computers all talk to a central object called a hub. The hub is a device that allows each of the computers on the network to communicate with one another without actually being physically connected—the hub acts as a relay point for pieces of information being sent over the network. Hubs are a convenient mechanism for creating networks because they minimize the number of cables that have to be run between systems and because they are easy to configure and install.

Another way to allow computers to talk to each other includes making point-to-point connections between the machines. This will be used in several of the network topologies that will be described in the next section.

Lastly, the computers are connected to the hub by way of simple twisted pairs of wires that resemble telephone cords, which make these kinds of networks very easy to build and configure.

Network Configurations

There are a number of different kinds of basic network configurations, each used for a different size of network, or to achieve a different level of network performance.

Bus networks

A bus network is a network in which each node has one connection to a common, shared network resource via some piece of interconnecting hardware like an Ethernet hub, as shown in Figure 2-4. Each node generally can consume as much of the network as it wants, except when it runs up against another node attempting the same. In other words, each node on a bus network generally competes for the shared resources of the single network cable.

Switches

Switched networks are very similar to bus networks, except that instead of a hub that allows unmoderated communications between any and all hosts, the interconnection mechanism is a device that lets each connected device see an entire network worth of bandwidth. This device is called a network switch. Network switches are specialized forms of routers where the switch isolates each connected device and sends packets directly between hosts that wish to communicate.

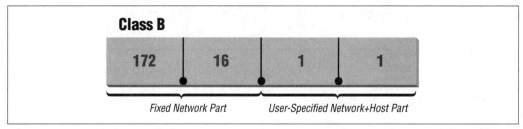

Figure 2-4. Simple bus topology

Cubes

Cubes of various degrees are also very common topologies for networks that need specialized communications, and for parallel Linux clusters. The "degree" of a cube represents the number of intervening nodes between any two endpoints. Hypercube clusters can be as simple as four nodes that are interconnected, as in Figure 2-5.

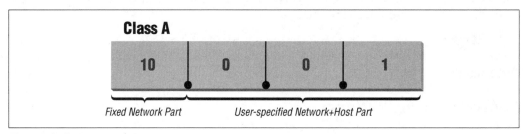

Figure 2-5. A two-cube

Figure 2-6 represents a three-cube. In a three-cube, there are eight processors. In such a cube, any processor can talk to any other with a maximum of three hops though intervening nodes.

Cubes of deeper dimensions can be created by connecting lower-order cubes into higher-order cubes; in effect, putting a cube inside a cube.

Meshes

Lastly, there are various forms of meshes. A mesh is a network topology where nodes are arranged on a grid, as in Figure 2-7. Grids should look familiar if you've ever taken high-school algebra; they're simply Cartesian planes with nodes along the vertical or y-axis, and along the horizontal or x-axis.

A mesh can be constructed out of combinations of the previous two kinds of networks described, hubs and switches.

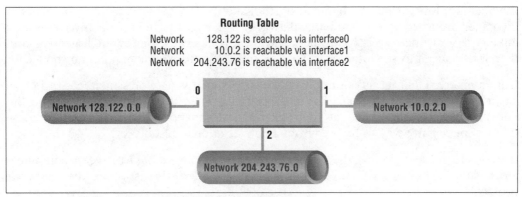

Figure 2-6. A first-degree hypercube

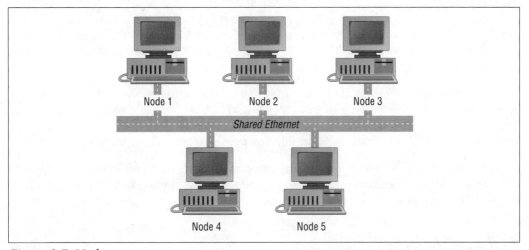

Figure 2-7. Meshes

The degree of connectivity between any two nodes can be described by the number of nodes between them. Interestingly, if you fold a mesh, you can change its connectivity and make what are, effectively, shortcuts or "worm-holes" that can move traffic between nodes across the mesh (and across a fold or curve) more quickly than routing the packet over the direct or Cartesian path.

Ethernet Communications

Ethernet is much like a room where a large number of people are talking, if everyone tries to talk at once, bits of conversation will be lost. In order for complete conversations to happen, people have to 1) listen before they speak and 2) back off and try again if they verbally collide with someone else who is speaking.

Ethernet employs a similar scheme to try to make its data conversations work. When a computer wants to transmit on the network, it listens first to see if anyone else is talking. If someone else is using the network, it backs off for a few milliseconds, and then listens again to see if the coast is clear and if its information can be transmitted.

Unfortunately, Ethernet as a protocol that is spoken by network interfaces is not as smart as human conversationalists. It doesn't guarantee that any packets put on the network will actually arrive at their intended destination. This low-level protocol doesn't specify any way to recover from a conversational misque.

In order to make sure that the conversations (data connections) between computers are reliable, a higher-level of communication is needed; this is where the "network protocol" comes in.

TCP/IP Networking

The networking protocol that is used in the design of Linux clusters is the Transmission Control Protocol/Internet Protocol, or TCP/IP. This is the same suite of network protocols used to operate the Internet.

TCP/IP is the *lingua franca* of the Internet. It is a communications protocol specification designed by a committee of people who, although they all worked for different organizations, sometimes with directly competing interests, were able to craft a set of standards whose effectiveness was proven by a set of examples of working software.*

It is an open standard, which means anyone can implement it and every implementation of TCP/IP can speak to every other regardless of who implemented it, as long as the TCP/IP implementor didn't deviate from the standard.

TCP/IP Addressing

An IP address consists of four numbers separated by periods. Each piece of the address represents eight bits. This allows 255 values for each of the four address components for a total of over four billion network address combinations.

These addresses are often called "dotted quad addresses" by old-timers. A typical IP address looks like this: 204.143.76.2. This is a convenient human-readable way of representing the 32-bit number that is used by computers in handling these addresses.

---

* In fact, because there were often so many competing interests involved in the creation of the Internet standards, the slogan of the main standards group for the Internet, the Internet Engineering Task Force (IETF), became "We reject: kings, religion, and presidents. We accept: working code." The result was standards that worked wherever implementors had the good sense to adhere to the IETF standard and resist introducing proprietary (read: incompatible) extensions.

Where Do IP Addresses Come From?

Internet addresses are not just "made up," they're allocated by a special group of Internet engineers who keep track of who has been assigned what numbers. This group is called the Internet Assigned Numbers Authority, or IANA. The reason that the addresses are assigned to individuals, network carriers, and corporations is to ensure that all Internet addresses are unique. If Company A connects to the Internet using address "1.2.3.4" and Company B does the same using the same IP address, neither of them is going to have a very good day. This is because Internet addresses are used to construct a kind of road map (called a routing table) of who's who, and more importantly who's *where* on the Internet. This road map is used by the Internet routers to deliver packets from one place to another. If an address shows up in two different places at the same time, it's impossible to know which is the "right" one, and so information would be lost by both Company A and Company B.

The designers of IP realized that networks that used their protocol might come in all different sizes. They split up the address space into several hierarchies of networks, called Class A, Class B, and Class C. Each represents sizes of networks ranging from really huge (millions of machines) all the way down to small office-sized networks of 255 machines and fewer.

Imagine organizing your mailing address in this fashion. It would look something like:

State.City.Street.House

Dotted quad notation can be read in this "largest to smallest" fashion, where the first byte indicates the largest area of the network, the second byte gets closer to the final destination, and so on. In fact, each number in the quad represents an address class.

Let's look at Class C type networks first.

Class C network numbers are addresses where all but the last eight bits are pre-specified. As in Figure 2-8, if you were given a network address that started out "192.168.1," you would be able to specify anything you wanted for the last eight bits of the address. An eight-bit number can be anything in the range of 1 through 254—the first address (0) and the last (255) are reserved address numbers. Class C addresses are very much like the address of an individual house on a street, such as 123 Main Street

Class C network addresses are identifiable by looking at the first byte of the IP address. If the first number is between 192 and 223 then you're looking at a Class C type address. The next two bytes are specified as the network numbers by IANA, and the third byte is, as specified above, available for whatever devices the user wants to address. In essence, a Class C allows you to address a Local Area Network of up to 255 machines.

Class B networks are the most common kind of network addresses given to very large organizations. For example, most universities and corporations have Class B network

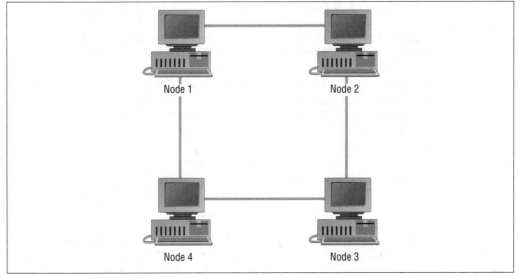

Figure 2-8. Class C network addressing

addresses. This class of network address allows you to make a network of networks, as shown in Figure 2-9. For example, you could have machines on the network numbered "172.16.1.*x*" and "172.16.2.*x*" where "*x*" is a workstation address.

Technically, these sub-networks of a larger network are called *subnets*. If we look at this simply, it is possible to view 172.16.1 and 172.16.2 as two different Class C networks, each of which can have up to 255 machines connected to them. Both 172.16.1 and 172.16.2 are subnets of the Class B network "172.16."

Class B addresses are like the street address of an office building, where the first two bytes specify the office building, the third byte specifies the floor, and the last byte specifies the mail-stop of a given individual.

Starting to get the picture? What a Class B network buys you is the ability to have 255 networks, each with up to 255 hosts on each of the networks. This comes in very handy when you are trying to network a campus or a large number of departments or even a company with offices in a number of cities.

Class B network addresses may also be identified by looking at the first byte of the IP address. If the first number is between 128 and 191 then you're looking at a Class B type address. The second byte is also assigned by IANA.

Finally there is the Class A network address type, pictured in Figure 2-10. The Class A address expands on the capabilities of the Class B networks by adding 255 more possible networks. So, a Class A network is a network that can have 255 networks of 255 networks of 255 hosts per network. This comes out to about 16.7 million possible addresses available to assign to individual hosts.

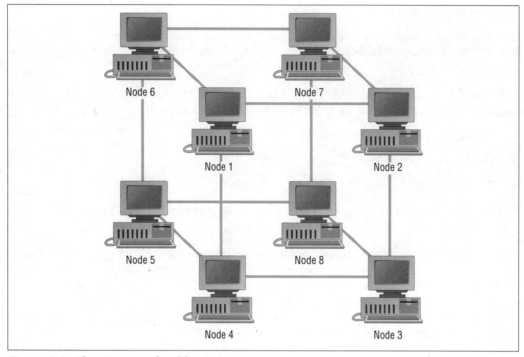

Figure 2-9. Class B network addressing

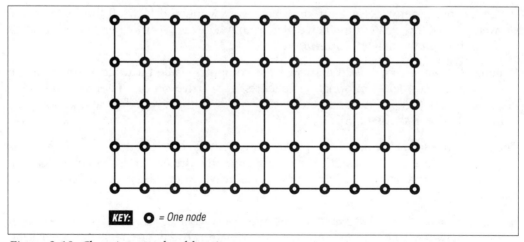

Figure 2-10. Class A network addressing

A Class A network number can be identified by its first byte; if it's between 1 and 127, then you're looking at a Class A address. The remaining three bytes are assigned by the user. This address class is very much like an inverted country-level postal address that specifies the state (the first byte), the city (the second byte), the street (the third byte), and the house address (the last byte).

The private networks

Some network numbers need to be absent from the publicly accessible Internet, so that anyone could use these numbers on a private network without the risk of conflicting with another group or organization.

IANA and its peer body, the Internet Engineering Task Force (IETF), set aside several large blocks of network numbers for such networks, specifically:

- The Class A Network: 10.0.0.0

- The Class B Networks: 172.16.0.0–172.31.0.0

- The Class C networks: 192.168.0.0–192.168.255.0

The zeros at the end of the addresses are a nomenclature that indicate the entire network. For example, 192.124.49.0 represents the Class C network 192.124.49.

Networking is at the very heart of parallel Linux clusters. At a minimum, you will need to be able to address machines on a simple Network of Workstations (a "NoW") which looks like a local area network of machines. Advanced cluster configurations will include dozens of addresses configured in complex ways that create multiple private networks across which the data processed by your cluster will travel. These IP basics will also help you with the next topic, routing.

Routing

If you are not a networking guru, and have ever wondered how all the bits you see on web sites or the email you receive gets from wherever *it* is to wherever *you* are, it's all done through the magic of *routing*.

Routing is a process by which a specialized computer (called a router) with multiple network interfaces, takes information (packets) that arrive on one interface and delivers them to another interface, given a set of rules about how information should be delivered between the networks.

The set of rules that defines how packets are delivered is called a *routing table*. As shown in Figure 2-11, it is simply a mapping table that the routing program looks at to determine where it should deliver packets that arrive from the networks to which it's connected.

In the old days of the ARPAnet, routers were just general purpose computers with multiple network connections and special software. Today, routers are specialized computers that run operating systems optimized to the task of routing packets.

Routing on networks usually is done in conjunction with routers. However, for use with clusters, we can use the network interface cards on our machines and some code in the Linux kernel to help us perform the routing function.

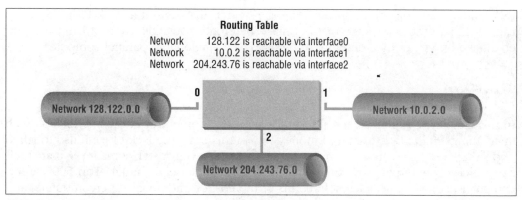

Routing Table

Network   128.122 is reachable via interface0
Network   10.0.2 is reachable via interface1
Network   204.243.76 is reachable via interface2

Figure 2-11. Routing

Depending upon the configuration you choose for your cluster, you will add multiple network interfaces to your cluster and make use of various routing mechanisms to allow the nodes of your cluster to communicate over that cluster topology. A number of these topologies will be discussed in Chapter 3, *Designing Clusters.*

Parallel Programming Systems

Lastly, the thing that makes a collection of machines on a network into a parallel computer is software.

There are dozens of different packages that have been developed over the years, but the two that we will be focussing on in this book are MPI and PVM.

MPI

MPI is a standard specification for message-passing libraries. MPICH is a portable implementation of the full MPI specification for a wide variety of parallel computing environments, including workstation clusters and massively parallel processors (MPPs).

MPI is the basis of much of the clustering work being done today. It's the result of an industry consortium comprised of computer hardware vendors, software vendors, and users of parallel systems.

MPI is installed by default on clusters built with the CD-ROM that accompanies this book.

PVM

PVM is another package that is installed by default on clusters built with the CD-ROM that accompanies this book.

PVM is the result of parallel programming research that started at Oak Ridge National Labs. It is a software package that permits a heterogeneous collection of Unix computers hooked together by a network to be used as a single large parallel computer.

Review

In this chapter, I explained the reason for the development of clusters, which as with many things in life boils down to money (or, in this case, the lack of it). I also touched upon the idea that clusters can be very powerful, even faster sometimes than their commercial counterparts (based on the rankings in the semi-annual "Top 500" supercomputer list). But clusters cost fractions of the cost of traditional supercomputers, and they can be made out of almost anything.

We explored the fact that clusters are so cost effective because they are really just computers that are networked in special ways. They run special software that allows them to solve problems that have been broken down into easy to compute chunks that run on the different nodes in the cluster.

This breaking down of large problems into smaller problems is also the basis of parallelism, which can be explored at levels ranging from the inter-system level (CPUs, disk channels, etc.), to the software level (data/control dependencies, granularity of execution, and program optimization), and up through the level of multiple systems connected by means of networks. At each level of parallelism, there are bits of performance that can be squeezed out that will make your programs run more effectively.

Finally, I covered the various kinds of hardware parallel processing schemes that you are likely to hear about, and introduced a number of networking basics such as IP addressing and various routing topologies that you will be seeing a lot more of in the coming chapters.

The next step will be to take all of the concepts and tools we have discussed here and see how to apply them to the design of an actual cluster.

CHAPTER THREE

DESIGNING CLUSTERS

This chapter deals with cluster design. We will explore what kinds of hardware choices are available to the cluster developer and discuss the hardware requirements for building a cluster system. This chapter covers all of the major hardware architectures (SPARC, Intel, and Alpha) with regard to how they could fit into either a homogeneous or heterogeneous cluster; it will also help you select a networking system to allow all parts of the cluster to communicate. Also covered in this chapter will be network architectures for clustered computing such as meshes, busses, cubes, and hypercubes. We'll talk about how these different configurations can be used to address various kinds of computing problems and how different configurations can also be used to speed the access to the data your problems will be working on.

Design Considerations

Before attempting to build a cluster of any kind, think about the type of problems you are trying to solve. Different kinds of applications will actually run at different levels of performance on different kinds of clusters.

Beyond the brute force characteristics of memory speed, I/O bandwidth, disk seek/latency time, and bus speed on the individual nodes of your cluster (which are all important, as we'll see in a bit), the way you connect your cluster together can have a great impact on its efficiency.

For example, if you want to use a cluster to speed up the rendering of computer generated imagery (CGI), a simple Network of Workstations (a "NoW") will generally suffice. This is because rendering is usually done by splitting up parts of a frame into smaller units, then giving each unit to a node on the cluster to process and then, finally, merging the image back together when the frame is complete. There is usually no reason for any one node in a cluster to have to talk to another—none of the subparts of the picture is dependent on another. This kind of problem is simply solved with a computational form of divide and conquer.

On the other hand, if your application is something like weather modelling, it's a whole different world. With weather, every interaction of a weather phenomenon affects every nearby phenomenon, and so on, ad infinitum. Now, even with the largest cluster or most advanced supercomputer, it's impossible to simulate weather accurately down to the smallest detail in any reasonable time. But even for small-scale weather prediction, the number of interactions is immense.

In this case, a simple NoW will work, but it is terribly inefficient since communication among processors and elements of the simulation is limited to the single network connection each node has. A more efficient system would allow different processors, as well as the simulation processes themselves, to interact by sending messages between "adjacent" parts of the simulation over some sort of network mesh, where each cluster compute node has *multiple* connections into the network.

There are also other uses for clusters that have less to do with supercomputing in the classical sense of a big fast machine running monstrous simulations. These are more about taking advantage of the power of distributed computing to provide services like very high-bandwidth file service (for example, to force feed data to another parallel Linux cluster running a monstrous simulation) or even a high-availability web server that can handle one million hits per minute.

We'll cover all of these varied uses for parallel Linux clusters after we look a little deeper into the hardware and connectivity you might use to build one.

Cluster Styles

Just as there are many kinds of computers for different applications, there are also many kinds of clusters that may be used for different applications. The original Beowulf cluster designed at NASA was, in essence, a simple network of workstations connected by an Ethernet cable via a hub. Since that first cluster, many cluster builders have experimented with a variety of configurations and have built a number of different kinds of clusters, each with different applications in mind.

One of the first things you should think about when designing your cluster is whether yours will be a homogeneous or a heterogeneous cluster. Simply put, this means that you have to decide if you are going to be working with hardware that's all of the same type or if you are going to acquire a variety of hardware resources. These may come from what's available in your environment or what you can acquire inexpensively from used or other aftermarket sources, which usually means an interesting mix of various makes and models of machines.

Homogeneous clusters

If you have a lot of identical systems or a boat-load of money at your disposal, you will be building a homogeneous cluster. This means that you will be putting together a cluster in which every single node is exactly the same, from the motherboard and the memory, to the disk drives and the network controller cards.

Homogeneous clusters are very easy to work with because no matter what way you decide to tie them together, all of your nodes are interchangeable, and you can be sure that all of your software will work the same way on all of them.

Heterogeneous clusters

Heterogeneous clusters come in two general forms. The first, and most common, are heterogeneous clusters made from different kinds of computers. For example, a few Sun SPARCstation IPXs, a few Intel 486 machines, and a DEC Alpha. It doesn't matter what the actual hardware is, except that there are different makes and models. A cluster made from such machines will have several very important details that you will have to keep in mind that will affect your cluster use and programming. The most important issues are:

Cluster networking
> If you are mixing hardware that have different networking technologies (such as 10Mbit/second Ethernet and 100Mbit/second Ethernet), there will be large differences in the speed with which data will be accessed and how individual nodes can communicate. Older machines may have built-in network adapters and may not be upgradable or even work with newer NIC cards. This is a common problem on old Sun equipment such as the IPC and the IPX where newer, faster network cards are not compatible with the older version of Sun's SBUS interfaces. It can apply to all sorts of systems that pre-date whatever fast, new networking cards you might like to use.
>
> If it is within your budget, you should make sure that all of machines you want to include in your cluster have similar networking capabilities, and if at all possible, have network adapters from the same manufacturer.

Clustering software
> You will have to build versions of clustering software for each kind of system you include in your cluster. Since the software I'll be describing in this book will run on any current Linux box, building the clustering software itself will not represent a problem, but keeping all of that software up to date and in sync can be quite an administrative hassle. You will also have to build copies of *your application* for each system in your cluster. I'll offer some guidelines and strategies on how to handle these aspects of heterogeneous clusters in Chapter 6, *Managing Clusters*.

Programming
> Your code will have to be written to support the lowest common denominator for data types supported by the least powerful node in your cluster. With mixed machines, the more powerful machines will have attributes that cannot be attained on the least powerful machines. For example, in the collection of machines that I specified above, the DEC Alpha machine is a 64-bit machine. All of its data types

default to be 64-bit (for integers) and even larger for most of its floating-point operations. The Sun IPXs on the other hand are 32-bit machines for all of their data types, and lastly the Intel 486s are 16-bit machines with some 32-bit operations. This is a kind of problem that can also lower the accuracy of whatever it is you are using your cluster for, if you are going to be computing numbers that require extreme levels of floating-point accuracy. There are ways around this with libraries that normalize data representations, but for the purpose of cluster building, they are probably more trouble than they're worth since they often add significant overhead to your programs.

Timing

This is perhaps the most problematic aspect of a heterogeneous cluster. Since these machines have different performance profiles, your code will execute at different rates on the different kinds of nodes. This can cause serious bottlenecks if a process on one node is waiting for results of a calculation on a slower node.

The second common kind of heterogeneous cluster is made from different machines in the same architectural family: for example, a collection of Intel boxes where the machines are of different generations (e.g., a mixture of 486s and Pentiums and PentiumIIs) or machines of the same generation from different manufacturers (e.g., Compaqs and Dells). This kind of machine mixture doesn't present that same radical problem of software versioning, but it can present some issues with regard to driver versions, or little quirks that are exhibited by different pieces of hardware. For example, if all of these machines have different network interface cards (NICs), you may find that those machines with cards from manufacturer "A" perform better than those from manufacturer "B," or that there are differences in the performance of the on-board SCSI chips on different motherboards, and so on.

These are just some of the issues with heterogeneous clusters. However, all is not lost if this is the kind of hardware you have at your disposal, and in fact these are just considerations and issues to be aware of and not show-stopping problems at all. Some of the most interesting cluster work is being done with collections of old "castaway" machines that cover the range from 386 machines to high-end UltraSPARC workstations—one of the coolest things about clusters is that you *can* make them out of almost anything!

Hardware for Clusters

When considering what hardware to use for your cluster, there are three fundamental questions that you'll want to answer before you start:

1. Do I want to use existing hardware?

2. Do I want to build all my hardware from components?

3. Do I want to use commercial off-the-shelf components?

You can build a cluster out of almost any kind of hardware. The factors that will probably play into your decision are a trade-off between time (i.e., convenience) and money.

If you are going to recycle older or unused machines into your cluster, you probably already have almost all the components you need to start building, and can skip over the next sections.

If you are going to use new systems, whether built from components or complete systems from a vendor or integrator, you'll probably want to look at some of the hardware descriptions below, as they will help you make some informed choices about which systems to include in your cluster designs.

Common Systems Used in Linux Clusters

Linux can and does run on almost every imaginable architecture and hardware platform. Even though the first Beowulf cluster was designed to run on the Intel x86 platform, people have built clusters out of a number of other architectures.

Unless otherwise specified, the design strategies in this book focus on Intel-based hardware, not because it is the best for every application, but because it is ubiquitous and it is easy for aspiring Linux cluster developers to get their hands on Intel boxes quickly and, often, very inexpensively.

It is possible to build clusters out of almost any kind of system, so I will discuss some of the most common non-Intel systems, what their general characteristics are, what to avoid, and where to get your hands on them.

SPARC-based systems

Sun Microsystem's SPARC architecture is almost ubiquitous. Most banks, brokerages, and technology-oriented firms use Sun systems in many areas of their organizations for everything from online trader workstations to CAD systems. Sun has also, in the late 1990s, moderated their prices in order to better compete with the increasing performance of Intel-based servers and workstations, so they are not completely out of reach of many budgets.

The SPARC architecture has been around since the mid-1980s. It was introduced as a replacement for Sun's Motorola-based 68000 family of VMEbus machines. With the SPARC architecture came a new peripheral interconnect system called SBUS which allowed Sun to make self-configuring peripherals that took up less space than their older VMEbus predecessors. Since its introduction, Sun has released a number of versions of the processors, at each stage gaining an order of magnitude in performance. The latest processors, the UltraSPARC series, come in a range of different CPU speeds and cache sizes and are used in everything from small desktop/side machines with PCI backplanes to huge "Enterprise" class Enterprise10000 systems that can have dozens of processors and cost many hundreds of thousands of dollars.

This has all led to a very good aftermarket in these machines that is a boon to the cluster builder since many organizations are buying new systems and selling their older, no-longer state-of-the-art systems into the used systems market.

Some easy-to-get systems are the SPARCstation-2 and SPARCstation-IPX systems. I would tend to avoid these systems because, even though they can be purchased for very small amounts of money (less than $700 as of early 1999), their performance is so poor that even a slow Intel Pentium will outperform them. There is also no upgrade path that will allow you to put faster CPU cards into them. Since the name of the game in building a cluster to squeeze performance out of a whole mess of systems, these would not be a good choice.

On the other hand, Sun's later machines, such as the SPARCstation-20 family and the SPARC-5 are very good machines to use for clusters. Both families of machines are new enough that there is a plentiful supply of new, fast CPUs that will turn these machines into good performers for a relatively small investment.

Appendix A, *Resources*, lists a number of resellers of new and used Sun equipment.

Alpha/AXP-based systems

The Alpha (AXP) architecture, developed by Digital Equipment Corporation (DEC), which is now part of Compaq Computer, is the first of the 64-bit generation of computers. It was introduced with great fanfare in 1991 by Digital and was intended to be both a replacement for that company's aging VAX line of systems, as well as a next generation server product in its own right.

Alpha processors were the fastest available machines for the entire decade of the 1990s. The first machine out of the door was a 100MHz processor that could process 64 bits of data at a time, and had a very large pipeline and cache. Since it is a RISC machine, its clock speed is pretty close to its MIPS rating. At a time when the common machine on most end-user desktops was a 25MHz Intel 80486, the difference was amazing. DEC also engineered the chip to be able not only to scale multi-CPU configurations (as in symmetric multiprocessors) but also to have multiple execution units on the same chip. Later generations of Alphas would use this feature to great advantage.

Due to a series of unfortunate mis-queues, DEC had trouble marketing the machine to a wider audience than those organizations already using VAXes that were looking to retain their software investment. (OpenVMS, the Alpha version of VAX/VMS, has a binary compatibility mode that can run older VAX applications.) Unfortunately, porting software was not a trivial affair. Most programmers did not write their software with 64-bit integers in mind, and a lot of rewrites were needed. To make matters worse, DEC placed a very high premium on the machines based on the Alpha and its peripherals, which priced it out of the market for all but the most well-endowed budgets.

In an effort to compete with the industry leader in workstations, Sun Microsystems, DEC came out with a large variety of Alpha machines, ranging from something code-named the "Universal Desktop Box" on the low end, to professional engineering workstations, super high-end multi-CPU servers, and even bare motherboards that were available for sales to system integrators. DEC failed to price its hardware competitively enough soon enough, though, and Intel and Sun wound up with 80% of the workstation market. Generally the Alpha is only used in high-end applications, but it is still the top-performing mainstream chip in the industry with the low-end systems in the 500MHz range.

Since DEC produced so many different models, there are dozens of kinds of systems available to the cluster developer. Alpha processors are a sheer joy to work with in terms of the performance; they are exceptional performers in the floating-point arena.

In the new equipment market, the price of Alpha motherboards is still quite high. This is because Compaq (the new owners of the former DEC) place a high premium on their performance and don't seem to want to cannibalize their existing Intel-based markets. Pricing for the top of the line systems is a few thousand dollars (US) for a motherboard with a 667+ MHz processor. That's extremely pricey, compared to the cost of Intel-based motherboards, but you get a lot of bang for the buck.

A Word About Used Alphas

In the used market, there are processor speeds ranging from 166MHz all the way up to 500MHz for varying sums. Almost all of them would be worthy additions to any cluster, but there are a few systems that one should steer clear of.

The "Universal Desktop Box" or "UDB" is the very low-end system that can be found at online auction sites and other aftermarket computer distributors; it is #1 on the "to be avoided" list. This machine was originally designed to be an extremely inexpensive consumer-oriented PC-type machine. It features a 166MHz "21066" processor. At first glance, these machines seem like a good deal. However, when you look under the hood, you find that there is no upgrade path possible with these machines—the CPU is soldered to the PC board. This machine also has a very slow memory bus, only one slow PCI expansion slot, and a very small power supply. So, unless you want to buy new systems whenever you want to increase your cluster's performance, look at the higher-level AXP systems.

Another system to avoid (although they are pretty scarce) is the "Jensen" motherboard. This was another low-end system that will not make a very good addition to a cluster because of its slow CPU speed and ISA backplane.

Finally, the DECSystem "LX" series are often available very inexpensively, but they were designed with a slow bus and a memory system that has a large number of wait states, which really slows these systems down.

The only downside to most of the Alpha systems on the marketplace is that the older systems have only 10Mbit/second Ethernet on the motherboard, and it can be difficult to find newer NIC cards since older systems usually were based on a close, proprietary expansion bus called TurboChannel for which peripherals are no longer made.

StrongARM-based systems

This family of processors was originally developed by Advanced RISC Machines ("ARM") of Great Britain. The StrongARM is the 32-bit version of the ARM architecture and was co-developed by ARM and Digital Equipment Corporation. The "StrongARM-110" is the basis for machines such as the Apple Newton and the eMate. Other ARM chips can be found in Acorn machines, which are found mostly in the UK.

One very interesting machine that uses the StrongARM-110 is the Netwinder network computer originally made by Corel Computer, which sold the rights to the Netwinder to Hardware Canada Corp. This company is assuming development and marketing for the Netwinder, and is selling the machine under the name "Rebel computer."

The Netwinder is an amazing little box. It's not much bigger than a medium-sized hardback book, but has within it 32–64MB of memory, 4GB disk, a video card, video processor (suitable for use in video-teleconferencing), stereo sound, and two twisted-pair Ethernets—one 10Mbit/second and the other 100Mbit/second. Corel priced them at very aggressive price-points, and they rate at about 200MIPs.

In 1998 when the machine was first announced, some engineers at Corel even made a custom backplane for these machines that connected ten of them in a simple cluster that they ported the Apache web server to. They then added some custom code to Apache to allow it to track web connection states and keep HTML "cookies" in sync across the cluster of Netwinders, and made a fault-tolerant machine that could handle close to one million web hits per minute. All of this came from a cluster the size of a bread box.

Unfortunately, despite the incredible number of features to be found in the box, there is a downside: the StrongARM processor doesn't have a Floating Point Unit (FPU) so its performance numbers are relevant only for integer-based calculations. This means that although most programs will execute extremely quickly on a Netwinder (or other StrongARM-based system), floating-point programs, such as the graphics rendering or weather simulation mentioned at the start of this chapter, will perform at some fraction of the integer performance since all of the floating-point calculations are done in a software package as opposed to in hardware.

Intel-based systems

Lastly, of course, we come to the ubiquitous Intel family.

Since there are so many Intel-based systems on the market, and so many vendors of Intel-based motherboards, I'll go into the most detail about the choices available with this platform. Fortunately, the peripherals originally built for commodity Intel-based PCs (such as PCI cards) work perfectly well in most modern workstations like the newer Alpha motherboards and Sun's PCI-based machines, so a large portion of the design elements that seem at first just to be Intel-oriented are actually applicable to almost any design.

Do-it-Yourself Versus Buying Off-the-Shelf

One of the ways to build a high-performance cluster is to have control over every piece of equipment that goes into the individual nodes. This usually means building the machines yourself from components that you purchase from a component vendor. This approach is not for everyone and requires that you literally put all the pieces together and understand how systems work at a deep architectural level to make sure that all of the subsystems work together correctly.

If you are not comfortable plugging in cables, mounting disk drives, and attaching motherboards into cases, then you will probably want to buy ready-made systems that you'll connect to a network and onto which you will install your selection of cluster software.

If you choose to go the do-it-yourself route, you will want to shop around. Do not buy the first thing you see in a catalog, and especially do not take recommendations from friends (unless they're expert cluster designers) who assure you they have the "hottest box around." Their "hottest box" may run impressively with Quake, but may perform very poorly running your application code.

There are five major components of any system, clusters included:

- System-board
- CPUs
- Disk storage
- Network adapters
- Enclosure (cases)

You should do a lot of research on the different components that you want in your system, especially the system-boards since this is the component that will tie together all of the peripherals in your cluster nodes. Fortunately, all of the major name-brand manufacturers have specification data sheets (this goes for all aspects of hardware, including disks and NIC cards) on their web sites, and these are excellent starting points for surveying what kind of equipment is available.

There are also excellent online resources where cluster builders share their experiences. Cluster-related mailing lists and other online forums are listed in Appendix A. I strongly recommend monitoring as many of these lists as you have time for—some of these lists generate several dozen messages per day.

Once you have some ideas about the kind of system-board you want to use as the basis for your cluster, you will need to make sure that all of the peripherals you choose are capable of taking advantage of whatever features come with the system-board. This, of course, should be done *before* you buy any system-boards.

By looking at the manufacturers' data sheets, you can usually get all of the information you need to figure out what kind of devices will work well on a given system. For example, if a particular system-board has a built-in "UltraWide" SCSI controller, it would be a waste of resources to plug a slow SCSI-2 disk into the system. Such a disk would work perfectly well; however, it would not take advantage of the high performance that an UltraWide SCSI controller is capable of.

Another part of looking at various system-boards involves deciding how many CPUs you want your cluster nodes to support. Fortunately, most system-board manufacturers build dual- (and sometimes quad-) CPU boards at very aggressive price-points. You can start out with such system-boards as single-CPU systems, and then when your computing needs expand, add the additional CPU (or CPUs) to gain more performance.

When looking into network connectivity, you will have to decide what kind of network topology your cluster will have. This will drive your choice of networking hardware. I'll get into network topologies for clusters in a little while, but you should make sure that if there is an on-board interface on your system-board, it is based on a current networking technology (which in 1999 was 100BaseT or 100Mbit/second) and there are enough expansion slots in the system to support additional NICs.

Finally, the choice of enclosures is critical. If you are buying machines from a vendor such as Dell, Compaq, or Micron, you are pretty much stuck with whatever size case they are shipping for the computers you are buying. If you are building a small cluster of, say, 8–12 nodes, this might not be a major hassle. 8–12 PC type "tower" cases will fit onto shelves, or can even be lined up on the floor, but that's not particularly elegant, portable, or serviceable. When you build your own systems, you have a lot more latitude in how your systems are packaged.

I build all of my clusters into 19-inch rack mount cases. These are the typical huge metal boxes you see in computer rooms. They range in size from 43 inches high all the way up to 83-inch tall units. For many of the systems I build, I install the system components into something called a "2U" rack mount case. The "2U" or "two-rack unit" designation is a reference to how much vertical space the case takes up in the rack. One rack unit is 1.75 inches high, so a 2U case is 3.50 inches high. There are multi-CPU system-boards that cannot be squeezed into such tight spaces, but rack mount cases will give you a way to put a lot of power into a very small, well-stacked space. For systems that fit into 2U cases, you can get up to twenty cluster nodes into one 83-inch rack. As you can imagine, it would take up significantly more space if all twenty of those nodes were in tower-style cases lined up against a wall.

One of the other nifty things you can do with a rack mount system is to acquire a rack mounted monitor/keyboard/mouse switch. This is a device that allows you to control multiple computers with one monitor/keyboard/mouse. There are several different manufacturers of these devices, and they can manage anywhere from four systems on the low end up to 1,024 systems on the high end.

Lastly, there are displays that are built especially for rack mounting where the display is an LCD flat-panel device that is built into a tray that can retract right into the 19-inch rack. Put this together with a similarly equipped keyboard/mouse, and you can build a very compact and amazingly powerful system.

System Performance Analysis

Part of any good design is a thorough understanding of the problem(s) you are trying to solve. Of course, if your goal is to build a general-purpose Linux cluster to solve a variety of problems, it will be difficult to hone your hardware and software choices too tightly, but there are a number of factors to consider in every case. The most critical are:

Code size

If you are going to be writing code that is very complicated, meaning that there is a lot of branching to subroutines and calling of libraries to perform your calculations, you are going to be concerned most about the size of the system cache in the nodes on your cluster. For large codes, a large portion of the program time is spent on the program rather than the processing of the data. Well-engineered programs (and programmers) do their best to avoid letting a program become an end unto itself (as opposed to the work the program is supposed to be doing) and try to minimize the program logic so that the code is efficient and as small as possible. This way more of the data (as well as the critical sections of the program) can fit into the CPU cache, and the program spends the majority of its time doing productive work.

Data size

With high-performance computers, the focus is on arranging data so that it can be processed in the most efficient manner possible. If your program spends 60 percent of its execution time deciding what to do with data rather than processing it, there's a problem that needs to be fixed. In looking at the problems you wish to solve with your parallel Linux cluster, you should look carefully at the data. How big are your data sets? How can the data be aligned (grouped) so that a small program can operate on it efficiently? Does your application lend itself to decomposition?

I/O

Lastly, you need to consider I/O. How much data do you have, and where is it coming from? Can it all fit into a flat file on a hard disk? Or does it have to be extracted from a database of some kind?

These are decisions that you should explore before spending a lot of money and time on hardware. As you'll see below, sometimes that "hottest" machine might not be the best machine for your application.

CPU Speed Is Not Enough

One of the most amazing things about the computer business is how quickly things change. There's an old adage in the computer business that goes something like this: if the car business changed as quickly as computer technology, then cars would double in gas mileage every eighteen months, cost a dollar, and travel at the speed of light.

CPU speeds are always on the rise. As of this writing in late 1999, the hottest chips are 500MHz Pentium III chips that are approaching traditional RISC processors in terms of their instruction rate per clock cycle. However, sometimes just the CPU speed isn't enough.

Something to consider when coming up with specifications for your cluster is that you want a CPU that has good performance across the range of its instructions. As strange as it sounds, not all machines have the best performance across all of their models. Intel, for example, adds special instructions to several flavors of the CPUs that make them into enhanced graphics performers. They call this the "MMX" line for Multi-Media eXtentions. CPUs like the Intel Pentium MMX line have instructions that are good for graphics rendering but might not add anything to general computing ability—in other words, you will have to write code specifically for these added instructions in order to get any value out of them. Companies such as Intel often add these new instruction sets into their high-end consumer machines to give them that added little kick that makes a difference if you are playing a video game or a flight simulator but won't add a lot to your cluster. So in general, unless you plan on writing a lot of assembly language code (which I would advise against, unless you are completely unconcerned about portability) it's a good idea to steer clear of CPUs with extensions that you don't need.

Digging Up Information on Performance

An excellent source for information on the capabilities of CPUs can be obtained from manufacturer's data sheets. Most manufacturers will send you free copies of their data sheets.

Intel is nice enough to send out quarterly CD-ROMs to anyone who asks. These CD-ROMs contain the complete set of data sheets for all Intel CPUs, networks, PCI products, and graphics processors. More information on finding concrete data on systems and components can be found in Appendix A.

One of the best resources for information on exactly how a particular CPU performs is called *The Microprocessor Report*, published by Micro Design Resources. This is a computer industry publication, shown in Figure 3-1, that focusses on the design and performance issues of microprocessor design.

VOLUME 13, NUMBER 7
MAY 31, 1999

MICROPROCESSOR REPORT

THE INSIDERS' GUIDE TO MICROPROCESSOR HARDWARE

IA-64: A Parallel Instruction Set

Register Frames, x86 Mode, Instruction Set Disclosed

by Linley Gwennap

Finally allowing a full evaluation of their new instruction set, Intel and Hewlett-Packard have released a full description of IA-64's application-level architecture and instruction set. The disclosures address some previous criticisms of the architecture and provide more details concerning how IA-64 processors will execute both x86 and PA-RISC binaries.

The disclosures show a thoroughly modern instruction set with a range of multimedia instructions and prefetch capabilities. Although IA-64 includes many RISC concepts, the architects added some rather complicated and specialized instructions. Concerns remain, however, about code density and just how much of an advantage these new features will provide over a standard RISC architecture.

One criticism had been that the large register file, while effective for compute-intensive routines, would cause excessive overhead on subroutine calls, due to saving and restoring the contents of the registers. The vendors disclosed that IA-64 supports register frames that alleviate much of call/save overhead.

Register Frames Are Dynamically Sized

With IA-64's 128 integer registers plus predicates, saving and restoring the entire register file takes more than four times as long as on a standard RISC processor. To ease this problem, IA-64 implements register frames, which take advantage of the large register file to efficiently handle multiple levels of subroutine calls. Register frames are similar to the fixed-size register windows in SPARC (see MPR 12/26/90, p. 9), except that IA-64 allows software to dynamically specify the size of each frame using the ALLOC instruction.

In the example shown in Figure 1, the top-level routine has specified a register frame with 19 registers, divided as 12 for local use and 7 for parameter passing (output). In addition, the routine can use the first 32 registers, which are designated for global use. When this routine calls a subroutine, the register frame pointer is advanced by 12 (the number of

local registers) to create a new register frame. This subroutine uses ALLOC to set up 15 locals and 8 outputs. The first 7 locals overlap the outputs of the previous routine, providing input parameters to the subroutine. The subroutine also has access to the 32 global registers.

From the subroutine's viewpoint, however, the registers in its frame are numbered from 32 to 54, even though they occupy physical registers 44 to 66. Thus, the compiler doesn't have to know which registers are unused by previous routines; it simply arranges each routine within its own virtual register space. This technique simplifies situations in which a subroutine can be called from various places in a program, and it can avoid saving and restoring registers, even when a subroutine is called through a dynamic link.

Register Save Engine Spills and Fills

Even though the IA-64 register file is large, it is finite. The architecture defines a register save engine (RSE) that automatically spills registers to memory when the register file is fully allocated, creating the illusion of an infinite register file. For example, if ALLOC must create a 20-register frame starting at physical register 120, the frame will go to register 127 and then wrap back to register 32. To avoid destroying state, the contents of registers 32–43 are stored to the memory stack. The RSE can save and restore registers before they are

Continued on page 6

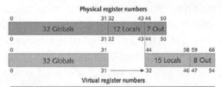

Figure 1. In this example, a top-level IA-64 routine calls a subroutine and allocates a new frame with 23 registers that overlap the output registers of the original routine. The subroutine uses virtual registers 32–54, but these are mapped to physical registers 44–66 by the hardware.

Inside: Cyrix R.I.P. ◇ Rise Roadmap ◇ IBM Gekko ◇ ARC V3 ◇ MIPS Jade ◇ SiS 630

Figure 3-1. The Microprocessor Report (cover image used by permission of Cahners Publications)

Each issue of *The Microprocessor Report* usually contains a feature article about a particular processor (such as the Intel StrongARM) or developments in a particular area of processor design (such as embedded systems). Other articles often cover how manufacturers are using a given chip in a given class of systems, and how different manufacturers are responding to the moves of their competitors. Contact information and subscription information for *The Microprocessor Report* can be found at *http://www. MDROnline.com.*

Memory Access Time

Another component worthy of strong consideration is the selection of memory for your cluster nodes. With fast CPUs, one of the limiting factors in overall performance is the memory system. CPUs can process information in the instruction cache and the pipeline at near-register speeds. This means that there is almost no difference between information being operated on in CPU registers and that which is fetched from the pipeline or stored in the CPU cache. Getting more data from outside the cache is a different story. Main memory is orders of magnitude slower than either of the previously mentioned forms of memory.

In your cluster hardware, you will want to make sure that your motherboards support the fastest memory access speeds currently available on the market. The actual memory you put into the motherboard should be matched to the system speed, and if your budget allows, you should include ECC (error-correcting) parts.

Single Versus Multi-CPU Performance

One of the hardest decisions to make is whether or not to make your nodes SMP (symmetric multi-processing) systems or just to stick to a single-CPU architecture. SMP systems are tempting. It's easy to come to the conclusion that "more is better" when it comes to the number of CPUs you have at your disposal.

Unfortunately, this isn't always the case. There are a number of different kinds of hardware designed for computers in general, and for parallel machines in particular. SMP machines, like most multi-CPU systems available today, are shared-memory multiprocessors. As with anything that is shared, someone must make the decision of how things are divided up. With all of the commodity machines that implement SMP, there is a master or primary processor, and one or more slave or secondary processors.

An SMP system starts up the primary processor (which is in a designated, logical place on the system-board), gets bootstrapped, and then initializes the second (and subsequent) processor(s). Interestingly, even though there is a second CPU, it is not automatically used. It is the job of the operating system both to schedule jobs (processes) to run on secondary CPUs and to allocate memory to them from the pool of available system memory.

This means that there is some overhead in using an SMP machine. It's not like having a whole bunch of extra processors that all work independently from one another without interference. For programs that are fairly static and don't need a lot of calls to the memory allocation system, or for those that perform a lot of I/O, SMP is a real win. You'll see an increase in terms of increasing the performance of a multi-threaded program. But if your code needs to make use of a lot of system resources after it's launched, there can be negative performance ramifications on an SMP system.

The news is not at all grim; the performance penalties for the use of SMP under Linux are nominal compared to the performance penalties under other operating systems such as WindowsNT. Since Linux is an continuously evolving operating system, its SMP performance gets better with every release.

If you are using SMP on other architecture such as the Compaq, Alpha, or the Sun UltraSPARC, performance is often better than on an Intel platform since board designers for these systems have more experience with multiprocessor environments. And there is more hardware on the system-board (and, frankly, on the CPU) to support such processing. Linux presents a single interface to the programmer, so at the end of the day, your programs will generally not know whether they are running in a uniprocessor or a multiprocessor anyway.

Backplane Interconnect

Most hardware these days have a number of the PC standards in common. For example, Compaq, Sun, and IBM all produce machines (Alphas, SPARC, and PowerPC, respectively) that sport some kind of PCI bus. Some might be standard 66MHz bus speed and others are the newer, faster, 100MHz version. But all kinds of commodity hardware such as SCSI interfaces and multiport network cards can be used on these systems under Linux.

Other systems, such as non-PCI SPARC machines, RS/6000s, and older DEC Alphas, make use of closed, proprietary backplanes for which peripherals can be hard to find, and will be much more expensive than their PCI bus counterparts.

Disk Selection

The selection of a disk subsystem on any computer is both a religious issue and a cost issue. All Intel PC-type motherboards come with an on-board IDE, or Integrated Drive Electronics interface. IDE is one of the two commonly used disk drive connection standards. The other is called SCSI, or Small Computer System Interface (often pronounced "scuzzy"). If you have been working with computers for any length of time you have probably heard of both of them. Often, SCSI interfaces are built into Intel (and other) systems by manufacturers as on-board features; on some system-boards, add-on SCSI adapters must be added in order to be able to use SCSI disk drives.

IDE and SCSI are both good interconnection schemes for connecting disk drives into systems, and depending upon your performance needs and budget, either can be used in the design of your cluster. However, SCSI has some distinct performance advantages over IDE, so I will be emphasizing it over IDE in the designs presented.

IDE disks are relatively fast and amazingly cheap. At 1999 prices, a 3.5-inch, 7200RPM 4GB IDE disk can be bought for less than $200. One of the principal drawbacks to IDE disks as a rule is the number of devices that can be supported by the average motherboard. Most motherboards have a primary and secondary IDE interface built in. Each of these interfaces can address two IDE disks, a master and a slave, for a total of four IDE disks in a single system. It is possible to add more IDE controllers, but only at the expense of interface slots that you might need for other purposes.

Another problem with IDE devices is their interrupt rate. An interrupt is a signal to a CPU that some peripheral device needs its attention. IDE devices present a very high interrupt count to the CPU. The more interrupts a CPU must service from a peripheral, the more time it is taking away from your code to deal with that device.

SCSI devices on the other hand have none of these limitations. The oldest SCSI controllers can address six devices (seven, if you include the host the controller is attached to) and newer "fast-wide" controllers can address fifteen devices per controller. One of the biggest wins in using SCSI devices is that they can perform a large number of operations (such as block moves of data) all by themselves without having to pester the CPU.

Linux supports well over fifty different kinds of boards from almost every known manufacturer.

For use in a Linux cluster, I would recommend using a board that supports a version of SCSI called "UltraWide." UltraWide SCSI is a very fast version of the SCSI protocol that allows a large number of devices to be connected to a system and supports transfer rates as high as 10Mbits/second.

The faster the interface you get, the faster data can be moved into and out of memory. This means that your programs will start up faster and that your programs will spend less time waiting for I/O to complete.

Diskless Versus "Diskfull" Configurations

Before we go any further and get into networking, it's a good idea to think about whether you want your cluster to be of the diskless variety—that is, where your compute nodes boot off of the network and have no local disk—or whether they should be "diskfull" systems—where nodes have their operating system and data stored locally. This decision will strongly influence what kind of networking system you choose for your cluster.

In the not-too-distant past, it was common practice to run large installations of computers in a diskless mode of operation. Until the early 1990s, disk drives were very expensive, on the order of several thousand dollars for less than 2GB of storage, so larger centralized machines were the norm.

Also, running large numbers of systems can be a major hassle in terms of system software updates, account administration, and backup. On workstations that have local disks, these tasks have to be attended to almost every day to ensure that no work is accidentally lost. So, to save on disk storage costs, running client workstations off of a larger, better endowed server-style machine made a lot of sense. It allowed the system administrator to build a common file system and applications directory tree for systems of the same architecture, and most importantly, it allowed user files to be stored in one central location where they could be easily backed up to tape or some other long-term storage medium.

There are downsides to diskless operation, though. Diskless systems are, by their very nature, slower performers than machines that have local disks. This is because no matter how fast the CPU is, the limiting factor on performance is how fast a program can be loaded over the network. Since all of the machine's activity is driven through the network, there are limited numbers of systems that can be run in a diskless configuration before the intensity of activity saturates the LAN and causes client workstations to slow down or even crash.

Even when systems are run in a semi-diskless state, where workstations have a local root file system (and the */usr* filesystem, applications directories, and end-user files are available via NFS) there is tremendous overhead in serving up files over the network. Diskless and semi-diskless configurations are excellent for users, where the kinds of applications that are run are word processors, spreadsheets, and low-overhead applications that will not place too much stress on the network that connects everything together.

What does this have to do with Linux clusters? Well, many of the same management issues that apply to general-purpose systems also apply to Linux clusters. If you have local disks on all your machines, you will have to be concerned about exactly what is stored on them. For example, if the users of your cluster log in to a node, put files there, and start editing then, and then the system crashes and destroys their work, they'll be pretty unhappy.

A Linux cluster is supposed to be a fundamentally different kind of machine than a general-purpose workstation. The goal here is speed and performance. Anything that stops a cluster node from operating at peak performance should be engineered *out* of your cluster. This means that you can set the ground rules of the operation of your cluster in such a way that you no longer think of it or treat it as a collection of workstations. You can ensure that user files are not put in places where they can be destroyed either by accident or by user negligence and that the compute nodes are optimized to be able to devote all their compute cycles to solving problems and not loading in programs over a shared LAN, etc.

As a general rule, I recommend that, unless resources are extremely scarce, all of the nodes in your cluster—no matter how large or small a cluster you plan on constructing—have disks installed that are large enough to hold a complete copy of the Linux operating system, the clustering software, as well as a sizable area reserved for running user jobs. In other words, all of your cluster nodes should be "*diskfull.*"

Part of the management application that we will discuss in Chapter 6, *Managing Clusters*, will help you set up the compute nodes of your cluster so that you can both manage your systems effectively and construct things so your users cannot put files onto a compute node in such a way that they could be accidentally deleted or do other things to inflict suffering upon themselves (and you).

Network Selection

Apart from the raw computer power of the nodes in your cluster, the most important choices you will make are in the area of network selection.

Since a cluster is nothing more than a network of computers, the network will be the main mechanism that enables—or limits—the communication across your cluster.

As mentioned in Chapter 2, *Basic Concepts*, there are a number of different kinds of network topologies, including buses, cubes of various degrees, and grids/meshes. These network topologies will be implemented by the use of one or more network interface cards, or NICs, installed into the head-node and compute nodes of your cluster.

Bus networks are straightforward. Each node has a single point of communication with the common communications network. A single NIC card in each node will suffice, with perhaps a second NIC in the master node. The second NIC would enable you to keep your cluster on a separate network from the master node's access point.

For anything more complicated than a simple Ethernet network, you will want to look at specialized cards called *multiport NICs* that have more than one Ethernet device per card.

Multiport NIC cards are very useful since they save valuable peripheral slot space, and on most commodity hardware there is a limited number of these slots (on Intel-based boards, there are usually 4–6 PCI card slots on the motherboard). For large clusters, you may have to have 3–4 of these multiport NICs installed to be able to fully connect the compute nodes.

Speed Selection

No matter what topology you choose for your cluster, you will want to get the fastest network that your budget allows. Fortunately, the availability of high-speed computers has also forced the development of high-speed networking systems.

For many years, from the early 1980s through the mid-1990s, there were very few choices in the network arena. You had Ethernet with a choice of thin-wire or some form of base-band cable, or you ran a token-ring network. For the most part, speed wasn't an issue: in the Ethernet world, there was 10Mbit/second, which was shared among all stations on the network, or 4Mbit/second (and later 16Mbit/second) for token-ring.

Other networking formats were available such as FDDI (Fiber Distributed Data Interface), which could move data at 100Mbit/second and was based on then-expensive fiber-optic technologies, and HPPI (the High-Performance Parallel Interface), which was based on a souped-up version of something like a parallel printer port. These options were usually prohibitively expensive, except for all of the most cash-rich budgets, and so they did not see wide acceptance outside of government labs and academic circles such as supercomputer centers.

Fortunately in the late 1980s, the development costs for specialized application specific integrated circuits (ASICs) dropped dramatically and allowed more power to be put in smaller spaces. This enabled the development of fast and really inexpensive network cards for high-speed networks, such as 100Mbit/second Ethernets.

Interestingly, the development of 100Mbit Ethernet cards also largely put to bed a long-running war between proponents of Ethernet (an open standard) and proponents of token-ring (a closed standard whose owners demanded patent royalties for every token-ring product sold in the world). Ethernet (at 10 and 100 Mbit/second) is the de-facto networking standard used in 99 percent of all local area networks. Token ring has been relegated to the status of a "legacy system" in most parts of the computer world.

Choosing what speed to run your cluster on is a matter of coming to grips with your budget versus the problems that you plan to solve with your cluster, but there are definite economies of scale to be examined with each level of performance.

10Mbit Ethernet

10Mbit Ethernet is probably the most ubiquitous form of networking available today. Thanks to the aforementioned advances in ASICs, 10Mbit cards can be bought for as little as $10 each depending upon what kind of cards you look at. Suggestions about places to look for these cards can be found in Appendix A.

If you decide to use 10Mbit networking, either because of cost or for reasons of compatibility with hardware in your cluster, you should buy the fastest card that your system can support. In this case, "fast" is related to the kind of I/O interface on the card and means that if the system-boards in your cluster support PCI connections, you should use PCI-based NICs rather than the older ISA (Industry Standard Architecture) cards. Using the state-of-the-art card, even though you are using a relatively slow Ethernet (compared to what will be discussed next) will ensure that the NIC card operates efficiently and doesn't bog the CPU down with unnecessary interrupts.

One of the drawbacks to using 10Mbit technology is the limitation on the amount of information you can carry over your cluster network. If you are planning a small cluster (say, less than 16 nodes) that is going to be a bus style network, and the total amount of communications between nodes of the cluster is going to be less than 60K/second per node (which is actually a lot of data) on a single interface, you should have no problems. If you need more bandwidth so that your nodes can communicate more, the addition of more interfaces and a technique known as "channel bonding" (covered below) can make things more efficient.

100Mbit Ethernet

100Mbit Ethernet cards are becoming more readily available. Almost every manufacturer that makes a 10Mbit board also makes a 100Mbit NIC as well. One of the nice things about these cards is that they will seamlessly interoperate with 10Mbit cards as well as 100Mbit ones. For the most part, such cards come only (for PC-style systems) in PCI format, so if any of your systems supports only the older ISA type cards, you will have to either rework your cluster or run your network in a mixed-speed configuration.

100Mbit interfaces are also often built into the motherboards of various commodity systems.

Suggestions about places to look for these cards can be found in Appendix A.

Gigabit networking

The hottest and fastest cards available are the 1000Mbit/second or gigabit network cards. Gigabit cards provide performance that was in the realm of science fiction in 1980. Unfortunately, these cards are available only from a handful of vendors, and are often, because the standards for gigabit networking are not yet finalized, incapable of interoperating. So, you will have to choose one vendor for all of your equipment to ensure that all the nodes of your cluster can communicate.

Channel bonding

One of the big features of commercial supercomputers is that they usually have a blazingly fast communications path that connects all of the CPUs and peripherals. NUMA machines make this communication possible by use of crossbar switches. Other architectures use variations on this theme to allow large amounts of data to be moved quickly around the machine.

For many years, the high cost of networking made the interconnection of workstations prohibitive. In 1993–1994, with the cost of 10Mbit Ethernet hardware declining, the original Beowulf built by Don Becker at NASA took advantage of multiple 10Mbit Ethernet cards to give their cluster a distinct advantage over a simple LAN: channel bonding.

Channel bonding is a software trick that allows multiple network connections to be tied together to increase the overall performance of the system. The Beowulf team, using the freely available source code that comes with Linux, reworked part of the networking code to allow for this networking enhancement, which "stripes" data across available network interfaces to give the effect of a wide communications channel. The result was a set of machines with an almost arbitrarily scalable network capability.

Channel bonding is a facility that may come in handy in your cluster building if you find that you have limited options in terms of the purchase of high-speed networking gear, or if you need more network capacity and don't want to dive into the still extremely expensive arena of gigabit networking. Since the price of higher-bandwidth networking has decreased so dramatically, channel bonding is not as important a capability as it once was.

The software for channel bonding is one of the tools that comes on the CD-ROM that accompanies this book.

Hubs, Routers, and Switches

The central component of every cluster is the networking hardware that ties it together. The amount of hardware you'll need depends upon the complexity of the configuration you plan on building. If you are thinking of a small-scale cluster, you can get away with a simple hub or switch. Or, if you are planning some kind of meshed system like a cube, you will need more hardware both in terms of interfaces for each of your nodes, and enough switches or hubs to make the order of connection called for in your design.

A minimal cluster configuration, such as the one used on the original Beowulf, was a simple network hub that allowed the cluster nodes to speak to each other. Since the original Beowulf was a simple network of workstations (a NoW), the only means of communication off of an individual node was via the Ethernet that all of the nodes shared. An example of this can be seen in the later section, "Cluster Configurations."

As Beowulf clusters started to get more complicated, and more channels of information-carrying capacity were added, there needed to be more complex connections between the cluster nodes. This called for the addition of routing systems to direct the traffic.

Once your cluster gets beyond a simple NoW, configuration gets complex. You're building a system that requires more attention to the infrastructure side of the cluster before you can actually use it to solve problems. For example, let's say that you want to implement a cluster in which you have four nodes in a fully meshed fashion, as shown in Figure 3-2. In order to allow each node to have essentially a dedicated channel over which to communicate, each machine would need to have three network interfaces.

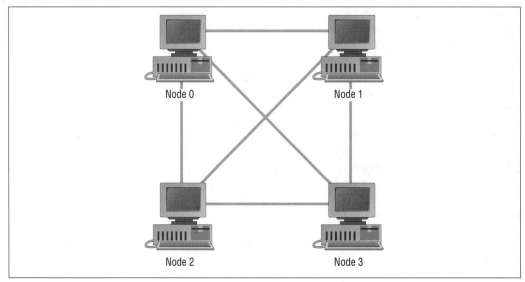

Figure 3-2. Fully meshed nodes

This presents an interesting problem in terms of how to connect the machines together. With a shared medium such as Ethernet, there is no way to allocate a private channel over something like a hub. Each node has the same access to the hub and can speak over it any time it wants. The only mediating factor is something called *collision detection*, implemented in the Ethernet hardware, that senses when two or more stations try to talk simultaneously and causes the network card in each computer to "back off" and try again.

In recent years, devices called *switching ethernet hubs,* or "Ethernet switches" for short, have come on the market that allow multiple computers to be connected to a hub-like device and that give each device the illusion that it has a whole Ethernet to itself. This is done by having a very fast routing chip in the switch. It knows exactly which device is on which port on the hub by keeping track of the hardware address and the source and destination addresses in the IP layer. With this information, the switch can route packets between devices that are actually talking to each other and not flood other objects connected to the hub with extraneous packets that are not meant for them.

This is a very effective way to allow cluster nodes to communicate, but it also costs a lot of money. There are also other ways to get the same effect.

Hub versus crossover routing configurations

If you wanted to make a cluster in which nodes could communicate over dedicated links, but you didn't want to spend a lot of money on hubs or switches, you could achieve the same effect using software. You would still need to buy enough network interface cards to build a fully connected mesh, but instead of using Ethernet switches or hubs, you would simply connect the nodes to one another using a special kind of cable called a "cross-over cable."

A cross-over cable is the network equivalent of a "null modem." This kind of cable has its data transmission and data reception wires twisted so that you can plug one end into a network card of one workstation and the other end into the network card of another. Normally, network cables are "straight-through," meaning that the wire on pin 1 at one end of the cable goes to pin 1 on the other end. The hub that the cable is connected to does the actual work of moving the packets from the transmit to receive sides of two communicating ports on the hub.

Using cross-over cables works only for making point-to-point connections between pairs of computers. For small clusters, building a cluster of machines where you want to make a set of dedicated communication paths between nodes, the cross-over cables solution is an elegant solution.

Once you get into large meshes or third or fourth degree hypercubes, the number of network interface cards and the sheer number of cables that must be connected become very difficult to manage. Larger clusters are usually built around Ethernet switches.

A Cluster Design Philosophy

I like the "do it yourself" way of doing things. I tend to build things, whether it's a piece of software, or a cluster, in such a way that it's a bit over-engineered with built-in expansion capability in case I want to push the limits of whatever system I am using.

The cluster designs presented here are, plainly, over-engineered compared to the very spartan designs that you may see written about in papers available on the Internet or in other books about clusters. Some people recommend a minimalist approach to building hardware in a cluster. I go in the opposite direction. My feeling is that hardware is pretty inexpensive, so you might as well make all of the processing elements in your cluster as highly powered as you can afford, because your computing needs will surely outpace your available resources before you even get your first application up and running.

The cluster itself should be viewed as a special, standalone entity. It should have its own networking facilities that are not shared with other systems. Trying to wedge a cluster into an existing network is a recipe for disaster—the cluster will most likely be hamstrung by the traffic on the existing network, and other machines on your network will feel the effects of network congestion from your cluster if it is doing any heavy network-oriented data crunching.

Lastly, a cluster should have head-node (which I also refer to as the "master node" at various places in this book) that serves as the central focus of the operational aspects of the cluster. The cluster also should include a high-quality graphics system so that the master node can be used as a visualization station.

The master node is where you, in the role of system administrator for this parallel supercomputer, will maintain all of the information about the cluster, and where the users of this system will log in, in order both to submit their jobs to be processed by the system, and to look at the results of their work.

The slave or compute nodes of clusters that I design have a *lot* of disk space. This is not solely so that Linux can comfortably fit on the machine; it is also so that all of the core applications that will be run on the cluster can be installed on each node. If the core applications, such as MPI and PVM, are stored on each compute node, there is no reason for extra network activity to be generated. Additionally, with large enough disks, it's possible to compile end-user programs in parallel even before they are run, which will further speed up the operation of the system as well as store large data sets that end-user programs will actually operate on.

Cluster Configurations

If you have decided what kind of hardware architecture to base your cluster on, whether you are going to go with the kit approach or work with pre-assembled systems, you should next decide how you are going to hook it all up in order to start the transmutation of your equipment from "pile of boxes" to "parallel Linux supercomputer."

There are any number of ways to connect a cluster of machines. The most simple ones are good general-purpose methodologies for making a straightforward parallel computing system; the really complicated ones are best for very complex applications that require complicated data sharing and communication strategies like weather simulation, which was mentioned previously.

The first kind of topology I will introduce is the classic network of workstations or NoW. From there, I'll spend time on more varied kinds of cluster interconnections and meshed architectures.

The Network of Workstations

A network of workstations is the most simple of cluster configurations. As shown in Figure 3-3, there is nothing to distinguish this "cluster" from a four-node local area network (LAN). And, at the level of a NoW, there is no difference except that a simple LAN is usually used by individuals and a NoW is used by clustering software, such as PVM or MPI, that allows this LAN to be used effectively as a parallel processor.

This is, of course, an extremely simplistic example. A "simple" NoW could in fact have dozens of nodes, which could make a very effective rendering farm if you were making computer generated imagery. You could even scale such a NoW up to a hundred

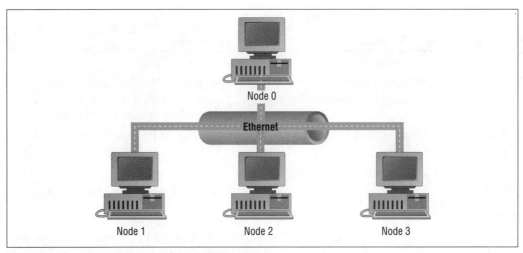

Figure 3-3. Simple network of workstations

nodes, but that would not be a good idea unless you had some really fancy networking to keep such a large LAN from getting congested.

Sample Designs

Before we look at any more designs, it might be good to put some concrete names and specifications together to see just what kind of system we're talking about.

The manufacturers and brands listed in Table 3-1 are for purposes of illustrating these examples, and are not meant to endorse any particular vendor. However, these are, in fact, some of the components I use in my own cluster designs. Bear in mind that by the time you are reading this book, these vendors most certainly will have: a) come out with newer/better/faster products, b) merged with some other company, c) gone out of business, d) any or all of the above.

Table 3-1. A Simple Network of Workstations

Quantity	Item	Description
4	Tyan S1836DLUAN	Dual CPU 440BX Motherboard, 100MHz Bus
4	256MB DIMM	256MB memory module
4	500MHz Pentium III CPUs	Central processor
4	Seagate ST39140W	9.1GB Fast-Wide SCSI Disk
4	Generic tower cases	Cases + power supplies
1	#9 Imagine 128 AGP video card	High-end graphics for head node
3	"el-cheapo" PCI video cards	Simple, cheap cards for the compute nodes

Table 3-1. A Simple Network of Workstations (continued)

Quantity	Item	Description
1	SMC 4-port 100BaseT Hub	
4	Twisted-pair cables	Cables to connect machines to the hub
1	Belkin OmniView 4-port KVM switch	Device to allow sharing of monitor and keyboard among all cluster nodes
4	PS/2 style keyboard/mouse cables	Cables for all four cluster nodes
1	PS/2 style keyboard	
1	PS/2 style mouse, 3 buttons preferred	
1	Viewsonic 15-inch LCD flat-panel monitor	Display for the head end of the cluster

Obviously, this is a very "do it yourself" little cluster. You could, if the "kit" approach is not your thing, buy similarly configured commercial systems from any of the well-known PC vendors and create a similar four-node cluster. As I write this book, this four-node cluster can be constructed for less than $6,000, a price that will surely drop very quickly as technology advances and hardware prices continue to decline.

Cubes and Hypercubes

Once you get into problems that go beyond the simple "divide and conquer" type of applications that are amenable to a simple Network of Workstations, you enter the realm of complex clusters. More complex architectures can be used to solve more complex problems that require more extensive communication capabilities.

The most common kinds of advanced clusters in use are based on some form of "hypercube." A hypercube is a geometric structure composed of one or more three-dimensional cubes, where all of the edges are connected as shown in Figure 3-4. In such a cluster, each node shares a common connection with every other node on one interface, yet has direct communication with the three adjacent nodes on three other interfaces. The particular hypercube shown here is called a "1-cube" because it is in fact just a cube. Higher-degree hypercubes are composed of successively deeper nested cubes, such as shown in Figure 3-4.

If you look carefully at Figure 3-5, you'll notice that as soon as we start adding more connected edges to a hypercube, the connection complexity increases dramatically. The "1-cube" connections were pretty straightforward; each node needs one set of common connections, and then three dedicated connections, one for each node that a given node can directly communicate with. The big advantage that is obtained by building a hypercube is the direct-path communications between adjacent nodes that is created by the use of the cross-over cables mentioned earlier.

You can make hypercubes of arbitrary degrees providing you have enough slots for multiport network cards, but maintaining all of these connections does get quite

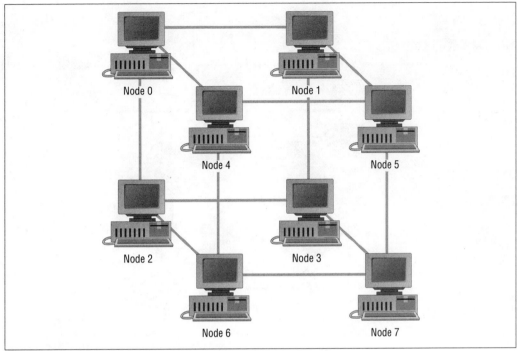

Figure 3-4. A cluster in the form of a hypercube

complicated. Furthermore, the cabling can be quite a challenge to keep in a maintain-able state unless you are meticulous in labelling everything properly. Despite all this, the biggest problem with large hypercubes is adding or removing nodes. If they are all connected together using cross-over cables, removing a machine for maintenance pretty much knocks your cluster out of action since the cross-over cables are the sole communication path between edges of the cubes. Fortunately, there is a way around this problem.

One common way to implement hypercubes is to connect all of the nodes to a com-mon, shared device, such as a hub on one interface per node. This effectively forms a NoW. To complete the picture for a 1-cube, you can connect the edge nodes using cross-over cables. This works well for small cubes, but a more robust solution would be to use an Ethernet switch. Ethernet switches, as discussed earlier, allow connected devices to have the effect of a clear channel of communication even though there may be many devices connected to the switch.

The benefit of the Ethernet switch, besides the clear communications channel, is the ease with which you can add or remove nodes either for maintenance or to add more nodes. The effect of the Ethernet switch in keeping the various interfaces apart is the same as though you had used point-to-point wiring in the form of cross-over cables.

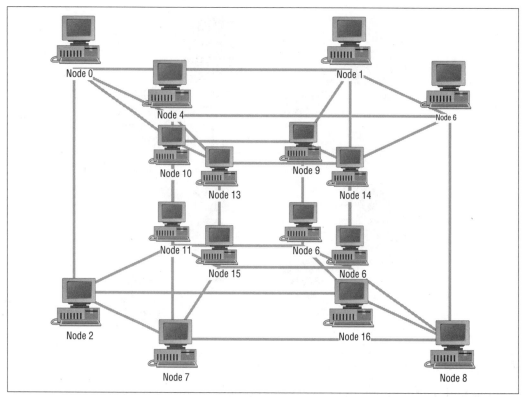

Figure 3-5. A "2-cube" hypercube

Meshed Designs

One of the most useful aspects of switched networking equipment such as Ethernet switches is that you can create a network that is fully meshed. This means that every node in the cluster can communicate with every other node directly. This may seem "obvious," but on a network where there are, for example, 16 nodes, each with four network interfaces, there is no way, without a switched network, to allow a node to have more than one interface on a given network without a complicated collection of hubs and routers. Because of the way packet routing works, most operating systems, including Linux, need to be able to differentiate network interfaces as being on unique networks.

For a 16-node cluster to be fully meshed, each interface must reside on a different network subnet. In the simplest terms, this would require four 16-port hubs and a large routing table on each cluster node to inform each node's TCP/IP stack on which network every possible interface resides.

As you can see from Figure 3-6, a fully meshed network is quite complicated.

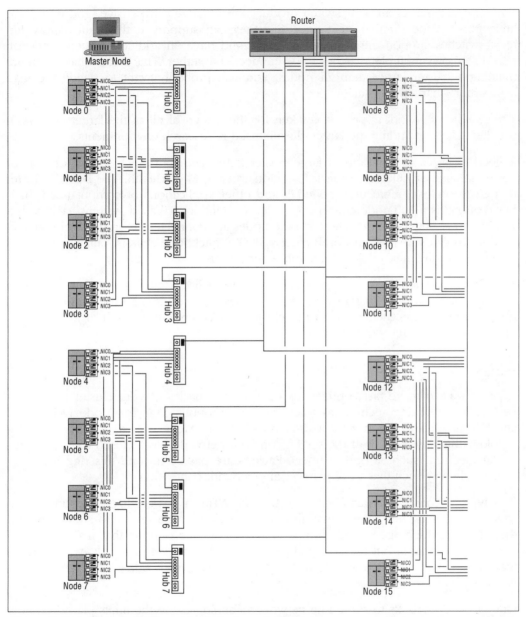

Figure 3-6. A 16-node, fully meshed cluster network

A more compact solution would involve using a switched network to achieve the same result. With a switch, all of the hubs, the routers, and three of the four network interfaces per node could be removed. As you will recall, a switch gives each connection the appearance of a clear channel of communication between nodes.

The only drawbacks are that switch products are relatively expensive, and they have limitations on the number of connections they can support at their full bandwidth. Most switches support either 16 or 24 ports, and have an additional interconnection port that allows multiple switches to be connected together. This means that if you are building a cluster larger than 24 nodes, you will probably want to divide the load across more than one switch.

The switched network approach is taken for the design of all of the larger clusters in use these days, including the larger clusters used in research environments.

A good example of this kind of large cluster is the *LoBoS2* (which stands for "lots of boxes on shelves") cluster at the U.S. National Institutes of Health. The LoBoS2 cluster is used to perform molecular modeling and other applications of computational biology. LoBoS2 is a 100-node cluster composed of Pentium II based systems each with a 1Gbit/second network card. The compute nodes are connected in groups to 1Gbit/second switch cards in a 3Com CoreBuilder 9000Gbit backbone chassis. This chassis gives the cluster a fully meshed set of network connections.

This chassis is connected to a set of ATM switches (discussed in the first section) that communicate with the cluster's four master nodes. The result is a fully connected 100-node cluster where each node in the cluster can communicate with any other arbitrary node at close to wire speed.

Rings

Another way to make fast connections between the nodes of your cluster is to use a very fast networking technology such as Asynchronous Transfer Mode (ATM) and attach your cluster together by a ring. As shown in Figure 3-7, a ring is a network topology that connects all of the stations on your network into a closed loop on a particular medium (such as optical fiber). Packets are passed around this ring in a very predictable way such that there is never any network contention.

Ring-type protocols, such as FDDI, SONET, and ATM, use specialized data-link protocols (the signaling mechanism that allows raw packets to be sent across the network) that allow for high speed and various quality of service options that make ring networks very effective. But they run TCP/IP as their higher-level protocols, which means that these networks can easily be made to interoperate with other TCP/IP-based networks such as Ethernet.

One of the drawbacks to some ring network technologies are the limits placed on how many nodes can be connected to the ring. These limits exist because, in order to provide quality of service, there are hard limits (depending upon both bandwidth and the protocol architecture) on available addresses. These limits may seem to hinder the usefulness of rings for clusters, but actually, the opposite is true. Rings such as SONET and ATM give very high performance and also give designers the ability to connect rings together, as shown in Figure 3-8, either with bridge systems or even with other rings to make larger networks that share the same performance and bandwidth characteristics.

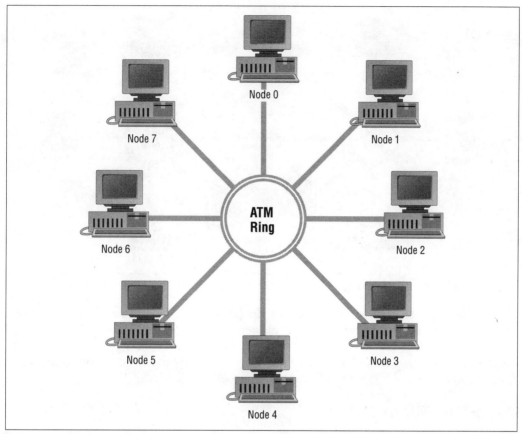

Figure 3-7. A generic ring

Front-Ended Systems

In the clusters described so far, there is no difference between any of the cluster nodes. In other words, one node is just the same as any other from the perspective of how they interact. As you'll see when we get into discussing messaging systems shortly, it is possible to let users log in to an arbitrary node and start firing up programs. One problem with building a cluster where a user can jump onto an arbitrary node is that the user's work can be lost if there is a problem with the node they've chosen to work on. And there is no central way for you, as the cluster owner/administrator, to impose order on the cluster.

A more structured approach is to add an additional node (or select one of the nodes already in the cluster) to serve as the master node of the cluster. Adding a system that is a central access point for your cluster will give you a lot of control over how the cluster is used. It also allows you to allocate resources depending on who is running jobs, and it gives you the ability to use the master node as a main repository for software installed in your cluster, which can make software maintenance easier.

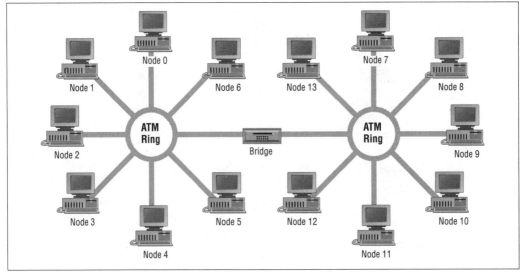

Figure 3-8. Interconnected rings

If your cluster gets large enough (more than 64 nodes), it might make sense to have multiple master nodes. Having multiple master nodes allows you to break up some of the users onto different machines (since, from their point of view, the cluster is "just" the master node that they log in to). This process can allow for better performance in terms of interactive editing, visualization, and so on.

To SMP or Not to SMP

The sample design above calls for motherboards that are capable of utilizing dual CPUs in a symmetric processing configuration. SMP systems are not required for cluster building, but using SMP-capable systems can give your cluster an even more powerful kick.

SMP systems introduce parallelism at the system level. The Linux kernel is able to distribute processes across the CPUs available in the system. Having cluster nodes that themselves are capable of parallel processing can double or triple the overall performance of your cluster.

At the time of the writing of this book, the most common SMP systems available in the Intel hardware family were dual CPU motherboards. There were also several four-way and even eight-way systems on the market, but their prices tend to be extremely high. One nice thing about Intel processors is that Intel comes out with faster CPUs every six to eight months, and the cost of the previous generation drops 12-20% with each new generation.

For other architectures, such as the Sun SPARC family, most recent-generation machines support SMP out of the box. The only exception to this are the low-end PCI-based enterprise servers; however, adding additional CPUs can be quite expensive.

For the DEC/Compaq Alpha family, choices of SMP machines are limited to their high-end workgroup servers, which are quite expensive. Adding additional CPUs will cost several times that of a similar SPARC CPU and perhaps ten times as much as an Intel CPU with similar clock speed. The benefit of the Alpha is its overall blazing performance. It will be up to you to determine if your needs justify the added expense.

Although two-way and four-way SMP machines can add a lot of power to a cluster, you should use them carefully. One of the drawbacks to using an SMP system can be the quality of the resource management that the OS supports. This functionality is called "lock management."

Lock management is a kernel-level functionality that allows resources to be shared by multiple processes but prevents a process from changing a value at the same time that another process is either accessing that resource or writing to it.

Linux is pretty good with two-way SMP resource locking but, as of the version 2.2, the kernel still has some problems with larger SMP systems. This can be a problem if the software you intend to run is very dependent upon having several processes access the same variable or array simultaneously. Linux kernel development is so fast and the interest in large-scale SMP is so high that it may be safely assumed that this will not remain an issue for very long.

If you are planning to use SMP in your cluster, be sure you have enough memory on board. For two-CPU Intel-style systems, 128MB of system memory is an absolute minimum. For SPARC processors, start at 256MB, and for the Alpha, 512MB is a good starting point. You should consider that the available system memory is divided up among the available processors, so if you have a two-CPU Intel motherboard with 128MB of main memory, each CPU will effectively have 64MB of memory to work with. If your programs use a lot of arrays or other in-core storage, you may find your application swapping to disk a lot in search of virtual memory. Any time your program is forced to swap to disk, your application will not be running at peak performance.

The bottom line is that, wherever possible, you should try to include SMP motherboards in your cluster designs. The cost differential (for Intel-type machines) compared to the single CPU equivalent motherboards is minimal. The performance boosts you can get by adding the additional CPU are potentially significant.

Recommended Configurations

The hardest part of getting started in clustered systems is putting a stake in the ground and deciding on an initial configuration to build. To help you get started, there are three basic configurations that represent three different levels, in terms of power and networking speed, that I would recommend.

Since clusters are built in a modular fashion, it is easy to start with a small cluster, in order to gain experience with these systems, and then add to it in a structured fashion to add either computation power or network bandwidth as your needs grow.

Entry-level cluster

A good cluster for experimentation is one where you have enough inherent CPU power and enough network bandwidth to attack real-work problems while retaining the ability to upgrade to a more powerful configuration without having to start building your cluster from scratch. The configuration described in Table 3-2 is very inexpensive to build.

Table 3-2. Entry-level Cluster

Quantity	Description
1	Dual CPU capable system as master node with a single 450MHz Pentium CPU
3	Dual CPU systems as compute nodes with a single 450MHz Pentium CPU
4	64MB memory modules
4	6.0GB EIDE disks
4	10Mbit/second Ethernet adapters
1	8 port 10/100Mbit Ethernet hub

The system units themselves can be purchased from most large PC vendors or through online auction houses on the Internet for less than $750 per node (as of 1999). The networking equipment and keyboard/video switch can be purchased for less than $600, and the EIDE disks and the system memory are usually included in the price of the systems when purchased from a vendor (as opposed to building the systems yourself from components).

This cluster configuration has several built-in upgrade scenarios; the first involves upgrading the network cards in the systems to bring them up to 100Mbit/second. This will give the cluster nodes almost ten times the bandwidth of the initial configuration.

A second-level upgrade would be to add a second CPU to each node in the cluster. Such an upgrade will effectively double the performance of the cluster. At the time you add the CPU, you will probably also want to double the amount of main memory, bearing in mind that as you add CPUs to an SMP system, the amount of memory available to each CPU is effectively divided evenly between all of the CPUs.

A final upgrade path for this system entails swapping out the 10/100Mbit network hub for an Ethernet switch. The addition of a switched network to this cluster will give each of the nodes a clear channel of communication so that there is no chance of network collisions getting in the way of internode communications.

Of course, it is always possible to upgrade the CPUs to higher clock speeds, which will give an additional boost to the cluster's performance.

You might notice that this design calls for the use of EIDE disks, something I asserted I would avoid. In general, I stand by my earlier statement, except in the case of an entry-level cluster where you may want to use either existing systems or entry-level equipment when you start out. Since EIDE disks are often included in package deals available from vendors, there's no reason not to take advantage of them. You can always upgrade to SCSI disks later on when you need faster disks and controllers with more expansion capability.

One node in this configuration should be designated as a master node in terms of a central place to allow users to log in and start their batch jobs, and then use the other three nodes as the primary computer systems. In order to get the most out of this configuration, it will be necessary to allow the "master" to act as a compute node as well.

A good thing about clusters is that you can use almost all of the parts from your first cluster to build your later clusters.

Mid-range cluster

The next step up from an entry-level cluster is a larger cluster, described in Table 3-3, which takes advantage of more powerful CPUs and more powerful networking to deliver greater performance.

Table 3-3. Mid-range Cluster

Quantity	Description
1	Dual CPU capable system as master node with a dual 500MHz Pentium II CPU
8	Dual CPU systems as compute nodes with a single 500MHz Pentium II CPU
8	128MB memory modules
8	Fast-Wide SCSI adapters
10	9.1 GB SCSI disks
8	100Mbit/second Ethernet adapters
1	24 port 10/100Mbit Ethernet switch
1	8 port KVM switch

The big differences between this cluster and the entry-level cluster are centered around the quantity/speed of the compute nodes and the addition of SCSI disks as opposed to the EIDE disks specified in the entry-level system.

Another difference from the previous clusters is the addition of a dedicated master node that is distinct from the compute nodes of the cluster. In the previous example, since there were just four nodes, there wasn't a big distinction between the nodes. In this cluster, the master node should be configured with the extra SCSI disks listed in the configuration. This extra disk space can be used to hold user files, production and test versions of cluster libraries, etc. If you are using the clustering software that comes with this book, you can also set up the cluster management system that will allow you to generate billing reports and handle other MIS tasks that will enable you to support a large number of users.

Logical upgrade paths for this cluster include faster CPUs, more compute nodes, and the addition of faster networking. These upgrades, especially the transition to Gigabit networking technologies, will give you a very advanced, state-of-the-art hardware platform.

Advanced clusters

The final cluster we will describe is in the domain of high-end clusters, described in Table 3-4. The main difference in this cluster is the addition of gigabit networking.

Gigabit networking is still a very new field in terms of market-tested products. The 1000Mbit specifications have just recently been ratified by the appropriate standards bodies, and fully standards-compliant systems should be available by the time this book is in print.

Table 3-4. Advanced Cluster

Quantity	Description
1	Dual CPU capable system as master node with a single 550MHz Pentium III CPU
16	Dual CPU systems as compute nodes with dual 550MHz Pentium III CPUs
17	128MB memory modules
17	Fast-Wide SCSI adapters
19	9.1 GB SCSI disks
17	1 Gbit/second Ethernet adapters
1	24 port 100/1000Mbit Ethernet switch
1	24 port KVM switch

Scalability

A number of different cluster styles have been discussed in this chapter. We've discussed simple Beowulf-style clusters that are interconnected by simple hubs, fully meshed systems that use advanced Ethernet switches to allow point-to-point communication between clusters, and even clusters built around ring-type media such as SONET or token-rings.

There is no "one true way" to build a cluster. The strength of Linux clusters is the great variety that can be applied in their design. Most cluster builders start out with a simple hub-based system and then expand their clusters as their needs change and their experience with parallel computing evolves. It is certainly even possible to combine different cluster architectures if your application requires a certain style of communication.

As you scale your clusters, you will eventually find that there are limits to what can be done with a single kind of media. For example, most high-speed 100Mbit and

1000Mbit switches are limited to 32 ports per switch. The logical way around this limit is to "go up a size" and use faster devices to make the interconnection between collections of nodes in the cluster. For example, if you need to make a 48-node cluster that needs 100Mbits of connectivity between the compute nodes, you might join two 12-node clusters each connected to 100Mbit switches and open them with a gigabit router or switch.

The only upper limits for scalability are the highest available network switching components available, the aggregate amount of traffic your cluster will generate, and the physical limitations of the speed of light with regard to the cabling between your nodes.

In regard to the master node, there is no reason that you cannot have multiple master nodes. Recall that the master node is a place where cluster users can keep their files and where they can launch jobs. If you have enough users that the master node is no longer comfortable (i.e., slow interactive response time is becoming painful), split the master node into two master nodes. The only major consideration will be ensuring that you load-balance any queuing systems so that one master doesn't monopolize the bulk of the cluster.

Data Access for Clusters

Now that we have some guidelines on what kind of systems go into a cluster, and how you might connect them together, there is one more big issue we have to deal with: data access.

There are whole classes of problems where it's possible to put the entire data set you need to work on the head-node of your cluster, launch some batch jobs, and come back after lunch to get the results.

If your data sets are small enough, all you need to be sure of is that you have enough disk space on your master node and slaves for the input data, temporary files, and output files that are generated. For larger data sets, say copies of the U.S. Census data set, Geographical Information Systems (GIS) data, or input to a data-mining system, things are more complicated. It might not be possible to keep either the input or output files on the cluster itself.

One of the hard parts of designing a parallel cluster comes into play when you are dealing with data sources outside your cluster. One of the big "wins" in a clustered environment is the ability to make a collection of machines that share a *private* network. On a private network, communication occurs in such a way that very little of the communications channel used by a machine is taken up by superfluous traffic. However, if your applications will need to access large off-cluster databases in order to have data to work on, you might have a problem if your compute nodes are competing with each other for network access in order to get to data that resides on another network.

One way to solve this problem is to give your master node an additional network interface on the network where your data resides, and have the master node take control of the data delivery problem, as shown in Figure 3-9. This entails, literally, adding another network card (or cards) to the master node. With additional network cards, this system can be connected to the network where your data sources are, and you can either write a program to parcel out data to the slave nodes, or you could use tools such as the Network File System (NFS) to allow the master node to make the file system available to the compute nodes.

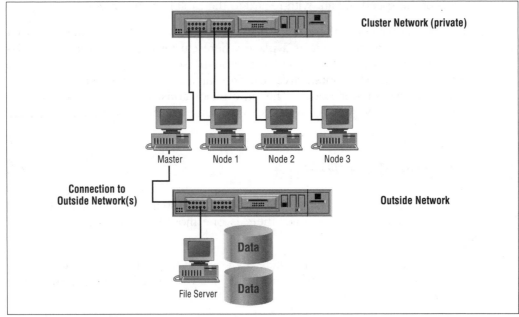

Figure 3-9. NFS data access through the master node

Another effective way to solve this problem is to add additional interfaces to the master node and all of the compute nodes, as shown in Figure 3-10. This approach will allow you to make a "data-only" network. A data-only network can be a channel over which your compute nodes access databases or other resources from which they gather their inputs, yet still have clear-channel communications over their private network for inter-node communications that are needed to solve whatever problem you are working on.

The potential drawback to this method of data access is the added expense of the additional network cards and the possible administrative issues relating to the security of your cluster.

Lastly, if you want to keep all of your data on your cluster, rather than import the data from outside, there is a software system that uses the inherent parallelism of the

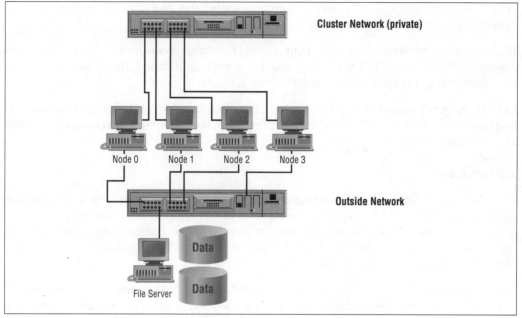

Figure 3-10. Data access via a dedicated network

cluster to make an efficient filesystem. The Parallel Virtual File System (PVFS), developed by Clemson University, is a way of using the nodes of a cluster to create a distributed RAID filesystem.

Using PVFS, you could create a large filespace that exists stripped across all of the nodes of the cluster and then allow individual compute nodes to access this filespace as though it was a coherent filesystem.

Security Considerations

The cluster system that is built from the software on the accompanying CD-ROM is configured to be an open system. No special efforts have been made to lock out access to compute notes to ensure that they cannot be accessed independently of the cluster's master node.

Security may be of concern to you if you plan on using your cluster in a commercial setting or if you have information that you wish to keep safe from prying eyes.

As with regular systems, clusters should be maintained according to good systems management practices. Keeping your cluster secure revolves around keeping the configuration of the master and slave nodes consistent, keeping the software up to date in order to ensure that as security holes are discovered they are fixed quickly, and controlling access to the services on the cluster nodes. Accounts should be secured with strong passwords, which should be changed regularly. Activities on your cluster should be monitored with system accounting tools, and you should regularly review system log files for unusual activity.[*]

If systems administration is not your forte, I would recommend *Essential System Administration*, Second Edition, by AEleen Frisch (published by O'Reilly). It's an excellent primer on how to take care of Unix systems.

One of the most common ways to secure Linux machines (and therefore your cluster) is to use tools such as *TCP wrappers*, written by Wietse Venema, a computer security specialist and researcher at IBM.

TCP wrappers

TCP wrappers allow a system administrator to control what ports on a system will allow connections and from what remote host those connections may originate. This can be as simple as setting up compute nodes to allow connections only from the master node of your cluster. Or it can be as complex as allowing only certain connections between certain ports on the destination host(s).

TCP wrappers work by modifying the */etc/inetd.conf* file that controls the activation of a large number of the daemon/server processes on Unix-type systems, including Linux. A wrapper program, called *tcpd*, is called, which then invokes the actual program for a given service.

The *tcpd* program checks a set of configuration files to determine which hosts may connect to the service that the wrapper program is protecting. All accesses, whether allowed or denied, are logged to the system log files so that they may be reviewed by the system administrator.

The TCP wrappers access control file can contain scripts to be performed under various conditions, such as an unauthorized access attempt. These scripts then try to determine the source of the attempted access.

TCP wrappers is shipped with and installed by default on most Linux distributions, including the one that comes on the CD-ROM shipped with this book.

IP chains

An alternative system security package is the *IP chains* system. IP chains is a set of filters that are installed at the network driver level of the Linux kernel. Rule tables are applied that define what kinds of traffic are accepted or rejected from a particular system.

---

[*] An excellent tool for automatically monitoring log files is *swatch,* an Open Source package written by E. Todd Atkins at Stanford University. *Swatch* is included on the CD-ROM that comes with this book, and is installed by default with the cluster software.

IP chains is a very powerful toolkit that is usually used to create firewalls on Linux. It is capable of performing some very involved network tricks involving checking of IP packet streams, proxying of connections, and network address translation.

Unless you have some extreme security concerns, or your cluster is, for some reason, going to be connected to the Internet or other public network, IP chains may be too much work to install and maintain.

IP chains is not installed as part of the clustering software's default installation, but it is included in the Linux distribution on the CD-ROM, should you decide to install it at a later point in time.

Messaging Systems

The parallel programming libraries are really the heart of what makes it possible to make high performance systems out of collections of individual Linux systems.

Parallel programming environments have evolved over years of professional and academic experimentation with parallel programming. Long before the existence of Beowulf clusters, people have been trying to pry more performance out of networks of workstations.

Until the early 1990s, systems that enabled parallel programming on networked workstations were proprietary commercial packages. They did not gain a widespread following because the user community was usually at the mercy of vendors who charged large fees for the use of their libraries, were slow to fix bugs, or did not support a wide variety of architectures.

In response to the need for a coherent set of tools that would work on a variety of architectures, a consortium of manufacturers, universities, and government labs came up with various working groups to help set standards that could be implemented by anyone and run the same way on any architecture.

The result was two systems for doing parallel programming: one focusses primarily on the use of heterogeneous systems and is called PVM or the Parallel Virtual Machine, while the other is designed to work primarily on large scale homogeneous clusters and is called MPI or the Message Passing Interface.

At the same time, outside the realm of consortia and standardization, other efforts to make parallel programming easier for networks of workstations were underway. One of the more popular systems that has emerged is the Bulk Synchronous Parallel (BSP), a computing model for parallel programming.

One of the really nice things about these libraries is that they are not mutually exclusive—you can run many of them simultaneously depending upon what kind of cluster you have chosen to build and what level of functionality you need in your applications.

PVM

The Parallel Virtual Machine was developed at Oak Ridge National Laboratory in Knoxville, Tennessee, and is a true virtual machine. It is a software system that allows users to set up a controlling workstation that spawns subprocesses on other machines. What makes PVM a unique parallel programming environment is that it allows for the creation of a truly encapsulated virtual environment for running parallel programs, and these parallel programs can be run on different hardware platforms.

The virtual environment offered by PVM looks a lot like the standard Unix programming environment: there are processes, command-line directives to access information about running processes, and so on. Each user can construct his or her own environment controlled from a single host on which subprocesses are launched on other machines via the *rhosts* access file mechanism.

PVM is not a kernel-level environment, so it can actually be run by any user who has enough resources to compile the package and who has available accounts on enough machines to make running parallel programs worth the effort.

PVM has quite a following since it has been around longer than its cousin, MPI, which is a larger system with more primitives and which runs on more platforms.

MPI

MPI, or the Message Passing Interface, is the current de facto standard for parallel programming, both on cluster systems such as parallel Linux clusters as well as on traditional supercomputers like the Cray T3E and the IBM SP2.

MPI is the result of a large consortium of interested supercomputing users representing both the parallel processing vendor community (such as IBM, SGI, and a number of compiler and tool vendors) and the parallel processing user community, which is composed of a large number of government labs, universities, and an increasing number of commercial users.

MPI is an open standard, which means that there is a published reference implementation. All of the members of the MPI consortium have the ability to take that reference implementation and optimize it for their particular hardware/software platform as long as the calling structure and API are unchanged. All manufacturers of commercial supercomputers provide an implementation of MPI with their systems. This has been a great boon to the development of parallel applications, since MPI can be used not just on a single vendor's system, but also as a bridging tool to allow multiple systems to be tied together using MPI to ensure that the integrity of the programming model is maintained.

The two most popular free implementations of MPI are "MPICH" and "LAM." Each of these is a complete version of MPI, based on the free reference implementation of the libraries.

MPICH was implemented by Argonne National Lab and Mississippi State University. It is a vanilla version of the MPI libraries and will port (and has been ported) to most flavors of Unix.

LAM stands for the "Local Area Multicomputer" project and was developed by Notre Dame University. This software is an implementation of an MPI programming environment with a twist: it contains a development system, and it is targeted at heterogeneous collections of workstations. LAM also comes with several nifty visualization tools to allow you to examine the state of the machine allocated to the cluster and to see the message flows between nodes.

The cluster software installed from the CD-ROM will install the two most popular messaging systems, PVM and MPI, by default. The MPICH and LAM versions of MPI are installed, since they are both guaranteed to work on almost any system. LAM comes with tools that make program development easier, especially for beginning parallel programmers.

These versions were chosen because they are complete and have the largest following and support in the mainstream of the parallel programming communities. Other parallel programming libraries and tools are available in the various tool directories on the CD-ROM.

As a matter of personal design taste, I try to stick to the KISS* method whenever possible, but if you find after working with your cluster for a while that there are functionalities that are not provided in either PVM or MPI, or if you want your users to have more packages to experiment with, you may want to install some of these other tools.

Queueing Systems

For a serious operating system, Unix is missing a very important capability: a decent batch processing system. Most Unix systems come with the same batch system that has been shipped with the operating system since the early 1970s. The Unix batch system is about as bare-bone as possible. It allows a user to submit a job to be run at a given time with two commands: *at* and *batch*. The *at* command allows a job to be run at a given date and time, while the *batch* command allows users to submit a batch job to a queue that has names from A to Z, where the higher the letter, the higher the runtime priority (and presumably the more CPU resources the job may use).

That's it—there are no resource controls, no way to allow for different-sized jobs, no way to pipe jobs to different machines, and no way to limit resource usage.

---

* KISS is, of course, "Keep It Simple, Stupid!" In a complex system, such as a cluster, simplicity is a good idea, with Occam's Razor being the limiting factor in any cluster design.

One of the most important features of your cluster will be the ability to set up systems by which your users can run jobs non-interactively. And, since this is a clustered environment, you will also want those non-interactive jobs to be able to be delivered to lightly loaded nodes in your cluster or even to be split up among nodes.

There are a large number of commercial load-balancing and queueing systems available for Unix systems including *Codine* from Genias Software, *LoadLever* from IBM, and *Clustor* from Active Tools. All of these allow users to have what could be considered a traditional batch system that might be found on an IBM mainframe or DEC VAX system. These are very good tools, but they can add greatly to the cost of a cluster as their cost is usually tied directly to the number of nodes you wish to run the batch system on.

Since the point of this book is to help you build a fully functional cluster, a system that can support a fully functional batch system is needed. Fortunately, Open Source software came to the rescue.

The batch system that is installed by default is the Generic Network Queueing System, or GNQS. GNQS is a branch of a package originally called COSMIC NQS, which was developed at Sterling Software under contract with NASA. It was placed in the public domain in the 1980s and has led to numerous different versions that, although derived from that same base, offer different features. Some of the offshoots of COSMIC NQS include: Monsanto NQS, the Distributed Queueing System (DQS), and CERN's NQS++.

GNQS was selected because it compiles on the reference architecture supported by the accompanying CD-ROM (i.e., Intel), as well as most current hardware from Silicon Graphics and Sun Solaris up though Crays.

As part of the software installation process, a series of queues are created—"SLOW," "MEDIUM," and "FAST"—as demonstrations of how to implement a number of queues that can handle distributed jobs of varying durations.

Parts of the cluster administration toolkit that also comes with the CD-ROM will help you set up and manage queues on your cluster.

Compilers

One of the biggest choices you will have to make will involve the compilers available on your cluster. By default, the CD-ROM that comes with this book will install the GNU C and F77 compilers. It's hard to find a better C/C++ compiler than gcc. The GNU F77 compile (g77) is another story. It is much newer than gcc. As a result, it isn't as robust, nor is there very much support for the parallel programming libraries as there is in commercial FORTRAN compilers.

For most applications, gcc and g77 will do quite nicely, but if your applications will use FORTRAN programming and FORTRAN-based parallel tools, you will probably want to invest in a commercial FORTRAN compiler. Among the most popular are:

Absoft FORTRAN
Absoft makes F77/F90 compilers that run on Intel/Linux systems as well as compilers for the Apple Macintosh and Windows systems. Absoft has been around for many years and makes a solid product; they also sell various math libraries for use with their compilers. They can be reached at *http://www.absoft.com.*

NAG
The Numerical Algorithms Group (NAG) is one of the oldest vendors of FORTRAN solutions. They have been around since the 1970s, providing libraries for high-performance computation as well as compilers. Their compilers run on a variety of platforms, and they have recently started supporting Linux. They can be reached at *http://www.nag.co.uk.*

The Portland Group
The Portland Group is a vendor of highly optimized F77/F90 compilers; they also have C/C++ compilers that are designed for use in clustered environments. They can be reached at *http://www.pgroup.com.*

Other Tools

The number of programming tools that are available right now under Linux is amazing, and growing every day. There are too many to even consider attempting to list them, but there are a few places that you should keep an eye on for tools that will be helpful in fleshing out the capabilities of your cluster:

The Parallel Tools Consortium
The Parallel Tools Consortium is a U.S. Government initiative to develop tools to aid in the development of tools for parallel programs. This includes timing libraries, parallel execution tools, and visualization tools. See *http://www.ptools.org.*

The Beowulf Underground
This is a site that tracks developments in Linux clustering, including announcements from commercial vendors and links to software, trial versions, and betas. See *http://www.beowulf-underground.org.*

Extreme Linux Web Site
This site is an offshoot of the Linux Expo that tracks the use of Linux in parallel computing. A number of interesting papers are kept here, along with links to cutting edge work on Linux clusters. See *http://www.extreme-linux.org.*

If this chapter hasn't scared you away, I have one more suggestion before I move on to the real meat of the book, which is centered around using the CD-ROM to actually build a cluster. That suggestion is: start small, you can always enhance your cluster later.

CHAPTER FOUR

BUILDING CLUSTERS

In the previous chapter, we discussed different kinds of hardware that can be used for clustered computing and covered a number of sample designs for various sizes of clusters. In this chapter, we will put the pieces together into a real cluster.

For the sake of consistency, our examples will deal with homogeneous components, but all of the principles are the same for heterogeneous cluster installations.

This chapter will cover the essentials of site planning, how to put your nodes together if you have decided to go the "do it yourself" route, and how to package your cluster into a data center ready package.

Selecting the Place

In business, it's said that the key to success is location, location, location. The same adage applies to clusters. Finding someplace to put your cluster will be half the battle of building it. Unlike a home PC, a cluster can be a very large collection of equipment. A four-node cluster made out of off-the-shelf PCs can fit comfortably on a table-top; on the other hand, a 32-node cluster can take up a 24"×24" room, and that doesn't include its air conditioning. Before you attempt to build the cluster you have designed, it would be a good idea to figure out exactly where you will put it.

The amount of space you'll need is directly proportional to the kind of cluster you're planning to build. If you are building a cluster out of commercial off-the-shelf ("COTS") systems, you will need a lot more space than if you are building your cluster from rack mount systems. Whichever shape your cluster will take, you will need to select a space that can accommodate the size of the system you are building.

Preparing the Environment

Preparing the environment that your cluster will be operating in is almost as important as the components you will use to construct it. Attention to details such as space, flooring, air conditioning, and power will help make your cluster more stable and will ensure that you can get the most out of the system's capabilities.

Space

If you are building a small cluster (2–4 nodes), you will not need a special room or much in the way of a dedicated electrical circuit for your cluster; however, you should use a circuit that is not shared with any other devices. A dedicated cooling system is not generally needed for a small cluster unless the space is already warm or tends to get warm due to sun exposure or an overly active building heating system. If you do need cooling for a small cluster, you can usually do well with the addition of one or more fans to help circulate air in the room.

If you are building any kind of large cluster, you will not only need to find an appropriate place to house all of the machines (or racks of machines), but you will also have to make sure you attend to the other important details relating to power and air conditioning.

The most important space considerations to keep in mind are:

- When you select the space for your cluster, make sure there is enough space for you to walk around the equipment. You will have to service these machines to add disk drives, replace network cards, and install cabling. Giving the machines enough space will ensure that you give yourself (or your staff) enough space to work safely.

- If your machines are too close together, there will not be adequate air-flow around the machines. This will lead to overheating; prolonged overheating can shorten the life of electronics.

- Make sure that there is adequate room for cabling and power cords and that these will not be stretched, crimped, or exposed to sharp edges that could cut into them.

- Whenever possible, install your nodes and networking equipment in racks or on shelving. Doing so will allow you to have easy access to components and places to run cables cleanly and neatly. If you plan on using rack mountable servers for your cluster, make sure that you use racks that have stabilizers. The last thing you want to happen is to have a 2000-pound rack tip over onto you if you pull out one too many nodes.

Flooring

Your floors' construction is very important from a safety and usability point of view:

- Individual computers might not seem very heavy, but ten of them can weigh as much as 500 pounds (227kg); 100 nodes could be well over two tons! Check with your building management or an architect to make sure that the flooring in your space can support the weight of the machines that make up your cluster. This is even more important if you are considering rack mounting your cluster. The weight of equipment in a rack is concentrated in a smaller space than with free-standing machines. If you are planning to put a large cluster in your house, you may need to add floor joists to support the additional weight. Regular home construction practices do not support weights in excess of 750 pounds per square foot.

- If you will be housing a large number of nodes, consider installing a raised floor like the kind found in a traditional computer data center. A raised floor will allow you to run cables under the floor rather than over it, which will reduce the chances of someone tripping over a cable (and improve the appearance of your cluster). It will also allow you to direct air from your cooling system up into the nodes, which will help them stay cool and prolong the life of the hardware.

Air Conditioning

Taking into account the need for air conditioning for a large computer facility such as a commercial data center is pretty obvious. Large data centers are designed to be controlled environments that support a large number of servers, disk farms, and other equipment that can generate a lot of heat. But, since many clusters are built from commodity hardware such as is found in desktop personal computers, many people would not immediately think that providing air conditioning is a top priority.

As you will see, even in the operation of a small Linux cluster, issues of temperature control are important for almost any size cluster, if you are to get the most out of your investment.

Small clusters

If you're building a small cluster, such as a four-node system for home use or office use where you don't have a dedicated computer room, it is possible to keep such a system cool in a regular room, providing the room is not normally excessively warm. Small air conditioners can be very helpful for rooms that are heated by sun exposure. This works well during the summer when home heating systems are usually turned off, or set to some minimum level where it would be unlikely that the heating system and the air conditioning for your cluster would be in a deadly (and expensive!) heating/cooling embrace. The cooling afforded by a regular air conditioner can be made more effective by strategic placement of fans around the room to help circulate the air.

In the winter months, when heating systems come on, it would be a good idea to turn off the heat to the room where your cluster is housed. If the room is heated, you will be forced to run your air conditioner (or open a window) to keep the systems from overheating; this can get very expensive if you find yourself heating the great outdoors.

Large clusters

If you are going to have any sizable number of nodes in your cluster, you will need to have commercial-grade air conditioning to keep everything cool. Next to water, heat is the number one enemy of electronics. The hotter things get, the shorter the lifetime of the components. Unfortunately, the effects of overheating on electronics do not happen all at once, rather it is the "death of a thousand cuts" as component after component and subsystem after subsystem slowly break down with no predictable pattern. Usually the cumulative cost of such failures far exceeds the cost of the appropriate air conditioning that could have prevented the problem in the first place.

Most computer rooms are kept between 65F and 70F (18C–21C). Make sure that the room in which you place your cluster can keep the environment at or below this temperature range. Installing your machines in racks or having good spacing between individual systems will help ensure that there are not hot spots or "heat islands" that can cause equipment to overheat.

Computing the exact heat flow in a given space for a given collection of heat inputs (i.e., computers) and the best way to cool such an environment is beyond the scope of this book.

A very rough idea about the kind of heat that can be generated by your cluster can be found by applying the following equation, using information about the power consumption of the equipment you plan on using:

Heat Generated (in BTUs) = Total Power (in Watts) $\times$ 3.412

The constant at the end of the equation is a conversion constant that approximates the number of BTUs (British Thermal Units) per watt of power.

In order to make this estimation, you will need to collect all of the power information about every device you will have in the room with your cluster. This includes information on the power consumption of:

- Each of your master/slave nodes

- Each standalone disk or tape device such as RAID boxes or tape libraries

- Each network switch, hub, and router

- Any display devices

- Lights in the room

- Power strips (surprisingly, these things generate heat)

- Any other devices (radios, coffee makers, refrigerators, dehumidifiers, etc.) in the room

This information about power consumption can be found near the power plug on most devices (even coffee makers). The power utilization information will be on a label like the one shown in Figure 4-1. For rack mounted computer cases, you may have to examine the power supply itself.

Figure 4-1. Power supply information

The example shown here has all the information we need. Some devices do not explicitly state the maximum power consumption of the device but it is very easy to calculate from the other information on the label. If you remember your high-school physics classes, you may recall that power ("P") is a result of the product of the current ("I") moving through a device and the voltage ("E") applied to that device. Mathematically, it's written:

$$P = I \times E$$

At first glance, it appears that this power supply uses 862 watts. That seems a bit high. From the label shown it would appear that this is correct given an input voltage (115 volts AC) and a maximum input current of 7.5 amperes: 115 volts×7.5 amps = 862.5 watts of power.

The difference is that AC (alternating current) power, which is the input supply, is not a constant 115 volts. Alternating current rises and falls between 50 and 60 times per second (hertz) depending on what power grid you are connected to (the U.S. uses 60 hertz while most of the rest of the world uses 50 hertz). The actual AC voltage is the *root mean of the squares* of input voltage, an effective value of the AC voltage or current that corresponds to 0.707 times the AC input voltage.

If a wattage is not given and you have to figure out power consumption on your own, look at the direct current supply output voltages. In Figure 4-1, the lines referring to "total power output mode" make things a bit clearer. If we multiply +5V DC by the 30 ampere maximum current listed, we can see that this power supply puts out an average of 150 watts of power. These are the power outputs that are actually available for use by devices connected to this power supply on average; the device in this example is actually capable of delivering 302 watts at a maximum, which allows for higher power draws when devices like disk drives are starting up.

Consider the example cluster components listed in Table 4-1.

Table 4-1. Cluster Components

Quantity	Description	Power Consumption	Total Power
33	1 master + 33 compute nodes	350 watts	11550 watts
2	24 port network switches	85 watts	170 watts
1	LCD flat panel display	35 watts	35 watts
1	Tape backup device	76 watts	76 watts
1	LCD flat panel display	35 watts	35 watts
		Total	11866 watts

In order to determine how much air conditioning would be needed to cool this cluster, we need an equation to convert electrical power consumption (measured in watts) into equivalent units of heat, which is measured in British Thermal Units (BTUs). There are many variables involved in the thermodynamics of power to heat calculations, but a working number can be obtained if we know that one watt of power is equal to approximately 3.412 BTUs. Therefore:

Heat Generated in BTUs = total power in watts × 3.412

In the case of our example cluster, this works out as follows:

Heat Generated in BTUs = 11866 watts × 3.412 BTUs/watt

We see that it generates roughly 40,487 BTUs per hour of heat that will need to be dissipated.

To give you an idea of how much cooling this represents, the largest home air-conditioners available for installation in windows max-out at around 15,000 BTUs or just 37% of the amount we have roughly calculated would be needed to cool our 33-node cluster.

Bear in mind that this example doesn't take into account all sorts of other heat generating objects that may be in the space in which you are planning to host your cluster. Other heat sources may include such seemingly innocuous items as the room lighting, heating pipes that may be running in the ceiling, walls, or floors, heat penetrating through the walls from other rooms, sunlight coming in through any windows, or even the heat carrying/transfer capacity of the walls themselves, as heat bleeds though from other rooms or even the outside environment.

Interestingly, you may need less cooling for the COTS cluster than for a rack mount cluster. This is due to the density of the components in rack mounted systems versus the amount of air that would be able to flow between the individual standalone systems. Again, it all depends on the size of your room, how much equipment there is, and how freely air can move in the room.

As you can see, cooling a cluster is a pretty complex issue to deal with. You should call on the services of a licensed HVAC* contractor to ensure that you get the best advice on your cooling needs.

Power

As you have seen from the discussion of cooling, power use quickly adds up. The 33-node cluster used in the example in Table 4-1 consumes almost 12 kilowatts of power each hour or 288 kilowatts of power per day. That's the equivalent of leaving twenty-nine 100-watt light bulbs running all the time.†

Because a large cluster uses so much power, you should enlist the skills of a licensed electrician to tally up the power requirements for all the components of your cluster and other equipment in the room such as networking equipment, lights, UPSs, air conditioning, etc. Then, have the appropriate circuits and circuit breakers installed for all of the equipment, making sure to evenly distribute the load. Make sure that you factor in excess capacity for expansion—you will certainly add to your cluster as you gain experience with it.

I cannot emphasize enough how important it is to have adequate power and circuit breakers installed. All of the nodes, networking hardware, and other components in your cluster should make use of three-wire grounded plugs and have power supplies with fuses or circuit breakers; these are safety features, and they should never be defeated or tampered with!

---

* HVAC stands for "Heating Ventilation and Air Conditioning," the catch-all name for environmental control systems.

† At an average of \$0.08 per kilowatt hour of electricity, that comes out to about \$23/per day to run this cluster.

Overloading electrical circuits is *extremely* dangerous and can lead to both fire and electrocution. As interesting and fun as supercomputing is, it is not worth dying for.

As if to make matters worse, most insurance policies will not cover damage caused by deliberately overloading electrical service or for installations that are not compliant with your local electrical and/or zoning codes. Also, in many localities, knowingly causing a dangerous situation, such as an electrical fire hazard, can be grounds for criminal charges.

You should also invest in an Uninterruptible Power System (UPS) to ensure that your cluster can be cleanly shut down in the event of a power failure. You can lose data if the power goes out without warning, since the nodes in your cluster will not be able to write their buffers to disks safely. Sudden, abrupt power failures can also cause the read/write heads on hard drives to impact the surface of the disk causing physical damage that destroys the device (this is often called a *head crash*). Head crashes will cause you to have to replace the disk drive, and you will also (most likely) lose any data that was on the disk at the time of the crash.

Most UPSs also function as power conditioning systems. One of the most common causes of equipment failure is as a result of power spikes or other fluctuations that can destroy system-boards, disk drives, and other components. Power surges can also damage components in such a way that they do not fail outright, but exhibit intermittent failures that can be very hard to track down.

Building the Nodes

While building cluster nodes can be a smooth process if you're using identical components or commercially made systems, building nodes from ad hoc components can be quite an adventure. Either way, a little planning can go a long way to make the experience interesting and fun instead of tedious and painful.

Information Gathering

Before putting your system together, there is a lot of information gathering you want to do. This is important, no matter how large or small your cluster is. Some of the information you need to gather is critical to actually building the cluster and will be required during the installation process that will be coming up in Chapter 5, *Software Installation and Configuration*. Other bits of information will ensure that you will be able to keep your machines up to date and be able to get speedy support from the vendors who made your equipment.

Serial numbers

Write down every serial number from each individual piece of equipment. This should include the systems units themselves, if you are using commercial off-the-shelf type systems, and motherboards, disk drives, and network cards if you are building your nodes from bare components.

Having records of these serial numbers will help you get faster technical support from your vendors should you have a problem with a system or a component inside a system, since you won't have to pull systems off of shelves or out of racks.

For systems built from components, keeping such records is even more important. Often you will want to ensure that new components you add to your cluster have the same revision as those you already have. Alternatively, if the manufacturer of some component like a disk drive were to announce a new firmware version that will ensure the safety of your data or a speedup that would cut your access time in half, you will want to be able to determine if your disk drives need to be updated as quickly as possible.

The cluster management system described in Chapter 6, *Managing Clusters*, will help you keep track of this information when your system is up and running.

Hardware addresses

The Media Access Control or MAC address is the hardware address of a network interface card that uniquely identifies that NIC on a network. Every MAC address is unique, and we will use it as part of the upcoming installation process, so that the master node of your cluster can automatically install and configure your cluster.

For each of your systems, you will want to write down the hardware address of the NIC card. The hardware address is usually found either on the back of the system box, near the network connector, or on the network card itself, as shown in Figure 4-2. If the hardware address is not on the back of the box, you will have to open the case and examine the card. For system-boards, the hardware address is often found on a label on a chip near the network connector, as shown in Figure 4-3.

Hardware addresses are usually written in a very stylized way that will help you identify them. For example, an Ethernet address is a 12-digit number that is written as a series of 16-bit hexadecimal numbers separated by colons (:). A typical Ethernet looks like this: *00:80:7E:00:12:01* and is often on a label on the network interface card. MAC addresses for other media (such as FDDI and ATM) have different lengths, but follow the same basic formatting conventions.

Figure 4-2. Network hardware address label

On system boards that have built-in network adapters, the hardware address is usually on a small ROM chip located somewhere near the network connector.

Figure 4-3. Hardware address on a system board with built-in Ethernet

These are, of course, just examples. The hardware addresses of your NIC cards will be different. Cards from the same manufacturer may well have the same first four digits (each manufacturer is assigned a unique ID code that becomes part of their hardware addresses). If you buy network cards—or system boards—in bulk, you may well get a run of sequential hardware addresses.

You should write down the hardware address for each node. If you are using muti-port NIC cards, make sure that you write down all the hardware addresses and indicate which hardware address belongs to which port. This should be clearly indicated on the card.

It's also a good idea at this point to create a label for each node, as shown in Figure 4-4. You should start numbering your compute nodes at zero. This will make things clearer when you actually write and run software on your cluster—most programming languages start arrays and other programmatic storage with indices of zero. When you are addressing compute nodes in an array, this will save you the confusion of an array that starts at index "zero," and compute nodes that are numbered starting with "one." You should also add the Ethernet address to this label, as well as other relevant information about the node. It's a good idea to make the label large enough to be seen at a distance and place it on the front of each node.

Node zero is, traditionally, used to designate the "master node" and will be the first one you install software on and the one that will enable all of the other nodes to be bootstrapped automatically. If you are planning on making a separate node your master node (which is a strongly recommended), you can place a compute node at the "zero-th" node.

The master node should be, if you've been following the design suggestions in previous chapters, configured with extra disk space to hold not only the clustering software but also end-user filesystems and the tools and packages you will be using to administer the cluster.

Node 0

IP Address: 10.0.2.8 (eth0)
Ethernet: 00:E0:81:10:34:2E
CPU Type: (2)PentiumII/450Mhz
Memory: 512MB
Disk: 36.46Gb (4xST39140w)
Vendor   Tyan
Model: S1836-DLUAN
Serial#:   AB-1234567-ZZ

Figure 4-4. Node label

Using Off-the-Shelf Systems

If your cluster design calls for the use of off-the-shelf systems in your cluster, you should try to make them identical systems. This will save you a lot of hassle if you run into any problems with your systems. You can use parts from one system to keep another going. It will also make upgrading them easier should you choose to do so.

There are several factors to consider when purchasing off-the-shelf systems.

Stability of the vendor

Is the vendor going to be around for a while? In the PC marketplace, price wars are wreaking havoc with older established vendors as they try to compete with low-cost upstarts. Make sure that the vendor you choose is stable, or at least will have support for the systems you are buying for at least 3–5 years into the future. There are cases of PC vendors who refuse to support systems if they discontinue selling them. This can leave you in a very uncomfortable position should you need parts.

Motherboard configuration

Some manufacturers design their own motherboards or create systems that are not standard sizes (also known as "form factors"). This can create a real problem if you need to upgrade the motherboards in off-the-shelf systems that were made with these odd-sized boards.

Here are the seven standard sizes of system boards that are commonly used in the PC industry:

AT form factor

AT form factor motherboards are modeled after the size of the original IBM PC/AT motherboard introduced in 1984, which was 12 inches by 13.5 inches (305mm by 342mm) in size with expansion slots that were spaced on 1.8-inch (45mm) centers. These motherboards are very large and usually require very large cabinets. AT style motherboards are not widely used anymore, having been replaced by the ATX and mini-ATX form factors discussed below.

Mini-AT form factor

The mini-AT motherboards are typically 13 inches by 8.7 inches (330mm by 220mm). The exact dimensions may vary from manufacturer to manufacturer. These motherboards were used for more compact systems that could still take advantage of the expansion slot characteristics of the full-sized AT motherboard.

LPX form factor

The LPX style of motherboard was developed to aid in the creation of low profile (the "LP" in "LPX") personal computer systems. These kinds of motherboards are small enough to fit into tiny system cases that could be put under a computer monitor or even in a desk drawer. The LPX motherboard measures 8.66 inches by 13 inches (220mm by 330mm), which doesn't seem that much smaller than the Mini-AT. The main difference is the kind of expansion ports that can be inserted into this style of machine—on these systems a special "daughter card" is inserted into the machine that allows one or more standard expansion cards to be installed parallel to the system board; this allows for a much shorter case than with standard cards mounted perpendicular to the system board.

Mini-LPX form factor

The mini-LPX board is a further refinement of the LPX family of boards that allows manufacturers to create even smaller systems.

ATX form factor

The ATX form factor is the first motherboard specification that a majority of PC vendors adhered to. The board size is 12 inches by 9 inches (305mm by 244mm). Previously these form factors were nice guidelines, but most manufacturers played with spacing and placement of connectors and so on that led to a big problem in finding cases that would house a motherboard from an arbitrary manufacturer. The ATX standard was introduced in 1995 and was developed by Intel, but published as an open standard. The ATX form factor standardized the placement of everything from where keyboard connectors could be placed to the placement of holes in the board itself to allow mounting screws to be inserted to secure the motherboard into a case.

Mini-ATX

The mini-ATX form is a slightly smaller version of the ATX board that measures 11.2 inches by 8.2 inches (284mm by 208mm). It allows printed circuit board makers to save a little money on the production of the fiberglass boards themselves in that they can get more blank boards out of the printed circuit board stock.

Extended-ATX

The extended-ATX form (sometimes called E-ATX) is a slightly larger version of the ATX board that measures 13 inches by 12 inches (325mm by 300mm). This form factor has become the standard for high-end servers and workstations. It is used primarily by Intel systems developed to support multiprocessor systems and those that need the extra printed circuit board space for extra power connectors and additional I/O connectors.

Confusing? You bet. The nice thing about standards is that you can have so many of them.

Fortunately, out of these seven form factors, only two, ATX and E-ATX, are of great interest to cluster builders since these motherboards support all of the new interesting features that will supercharge your cluster.

All of the boards that you might buy from a direct supplier would conform to one of these sizes; these last two size standards are so ubiquitous that most workstation suppliers such as Sun, IBM, and Hewlett-Packard make their workstation motherboards with these sizes as well—it's a lot easier to find case manufacturers to supply cases since they don't have to re-tool their manufacturing operations for an odd-sized board.

The manufacturer of any off-the-shelf system you consider for inclusion in your cluster should be questioned to make sure that their motherboards are compliant with one of these standards. If you purchase systems that don't comply with these specifications, the only way to upgrade your systems may well be to buy *brand new* systems because new motherboards will not fit into the cases properly, and you have to replace the cases in addition to the motherboards. This can be quite expensive if you want to upgrade your whole cluster. If the systems you purchase are based on ATX or mini-ATX motherboards, then you can simply buy a new, faster motherboard from either the original manufacturer or a third party motherboard supplier when you want to increase your cluster's capabilities.

Another item on your checklist for off-the-shelf systems should be system bus speed. You should make sure that any system you buy supports the highest bus speed available for the class of systems you are considering. As of mid-1999, this means that if you are considering Intel-based systems, you should only be considering systems with 100MHz or 133MHz bus speeds. Older systems used 66MHz bus speeds; these systems will function perfectly well but will limit the speed with which I/O and network devices can move information from the network or disk into memory.

Built-in versus add-on network cards

An important decision you must make with COTS systems is whether or not to buy systems that have a network adapter built in to the motherboard, or if you should buy the network cards as add-on components. The answer to this question is difficult: built-in NICs are very convenient, and many manufacturers hype this as a feature of their systems. But some manufacturers supply only low-speed (10Mbit/second) systems while others provide dual speed 10/100Mbit capabilities.

With the emerging standard of 1000Mbit/second networks just around the corner, I would lean toward network cards that you install in expansion slots. This is mainly because many COTS system manufacturers use components that will not be upgradeable to the new higher-speed standard. Some third-party motherboard suppliers use network chips that can be "flash updated" to support higher speeds.

Whichever route you choose, you will still be able to upgrade your systems at a later date by simply adding an additional network card to get the network speed you need.

Preparing COTS systems

There's not much to do in preparing COTS systems for cluster use unless the systems you have chosen do not have built-in network adapters. If this is the case with your systems, you will need to install these cards, taking care to record the hardware address (and serial number) information covered earlier.

One last thing to remember: the system you choose to use for your master node *must* have a CD-ROM drive in order to install the software supplied with this book. Compute nodes, however, don't need CD-ROM drives, only floppy disk drives. Since most computers come with CD-ROM drives, you may even get a price break from your supplier if you can get them to remove the CD-ROM.

Building from Components

If you are building your cluster nodes from components, you have the greatest control over what goes into your cluster.

When designing your system from scratch, you have to consider more pieces of the overall construction of a node at once. For example, do you want to put your nodes in tower cases? Will rack mounting allow you to get the most out of the space you have available to house your cluster? The answer to this last question will determine the number of network interfaces you will be able to put into each of your nodes, as tower cases will let you make use of all of the expansion slots on the motherboard while rack mount cases typically impose limitations on the number of cards you can install.

Although there is a lot more to consider when building from components, the flexibility and performance potential gained usually outweigh the hassle of doing the research. Creation of custom nodes can be broken down into four major decision points: motherboards, CPUs, memory, and cases.

Motherboards, CPUs, and memory

As with the off-the-shelf systems, you should make your motherboard selection based not only on your current cluster needs, but also with an eye toward the possible upgrade possibilities that you may want to implement as your needs and experience with clusters grow.

ATX or E-ATX family motherboards are preferable since they offer the most options from the largest number of vendors.

Using higher-end motherboards will also give you the greatest choice in terms of which CPUs you put into your nodes. On Intel-based systems, prices have been falling by about 30 percent per year for high-end CPUs for each new CPU introduction. For example, if a 450 MHz Pentium II CPU retails for $500 in January, you can expect to pay something like $350 for it by the end of the year as newer CPUs such as the 550 MHz Pentium III CPUs take the place of the older CPU.

Most higher-end motherboards also support several different kinds of memory systems. There's everything from vanilla dynamic RAM with no extra buffering or error correction circuitry, to fast Extended Data Out (EDO), Burst EDO, Synchronous DRAM, and a host of others. Since memory access times have a strong influence on the efficiency of the computer nodes on a cluster, you should make sure that you install the fastest memory available in your systems. When possible, error correcting (ECC) memory should be used; this will ensure that single-bit errors caused by heat, cosmic rays, or other unpredictable sources can be detected and corrected by the memory itself. But whatever memory system you choose, make sure that it is matched with the memory speed specified by the motherboard manufacturer to ensure that you do not introduce unnecessary wait-states into your systems.

Cases

The choice of cases can make a big difference in your options for motherboards or expansion cards. The two most common case styles are tower cases and rack mount cases.

Tower cases. Tower cases are the most familiar housings for PCs—they're the prevalent boxes that sit on, under, or next to many desks. Some tower cases, called mini-towers, are small enough to sit on an average desk and not take up all of the available space. Unfortunately, mini-towers are not very useful for cluster building because they are most often built to house non-standard motherboard sizes. Larger tower cases, such as the one pictured in Figure 4-5, are usually placed next to or under a desk, and are designed for ATX and mini-ATX motherboards.

Tower cases are quite large and are very useful if you need to install a lot of hard disk drives. Unfortunately, for use in clustered systems, most of this space is wasted. As stated in Chapter 3, *Designing Clusters*, the place you really want to put a lot of disk space is on the master node. All of the compute nodes need enough space to hold the operating system, and space to hold user applications and data when a job is running. Using tower cases in a cluster is a viable solution but will take up many times the space of rack mounted systems.

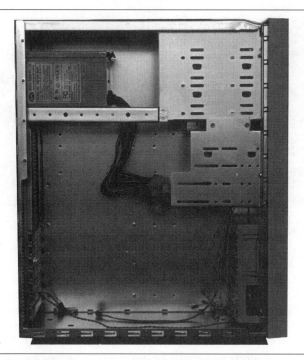

Figure 4-5. A typical tower case

Rack mounting. Rack mount cases, as shown in Figure 4-6, trade the spacious nature of tower cases for the space-efficiency of vertical stacking capability. Rack mount cases are measured in an odd scheme called "rack units," (abbreviated as "RUs" or just "U" when used with a number indicating how many rack units of height). Standard rack sizes are derived from military specifications that define standard sizes for equipment that is to be put into racks; this system has been adopted by the computer and telecommunications industry. Each rack unit is equal to 1.75 inches (44mm) of vertical space in a standard 19-inch (475mm) wide equipment rack. Equipment racks themselves usually come in 42-inch (1 meter), 63-inch (1.57 meter) and 80-inch (2 meter) sizes.

Unlike their tower cousins, which use a fan and the force of convection to draw in cool air from the bottom of the case and direct warmer air out of vents near the top of the case, rack mount cases are built to use forced air to create front-to-back cooling. This makes a lot of sense if you think about the fact that rack mount cases are meant to be stacked on top of each other, often with less than $1/4$ inch (6.25mm) clearance between each case. If convection were the primary way heat is removed, the rising heat from a rack full of equipment would allow the systems on the bottom to stay reasonably cool, while the systems on the top would cook.

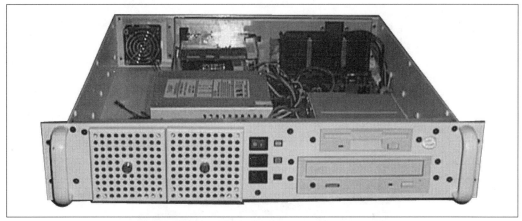

Figure 4-6. A 3U (5.25-inch high) rack mount case

Rack mount cases such as the 3U are a great space-saver for cluster building, but there is still a lot of space that goes unused, especially if you are going to include only one hard disk drive in the majority of your nodes, as would be the case with computer/slave nodes. This is a perfect case size for putting a master node into since the typical three-rack-unit rack mount case can comfortably house two to five 3.5-inch disk drives.

2U cases. An even more compact rack mount case style is the 2U or two-rack-unit case, shown in Figure 4-7. These cases are recent additions to the menu available to cluster builders. Building a cluster out of 2U rack systems would allow you to put twenty systems into an 83-inch high cabinet. That's an amazing space savings compared to the space a similar collection of tower cases would take up.

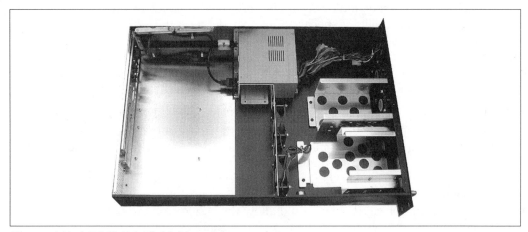

Figure 4-7. A 2U (3.5-inch high) rack mount case

The only drawback to 2U cases occurs when you want to put expansion cards into your system. Because a 2U case is only 3.5 inches high, full-height cards—including most network adapters—cannot be put into 2U racks without something called a "riser card." A riser card is an adapter that is inserted into a motherboard slot (usually a PCI slot) that then allows an expansion card to be plugged into the riser card at a 90-degree angle.

Most 2U case designs allow for the use of only one riser card per system if you intend on using a full-height expansion card, or two riser cards if you are using half-height expansion cards. For most system boards, this means that you will have to sacrifice up to half of your available expansion slots on your motherboard.

This should be a limitation only if you are planning to build some flavor of hyper-cube that needs a large number (greater than four) of network interfaces.

As with much in life, there are trade-offs for everything.

Assembling Custom Systems

One of the most fun (or most tedious, depending upon your temperament) tasks in cluster building is actually putting all of the components together. There are two basic strategies for taking a jumble of parts at the beginning of the day and, at the end of the day, having a ready-to-configure cluster.

The first strategy is best executed with a number of volunteers, each of whom has some experience putting together computer systems. The second strategy is expeditious in that it requires no work on your part at all but may add several thousand dollars to the cost of your cluster. (Some cluster building purists might even call it "the coward's way out.") The strategies may be explained as follows:

Strategy 1
> Assemble as many people as you have systems to build, or some reasonable divisor therein (i.e., three systems per person) and have each person assemble some set number of systems. Alternatively, make each person responsible for a particular subsystem. For example, one person unpacks motherboards and other parts, another installs memory and processors, while a third person puts assembled motherboards and disk drives into cases and connects cables.

Strategy 2
> Pay a third party company to build your systems out of parts of your choice. Most motherboard suppliers will gladly build systems to your specifications and integrate all the components for an added fee, usually between $100–$250 per system.

Racks Versus Shelves

If you are planning to build a system based on tower cases, you have limited options on where you are going to put them. Tower systems will need to be put into some sort of shelf system that meets all of the other criteria for space, air flow, and cable routing that were specified earlier.

Rack mounted systems can be placed within a 19-inch rack, or stacked one upon another on shelves. The benefit to using a vertical rack is the ease with which you can get to a system if you need to service it. If you pile rack mounted systems on a table or shelf, you will have to disturb (and probably power-off) systems in order to remove the system that needs your attention, instead of just sliding it out of the rack on a set of rails and doing whatever you need to do.

With tower systems, you will also need a place to locate the master node's display and keyboard. For rack mounted systems, there are parts kits available from many vendors for putting a keyboard and flat-panel display into a 1U slot in a rack. This can enable you to create a completely self-contained cluster (nodes, network fabric, display, and keyboard) all in one rack. As shown in Figure 4-8, rack mounting is the way to go if you can afford it, since it optimizes serviceability and space in a way that is not possible with nodes in tower cases.

I am a strong advocate for making life easy and thus am strongly in favor of rack-based systems.

Designing a Rack-based System

Rack-based housings are the most compact way to put together a cluster. You can buy rack cabinets in a variety of sizes depending on your available floor space or how many nodes you are planning for your cluster.

If you are using 2U rack mount cases, you can put up to twenty cluster nodes in an 80-inch high cabinet, with the remaining 13 inches of space available for the networking equipment that will tie the nodes together.

An 80-inch rack is a pretty big piece of equipment, and it is perfectly acceptable to split your cluster up across multiple cabinets. The only major issue you will have to deal with is how to run cables, or whether you should split up the networking hardware over multiple cabinets as well. This can add to the cost significantly, but it can also give you spare capacity for later expansion.

In addition to the nodes and networking, there are other things you might consider including in your cluster racks:

Power sequencer or power controllers

A power sequencer is a power-strip–like device that turns on power to different outlets on a power strip in a time-delayed sequence. Power sequencers are useful when you need to power up a large number of machines since they can ensure that all of your systems and their disk drives don't come on all at once. If you were to power up all of your systems at once, you could exceed the maximum rating of the circuit breakers for your systems—this is because the power-up current draw from devices such as disk drives can draw over ten times the average running current of a single system.

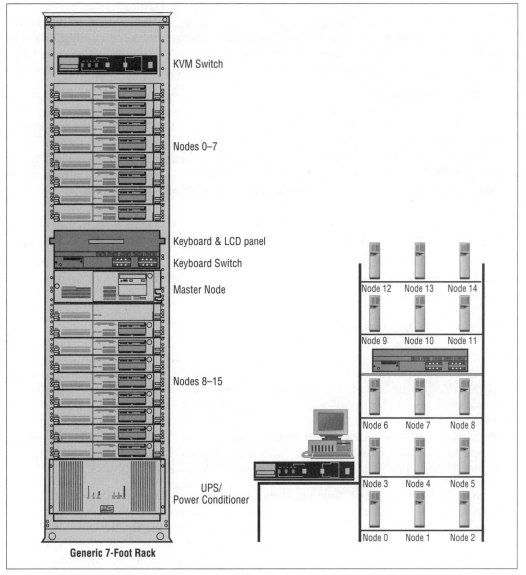

KVM Switch

Nodes 0–7

Keyboard & LCD panel

Keyboard Switch

Master Node

Nodes 8–15

UPS/
Power Conditioner

Generic 7-Foot Rack

Node 12   Node 13   Node 14

Node 9   Node 10   Node 11

Node 6   Node 7   Node 8

Node 3   Node 4   Node 5

Node 0   Node 1   Node 2

Figure 4-8. Clusters: Racks versus shelves

Remote access power control

There are several types of power strips on the market that can be controlled via a serial line or even a modem to allow you to actually power-cycle an individual outlet. This can be a life-saver of you have a piece of equipment that gets "wedged" and cannot be restarted any other way.

Internal fans to aid in air movement

> All of the individual rack mounted systems in your cluster will have fans that force air from the front of the case to the back of the case to help keep the system from overheating. You can also attach fans to the top of most 19-inch cabinets to help this process by forcibly pulling cooler air from the bottom of the cabinet.

Slide rails for computer cases

> Rack mount cases are usually designed to be permanently mounted in 19-inch racks. This works well for cases such as hubs/routers or KVM switches that rarely have to be removed for servicing. For compute nodes, it is helpful to add slide rails to the sides of the rack mount case and have matching rails on the inside of the rack that allow individual cases to slide in and out. This will allow you to open one case at a time without disturbing other cases should you need to work on a node.

Stabilizing bars

> If you have slide rails, you should also have stabilizing bars on the bottom of your rack. These bars slide out and provide greater support for the rack when cabinets are extended. This is a safety feature that can keep the cabinet from tipping over onto you as you work on or install systems.

Shelving Recommendations

If you must use shelving—because you are using tower cases, or you are using rack cases but don't like the look of data center style cabinets—the best kind of shelving is called "Metro Shelving." This is a brand name* for a very sturdy steel shelving system that can handle very heavy loads and is constructed out of modular mesh or grid. Using this kind of shelving material will enable more air to flow around your cluster. If you get Metro Shelving with wide enough spacing, you can also route network cables easily from shelf to shelf. There are also cable trays and other accessories that can be attached to Metro Shelving to help keep all of the odds and ends in order.

Of course, there are a lot of shelving options out there. Whatever kind of materials you decide to use to mount your cluster, make sure that you get a full set of specifications on what kind of load the materials can bear. Always err on the side of safety, and make sure that the shelves you build can bear the weight of your systems, so that people working on or around the cluster will not be hurt, or your machines damaged, by a falling system.

Installation and Cabling

Once you have all of your systems put together, the only task remaining before starting the installation is to cable everything up.

---

* Metro Industries can be found at *http://www.metro.com*.

Installing your systems on shelves or into racks is a pretty straightforward affair. You will probably want to arrange computer cases with the networking equipment near the center of the rack. Keeping the network equipment near the center will keep the cable lengths short and manageable.

You want to make sure that the Keyboard-Video-Mouse (KVM) switch is located as close to the master node and its display as possible. This makes logging into individual nodes easier should you have to, for maintenance purposes.

If you are using more than one network interface per node, it would be a good idea to tag the cables, or (even better) use color-coded network cables to ensure that you can easily identify different network segments.

It is also a good idea to make a set of pages that describe the hardware and software configuration of your cluster. This can be a useful tool when diagnosing system problems or when planning enhancements to your cluster.

If you will be running your cluster in a production data center type of environment, it would be a good idea to include the cluster configuration information in something called a "run book." Run book is a term used in the professional data center operations world to describe the documentation that is used as a day-to-day operations guide for a given system. This operations guide should specify all of the information that would be needed by the operations staff in order to keep the cluster running, such how to perform backups, how to check on the state of various hardware devices (such as disk capacity, tape drives, plotters, etc.), and so on. A good run book also includes a complete system hardware and software description so that if there are problems that come up, information about the system is readily available.

Summary

In this chapter, we have covered the essentials of selecting a location and putting together the cluster components you have chosen into a form where you can start treating them as an actual cluster. Here's a recap:

Site selection
A cluster must be housed in a space that has enough room to safely hold all of the components and whose floors can bear the weight of the entire cluster, which can exceed several thousand pounds. There should also be adequate space to allow maintenance to be performed on the hardware without creating a hazardous situation that could injure anyone working on the cluster.

Environmental requirements
Depending upon their size, clusters can require a lot of power and air conditioning. Wherever a cluster is installed, research must be done to ensure that the power connections are up to local building and electrical codes for the amount of equip-

ment being installed. The same goes for air conditioning. This chapter presented a simple way to calculate basic power and air conditioning requirements, but for complete details you should consult both a licensed electrician and a licensed HVAC specialist to ensure that your cluster can be installed and operated safely.

Building the nodes

Nodes can be obtained in two general ways: buying or building.

Buying off-the-shelf systems from a known vendor is the fastest way to get nodes for your cluster, but it's limited in the number of options available for mounting the systems in anything other than a shelf-based configuration because very few of the vendors provide such mounting options. Shelf-mounted systems can take up quite a bit of room and create interesting challenges for managing all of the various cables that need to be attached to all of the systems. Another issue with most commercial vendors of off-the-shelf systems is that they support only a limited number of hardware configurations. Many "stock" commercial systems have either more hardware or less hardware than you need for your cluster design, or they might not support specific features that you desire for your systems.

Building systems from commodity components gives you a larger number of options for cluster construction, not only in the mounting of the systems in that rack mount cabinets can be used to save space, but also in the exact configuration of the nodes in the cluster. With custom-built systems, you can apply the leverage of the "economy of scale" in building a cluster—better deals are often to be had when buying in bulk, and you can specify exactly the component you want in your systems.

Installation and cabling

The installation of the actual cluster system can come in two forms: shelves and racks. A rack mount installation is more space-efficient, but the racks and rack mount cases are expensive, while shelf-mounting is easier because off-the-shelf computer systems can be bought.

Information should be collected from all of the systems that will be added to the cluster, including the system serial numbers and all hardware network addresses. This information is useful as part of a cluster administration database, which can make cluster maintenance and administration a lot easier.

In either case, care should be given to the wiring to ensure that it is clearly marked and documented so that the cluster can be maintained adequately should there be problems or should enhancements need to be made to the cluster.

In the case of shelf-mounted clusters, special care needs to be given to the routing of network, keyboard/video/mouse, and power cables to ensure that these cables cannot be damaged by sharp edges or that they create a hazardous environment for people working on or near the cluster. 19-inch rack cabinets are usually built with "cable troughs" that can be used to route cables and keep them stored safely and neatly.

CHAPTER FIVE

SOFTWARE INSTALLATION AND CONFIGURATION

This section assumes that you have built a collection of nodes roughly according to the guidelines presented in the previous chapter. Your machines should all be built and connected to a network of some sort, depending upon the network configuration you have chosen. If you have your cluster all connected, the instructions presented here should work without modification. If you are using some very old hardware (for example, small disk drives of less than 1GB), you may have to modify some of the scripts presented here. Detailed information on the installation scripts may be found in Appendix C, *Installation Scripts*.

There are several ways to build a cluster. One way is to repetitively install Linux from a boot floppy and a distribution CD-ROM for each and every node in your cluster. This is a perfectly acceptable way of doing things, but since you are reading this book, I'll bet you're willing to look for ways to get the job done with a little more style (to say nothing of a lot less time).

The software installation methods I will demonstrate here are based on the standard installation methods used to build regular Linux systems. We will utilize all sorts of software tricks and utilities to help you build compute nodes quickly and with only two floppy disks. This is accomplished by using the following tools:

bootp/DHCP
> *bootp* is the boot protocol, a system by which workstations can load software over a network to bootstrap themselves. The Dynamic Host Configuration Protocol (DHCP) is a TCP-based protocol that works with *bootp* to allow client workstations to find out their IP address and other relevant information to allow them to bootstrap themselves over a network.

KickStart
> *KickStart* is a system installation and initialization scheme developed by Red Hat Software. It is modeled after a similar protocol called *JumpStart* by Sun Microsystems. KickStart allows client workstations to be completely configured over a

network by a master server that contains binary images and packages that will be installed on the client systems. These images contain a kernel and utility packages, along with configuration information that allows the KickStart system to set up the client machine.

With these tools, all of which come with the CD-ROM included with this book, and two floppy disks, you can build an entire cluster in a matter of hours.*

There are other variants of network installation and network booting. If you are using non-Intel machines, such as HP or SUN servers, it is possible to have the systems boot directly off the network, without using a floppy disk. This is commonly called "net booting." It requires that the machine you wish to bootstrap over the network have this capability built into the ROM operating system that is on the system motherboard.

In large workstation environments, like those usually found at banks and brokerages, systems are often set up so that when they are powered on, they query a well-known server to find out if there any updates or patches to be installed. Or, if the workstation being powered on has *never* been initialized, the master server may actually be configured to automatically format hard disk drives, install the operating system, make any required connections to application servers, and perform whatever other tasks are needed to get the workstation ready.

On these traditional workstations, network installation can be accomplished with relative ease because the machines have been designed from the beginning with network administration in mind. Unfortunately, commodity hardware such as Intel-based PCs typically lack these design features. More often than not, these systems do not have built-in network capabilities; a network card is an add-on device. Most ROM BIOS software on commodity hardware doesn't have the programming to support network booting without using a floppy-disk–based bootstrap program. Higher-end Intel-based machines, such as server systems, sometimes do have this capability, but this is the exception rather than the rule.

There is a way to get some add-on cards to support network booting, but it involves installing a specialized PROM chip on the network adapter card and loading that PROM chip with software that implements the network boot protocol. This is probably a major hassle unless you are really hardware-oriented or have a lot of machines that you want to add to your cluster.

Another way to install software onto a large number of disks (note, I said *disks,* and not *systems*) is to have a commercial initialization/duplication frame available. These devices look like something out of a science-fiction movie and contain a large number of slots into which disk drives are inserted. A controlling computer initializes the hard disks and copies the master-version of a disk image onto the blank target disks.

---

* In building a few clusters while writing and testing out techniques for this book, I was able to build a 16-node cluster, centered around a 100BaseT hub in under 20 minutes. Your mileage may vary, but that's not too shabby. If you're building a 128-node cluster, things will be significantly slower.

Initialization/duplication frames are used by PC manufacturers and other folks who need to make a lot of copies of a disk drive. They're expensive devices ($10,000 for a device that can copy four disks at a time, a lot more if you want to do a few dozen at a clip) and work only if all of the target disks are exactly the same model from the same drive manufacturer. These devices aren't very practical for most cluster builders since they're so expensive, and most people have a mix of different size/model disks that they use when building their clusters.

Since this book is aimed at allowing you to use commonly available hardware, I have chosen to use an installation method that I can be sure will work on the largest variety of hardware.

CD-ROM Overview

The CD-software that comes on the CD-ROM that accompanies this book is based on the Red Hat Linux version 6.2 distribution. For the most part, it's a "vanilla" Red Hat distribution, but there are several additional directory trees on the CD-ROM that have tools and applications containing clustering software, application libraries, and other software not supplied with the distribution available from Red Hat Software.

It should be noted that this is not an "official" Red Hat distribution and does not entitle you to any technical support from Red Hat. In effect, it is as if you downloaded this Red Hat distribution from any of the dozens of Linux archives on the Internet.

The CD-ROM is structured as shown in Figure 5-1. Each folder on the CD-ROM represents a particular area of tools or utilities for the installation and operation of a parallel Linux cluster. The software supplied on the CD-ROM falls into the following categories:

BootFloppyInfo
> The BootFloppyInfo direcory contains the source material needed to make Kick-Start diskettes for cluster building. These files will come in handy should you want to make boot disks for special systems (such as older computers with odd disk sizes).

ClusterTools
> The *ClusterTools* directory contains software that allows a group of computers to function as a cluster. These tools include the Message Passing Interface (MPI), Parallel Virtual Machine (PVM), and the Local Area Multicomputer (LAM) software packages. Each of these is a different set of tools for treating a network of machines as a single computation entity. Interestingly, none of these tools is mutually exclusive. In fact, many clusters run all of these tools simultaneously. Different applications are run with different packages depending upon the kind of application. We will cover these different packages and their applications in Chapter 8, *Programming in a Parallel Environment*.

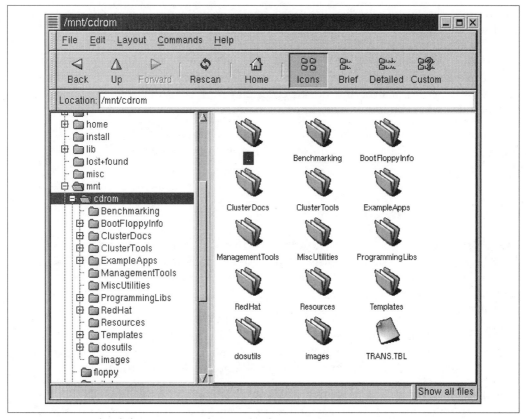

Figure 5-1. Top-level directories on the Linux Clusters CD-ROM

ExampleApps

The *ExampleApps* directory contains the complete source code to the example applications listed in this book, as well as many more examples from public domain sources of cluster demonstration applications. All of these examples, unless noted otherwise, are Open Source, which means that they can be used as the basis for your own applications.

images

The *images* directory contains the boot images that are used with RAWRITE.EXE under Windows/DOS or the Unix *dd* command to make the installation disks used to build cluster nodes. Also in this directory are the files that you need in order to construct your own custom boot floppies for making clusters that are more specialized than the generic cluster we will be building here.

ManagementTools

The *ManagementTools* directory contains tools that will assist you in the management of your parallel Linux cluster.

ProgrammingLibs

> The *ProgrammingLibs* directory contains a large number of libraries for parallel programming, as well as a number of libraries that will be useful in analyzing your applications to help tune them for high performance on a cluster.

Red Hat

> The *RedHat* directory contains a copy of the Red Hat Linux distribution.

Templates

> The *Templates* directory contains examples of various administrative files that will help you manage your cluster. Most of these files are copied onto the master node of the cluster at installation time; others are examples of how certain system configuration files are used (for example, there are fully commented examples of configuration files for the TCP wrappers application, DHCPd, and BIND).

Installation Overview

The installation of Linux and software that will allow you to operate a cluster is a two-phase process. The first part of the installation will be to install the Linux operating system on a system that you choose to be the master (or primary) node of your cluster. The second part of the installation will make use of the master node to automate the installation of Linux and clustering software on the compute nodes.

To install the Linux operating system and the clustering software and tools, follow these steps:

1. Create boot floppies for the master and slave nodes.

2. If necessary, adjust the partition sizes.

3. Install the base operating system (OS) on the master node.

4. Install the operating system packages on a special partition used to build the slave nodes.

5. Create the node management database on the master node.

6. Bootstrap the slave nodes.

7. Configure the OS extensions, clustering software, and management tools on the master node.

8. Customize the clustering software to the slave nodes.

9. Test the cluster.

Methodology

Since software installation can be tricky, I am going to present a series of well-defined steps that you can follow for most aspects of the installation procedure. These steps include:

Goal description
> This section provides a big-picture view of what you're trying to accomplish and how it fits into the overall plan of what you're doing.

Prerequisites
> This is a list of tools or tasks that you need to complete successfully before starting the current task. For some tasks, this includes a list of objects that you need to have on hand (such as blank floppy disks) or information that you need to have available (such as the Ethernet addresses of NIC cards).

Task overview
> I will spell out exactly how to complete a task, what you need to do, and the result you will get.

Task steps
> This section will list the specific actions that you need to perform in order to complete the task.

Screen shots/output
> If there is any relevant output in these steps that will help you understand what's going on or what you are likely to see, I'll include it here in the form of screen shots.

Testing the results
> For many of the tasks that you will perform while building your cluster, there are checkpoints along the way at which you can test the results of your work.

Review
> As a last step, we'll review everything that you have done, and tie it into the larger task of cluster building.

Your first task is to build the master node of your cluster so that you can configure it to build all of the other nodes. Once you have the master node built, you can move on to the slave or compute nodes.

Creating the Installation Floppies

Goal

The goal for this task is to create boot floppies that can launch the rest of the software installation tools. There are two installation floppies. The first floppy is for the master node, which will control the slave or compute nodes of the cluster. The second floppy boots and initializes each of the slave nodes.

Prerequisites

In order to start the installation, you will need two 1.44 MB 3.5-inch floppy disks. You will also need access to a machine on which you can create boot floppies. This can be either a Windows machine or a Linux machine. Once you have the installation floppies, everything else can be done on the bare machines you have built for your cluster nodes.

Overview

You will be creating floppy disks that will be used to bootstrap the nodes in your Linux cluster. You can find the images needed to create these floppies in the *Boot-Floppy* directory on the CD-ROM supplied with this book.

You can copy the disk images onto the floppy disks by using the RAWRITE.EXE program, supplied on the CD-ROM, under Windows, or by using the *dd* command under Linux, depending upon which kind of machine you have available for creating these floppies.

Task steps for creating boot floppies from a Windows machine

1. Place the CD-ROM provided with this book in the CD-ROM drive. Make note of what drive letter Windows uses to refer to the CD-ROM drive. Often the CD-ROM is a low-lettered drive such as "E:".

2. Open a DOS window; this can be accomplished by selecting Start→Programs→ Command Prompt.

3. When the DOS window opens, type the following at the prompt (replacing "E" with the drive letter of the CD-ROM drive on your system):

   ```
   e:\utils\rawrite e:\images\masternode.img
   ```

   When prompted, put a blank disk into the floppy disk drive and press RETURN. The process of writing the floppy should take about two minutes. This will create the boot floppy for the master node. If the RAWRITE program reports errors writing to your disk, make sure the disk isn't write-protected and try again. If the error persists, the floppy is probably bad. Throw it away and try a new one.

4. Remove this disk from the drive, label it *"MASTER-NODE BOOTDISK,"* and set it aside.

5. To create the second boot floppy, for the slave nodes, repeat the *rawrite* command above, but replace `masternode.img` with `slavenode.img` on the command line.

6. Remove this disk from the drive, label it *"SLAVE-NODE BOOTDISK,"* and set it aside; you will use it once you have finished building the master node.

If you are feeling very adventurous, you can make as many slave node boot floppies as you have slave/compute nodes, and run all of the installations in parallel. This will certainly be faster than doing them individually, but be careful not to overload your network (one to eight nodes at a time is probably a good limit); otherwise, some of the installations will time-out and have to be restarted.

Task steps for creating boot floppies from a Linux machine

1. Log in to your Linux system and become superuser (*root*).

2. If your CD-ROM drive is */dev/CD-ROM*, place the CD in the CD-ROM drive, and type:

   ```
   mount -r /dev/cdrom  /mnt/cdrom
   ```

   This will mount the CD-ROM at the standard Linux mount point for CD-ROMs.

3. Place a blank, formatted floppy disk in the disk drive, and then type:

   ```
   dd if=/mnt/cdrom/BootFloppies/MasterBootFloppy/masternode.img of=/dev/fd0
   ```

   This will create the boot floppy for the master node of your cluster. The disk-writing process should take about a minute. If the *dd* program reports errors writing to your disk, make sure the disk isn't write-protected and try again. If the error persists, the floppy is probably bad; throw it away, and try this step again with a new one.

   Once the process is complete, remove the floppy, label it "MASTER-NODE BOOT-DISK," and set it aside.

4. To make a boot floppy for the slave (compute) nodes, insert a blank, formatted floppy in the disk drive and type:

   ```
   dd if=/mnt/cdrom/BootFloppies/SlaveBootFloppy/slavenode.img of=/dev/fd0
   ```

5. Remove the floppy disk from the drive, label it *"SLAVE-NODE BOOTDISK,"* and set it aside. You will use it once you have finished building the master node.

6. Finally, remove the CD from the CD-ROM drive and put in a safe place; it will be needed for the next part of the installation.

Screen shots/output

Figure 5-2 and Figure 5-3 represent typical output on a Windows system and a Linux system, showing the processes of making the master and slave node boot floppies.

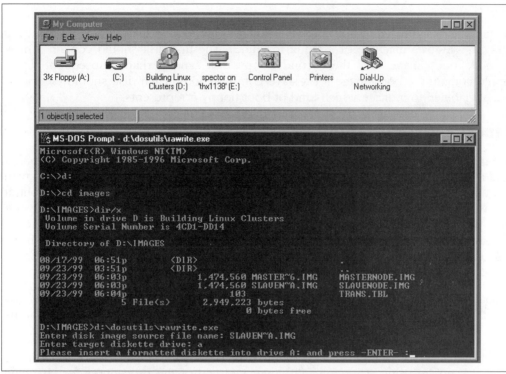

Figure 5-2. Making boot floppies under the Windows operating system

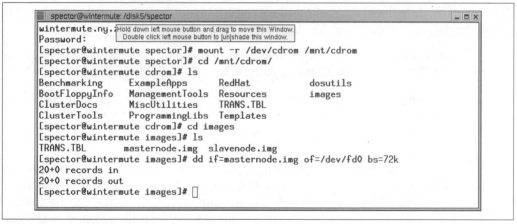

Figure 5-3. Making boot floppies under Linux

Testing the results

Assuming that neither the RAWRITE or *dd* programs returned error messages about the disk images, the only way to test these disks is to boot a system with them.

Review

In this task section, you should have made a minimum of two floppy disks (using either a Windows machine or a Linux machine). The first disk should contain a master node boot image, and the second floppy disk (and perhaps subsequent disks) should contain the boot image for a slave/compute node. Each disk should be appropriately labeled to indicate which kind of boot floppy it represents.

Adjusting the Partition Sizes

The boot floppies for both the master node and the slave/compute nodes are configured to install onto hard disks of 6GB or larger. Most hard disks that are shipped with prebuilt systems and most bare drives (both IDE and SCSI) sold after 1998 start out at at least this size, and most are even larger. If the primary hard disk drives on the systems you plan on using in your cluster are smaller than this, you will need to adjust the partitioning information on the KickStart files on the installation disks to match the size of your disk drives. You should not attempt to use disks that are smaller than 4 GB because the installation materials will not fit on a smaller disk.

If your disks are larger than 6GB, you may want to adjust the partition sizes. By default, extra space will be used by the */home* partition, which is where user home directories are created.

The information for changing the partition sizes is the same regardless of the kind of boot disk you're using. Therefore, I'll cover just one of the procedures for changing partition sizes.

The KickStart information controlling how a disk is partitioned is kept in the *KS.CFG* file on the master as well as on the slave boot disks.

There are three ways to edit the files that control the disk partitions, depending on your preferences and which mechanism you used to create the boot floppy:

- If you created your boot floppies on a Windows machine, edit the *KS.CFG* file on the floppy directly. This file is simply a text file and can be opened with any convenient text editor. Just make sure to save the file in text format, as opposed to a binary format such as Microsoft Word's format.

- If you are using a Linux or other Unix machine, you can copy the *KS.CFG* file off the floppy disks you have just created, edit the relevant information, and then copy the file back to the floppy disk. On a Linux machine, the file can be copied using the *mcopy* command, which is a utility for copying files to and from MS-DOS floppies. For other Unix machines, you will have to consult the documentation for your system, as there are too many different floppy disk access programs to conveniently list here. An alternate method is to make copies of the master or slave *KS.CFG* files that are on the CD-ROM, edit them, and then use *mcopy* to copy the files to the appropriate boot disk.

- On the CD-ROM, the *BootFloppyInfo* directory contains subdirectories named *MasterBootFloppy* and *SlaveBootFloppy*. These directories contain all of the component files that are on the floppy disk images. Included in each of these directories is a *KS.CFG* file that is tailored for the particular kind of system it is used to bootstrap.

Whichever method you choose, you will need to edit the "partition" lines in the *KS.CFG* file. These lines look like this:

```
zerombr yes
clearpart --all
part /boot --size 16
part / --size 250
part swap --size 127
part /usr --size 1024
part /tmp --size 450
part /var --size 750
part /usr/local --size 1000
part /home --size 1200 --grow
```

In the actual *KS.CFG* files, there are comments surrounding each line to explain what the line does. These have been removed from the example above to make it easier to read.

This example was taken from the configuration file for the master node; the slave node partitions are slightly different. The first two lines are very important and should never be changed—these clear out the master boot record and wipe out any previous partitions. Without these two lines, the installation will not be successfull.

When editing these partition sizes, please check carefully to make sure that the sizes (which are expressed in megabytes) add up to an amount equal to or less than the total size of the hard disks you are using. If you attempt to make a partition that is larger than the disk, the installation progress will announce an error, and the automated installation process will stop.

In general, if you are using fairly current hardware, you should not have to use these procedures. But if you are building a specialized cluster, you can use these facilities to more closely tailor the Linux clusters installation to your specific needs.

Building the Master Node

The master node is the "smartest" node in a cluster. In other words, it is the machine that has all of the software required to run the whole cluster. The master node has a large number of programs and configuration files that will allow you and other users of your cluster to treat the master node as if it were the entire cluster itself, for the purposes of running programs. The master node has various batch queues and other facilities so that a program can be submitted and run from this single point of control.

From a management perspective, the master node will be able to control and monitor all aspects of the operation of the cluster. The addition or removal of compute nodes will also take place through software installed on this node. Compute (slave) nodes, as we'll see in the next section, are minimal machines used primarily for computation.

The construction of the master node of a cluster is, for the most part, like the installation of a generic Linux system. The only differences are that most of the work is done automatically by the KickStart installation disk and by some of the packages that are installed in the base system.

As I mentioned in Chapter 4, *Building Clusters*, the master node of your cluster should be more heavily equipped than the slave or compute nodes. This situation occurs for several reasons. First, you want this node to be the central point from which all of the jobs on your cluster originate; this machine needs to have more software installed and needs more disk space than a compute node, where applications are stored in a more transitory fashion. Secondly, the master node is hopefully going to retain the state of all of the slave nodes. What this means is that if a slave node loses its hard disk, you should only have to replace the disk and reboot with the KickStart floppy to completely reinitialize that slave system.

Alternatively, if for some reason an entire slave node needs to be replaced or upgraded, or if you want to add new nodes, you should only have to add an entry to the */etc/dhcp.conf* file on the master node and boot the new system with the KickStart floppy to have the system set up and ready to use.

Master Node Linux Installation

Linux comes in a variety of different packages or "distributions." The package you'll be working with on the CD-ROM that comes with this book is based on the Red Hat 6.2 Linux distribution. If you are more comfortable with another distribution, it should be possible to use most of the techniques presented here to install software on your cluster, but you may have to modify a number of scripts. If this is your first foray into cluster building, I would recommend sticking with the CD-ROM. As you gain experience, you can modify and customize these procedures for your next cluster.

Goal

To install Linux on the master node of the cluster.

Prerequisites

Before beginning any of the steps in this section, you should have a computer designated as the master node with:

- A network interface card (NIC) installed

- A CD-ROM drive installed and attached to an appropriate interface

- A hard disk installed (with a capacity of at least 4GB)

- A keyboard and monitor connected to the system

You should also have the *MASTER-NODE BOOTDISK* floppy that you created earlier.

Overview

This section involves booting the master node with the master-node boot floppy and answering several questions that will be presented in dialog boxes on the attached monitor.

Note

If you have more than one hard disk installed in your master node, the installation process will automatically choose the first disk it finds as the place to install the operating system software. If you are using IDE/ATAPI disks, use the master disk on the first controller. If you are using SCSI disks, the installation disk should be the lowest-numbered device on the first SCSI controller.

Task steps

1. Power on the monitor and the CPU of the system that will be the master node of your cluster.

2. Open the CD-ROM drive and place the Linux Clusters CD-ROM into the drive but *do not* close the drive.

3. Insert the *MASTER-NODE BOOTDISK* floppy in the floppy disk drive.

   In a few moments, the screen should clear and a series of boot messages should appear.

   A Welcome screen will announce that this is an O'Reilly and Associates Linux Clusters CD-ROM and that this is the installation of a master cluster node based on Red Hat Linux.

4. Once the Welcome screen is displayed, close the door to the CD-ROM drive. Closing the CD-ROM drive at this point ensures that the system starts up from the boot floppy, as opposed to starting from the bootable CD-ROM.

5. If you have no SCSI controllers installed in your system and you are installing Linux onto an IDE/ATAPI disk, skip to task number 7.

6. If you are installing your master node with a SCSI based stystem, you might see a screen that looks like the one shown in Figure 5-4.

   This dialog, despite its appearance, is not an error. As I said earlier, this installation is almost completely automated, but there are a couple of instances where you may need to manually intervene in the installation of certain aspects of the software.

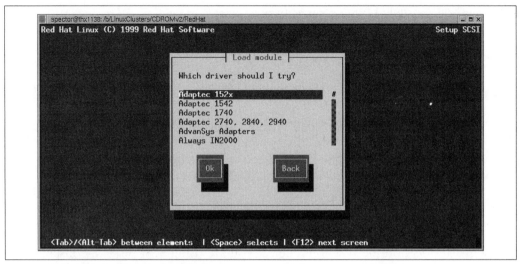

Figure 5-4. SCSI driver selection dialog

In a regular Linux installation, the system searches for a SCSI controller. If it finds one, it makes an internal note of it, and searches for additional controllers. This dialog is the result of the search for additional SCSI controllers and is caused by the system not finding any.

During a regular installation, without KickStart, this dialog would appear if the installation process needed you to tell it which SCSI driver to try to load to continue its search. In this case, it's just an artifact of a manual installation that's not handled by the KickStart part of the installation process. Although it seems like a bug, it's really not—you're just forcing the KickStart program to do something it wasn't *really* meant to do.

At this point, our aim is to tell the system to use the first SCSI controller installed in the system. Highlight the BACK button in this dialog by pressing the TAB key several times. Once you've highlighted the BACK button, press the RETURN key. This will take the installation process back to the previous dialog (which was not displayed because of KickStart) in the installation process, which is a dialog asking if there are any additional controllers in the system.

The SCSI controller card installed on the system pictured is an Adaptec-2940. The SCSI configuration dialog shown in Figure 5-5 might differ from the one you see on your master node depending on what brand of SCSI controller is installed on your machine.

To dismiss this dialog, you need to press the TAB key until the NO button is highlighted in the dialog, as shown in Figure 5-5. Once the NO button is highlighted, press RETURN. The installation will then continue.

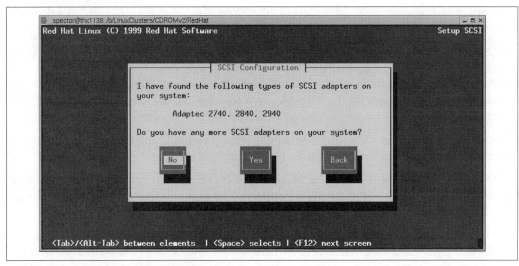

Figure 5-5. SCSI configuration dialog

7. The next point at which the installation process will require your input is when the installation process probes the video card in your system so that the X Window system can be set up. When the system determines what kind of video card is installed, you will see a dialog that looks very similar to the one shown in Figure 5-6.

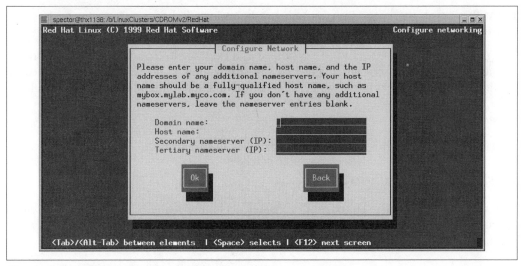

Figure 5-6. Video card probe results

Of course, the exact video card the installer discovers will probably be different from what is shown in this example. This information is used by the system in the final stages of the installation when you will make selections regarding other display characteristics of the video display. You should press RETURN to acknowledge this dialog.

8. Once this dialog has been acknowledged, the installation process will proceed by partitioning the hard disk drive and installing Linux. The installation process will then display a number of informational windows telling you about various activities such as disk partitioning and file system creation, and the installation of several hundred software packages that make up the Linux operating system.

9. After the package installation is complete, the system will display a dialog box asking you to choose monitor settings that will be used by the X Window System.

   Using the arrow keys on the keyboard, scroll down until you find the entry that most closely matches the monitor connected to your master node. Once you find the appropriate entry, press RETURN to confirm the choice.

10. The next dialog that appears will show what settings for the monitor and the display card have been selected as defaults by the X Window setup program—usually these are the highest resolution and greatest number of colors that the hardware will support. Pressing RETURN here will accept these settings.

11. Finally, the system will present three more dialogs regarding testing the X Window settings and whether or not the X Window System should be enabled at system boot time. You should press RETURN in response to each of these dialogs. When all of the boot activity is done, you will see an unassuming, rather plain screen.

12. At this point, the base Linux system has been installed on your master node. You should remove the floppy disk from the drive, and put it in a safe place.

13. Finally, press RETURN, and the system will reboot itself. You will see a lot of messages from the Linux kernel scroll by, mostly having to do with devices found on the system, available memory, versions of drivers, and capabilities of the kernel.

Screen shots/output

See Figures 5-4 through 5-6, which appear earlier in this section.

Master Node Configuration

Now that you've installed Linux on the master node, the really interesting part of cluster building can begin. You will start by installing the remaining packages that were not handled by the KickStart process.

Master Node Network Configuration

Because the KickStart process is meant to be automated, it skips over some details when performing an installation, such as the complete configuration of the target system's networking facilities. You may have noticed, if you looked at the *KS.CFG* file either on the CD-ROM or on the boot floppy, that the IP address was specified in the KickStart process, but this is just enough to get the process started. You will need to complete the processes by adding a number of entries into a number of configuration files.

Goal

To complete the network setup started by the KickStart process so that the master node has a symbolic name (a hostname) that is tied to the system's IP address, and to set up the other aspects of networking, including name services and routing information.

Prerequisites

In order to start this phase of the installation, you must have completed the installation of the basic Linux operating system detailed in the previous section.

Overview

You will be logging on to the newly created master node of your cluster as the superuser, or *root*. The superuser is the administrative owner of the entire machine and can execute any command whatsoever. This includes commands that can seriously damage the system (for example, removing the entire file system by inappropriately using the *rm* command).

Once logged in, your first order of business will be to change the *root* password from the default set up as part of the KickStart process.

After you change the *root* password, you will edit a number of system files to tell the system more about its networking environment. Finally, you will restart the networking system to implement your changes.

Task Steps

1. Log in to the master node by typing the username **root** and the password **mr.linux** at the login prompt. Note that both the username and password are lowercase, and that the password will not be echoed back to you as you type. The password **mr.linux** was set up by the master node boot disk as part of the KickStart process. For example:

```
Red Hat Linux release 6.0 (cluster)
Kernel 2.2.12 on an i686
login: root
Password: mr.linux
```

This is the default installation password for both the master node and all slave/ compute nodes.

2. Start an X terminal by clicking once on the terminal icon at the bottom of the screen (it's the icon with the footprint over what appears to be a monitor). This will launch a terminal session during which commands can be entered.

3. The *passwd* command is used under Linux to change passwords. At the command prompt (which should be a dollar sign [$]) in the X terminal window, type **passwd** and press RETURN.

   The *passwd* command will ask you to type the current password for the user *root*, and then ask you to enter a new password. Once you enter the new password, you will be asked to type it again. This is to confirm the password, and ensure that you did not make any typing mistakes.

   Make sure that you choose a password that you can remember. At this point, *root* is the only account that exists on the system, so if you forget the password, there is no easy way to break in to the system to change it. Your only solution will be to re-install Linux onto the master node from scratch.

4. Next, we are going to run a system management utility called *netcfg** that will allow you to customize the networking parameters of the master node. At the command prompt type the command as follows:

   ```
   $ netcfg &
   ```

   The & character tells the system to run this command "in the background," or detached from the terminal that initiated the command. This allows us to close the terminal if we want to, without stopping the *netcfg* program.

5. When *netcfg* starts up it will display a window. Since the KickStart process allowed us to specify the IP address for the master node, but not any name information, we'll fill it in here.

   In the first line of this network configuration dialog, we will enter the hostname for the master node of the cluster. You can call this anything you like, but for this first cluster I would recommend using the name *master*. If you make a mistake on the entry, just press the BACKSPACE key to erase the offending characters. If you accidentally hit RETURN, use the TAB key to step through the lines until you get back to the appropriate line.

6. On the next line you will need to specify the *domain name* in which this cluster will exist. For example, if your company is known on the Internet as *acme.com*, then you would enter **acme.com** in the domain name line. If your company

---

* One of the nicest things about Linux is the abundance of systems management tools; *netcfg* is a very simple tool for managing network parameters—it is also one of the oldest network administration tools available, and not well supported. However, for our purposes it gets the job done. The more up-to-date way to administer network settings (and almost anything else) is by using a program called *Linuxconf*. Linuxconf if a very comprehensive, and extremely complicated tool that really needs a whole book to cover its workings adequately, which is why I decided to have you use the easier, but less glamorous tool.

doesn't have a domain name, leave this line blank, and press TAB to get to the next input line in the dialog box.

I would strongly recommend that unless you have just a few machines on your network, you give your cluster its own subdomain on your network. A subdomain will allow you to logically separate your cluster from the rest of your machines. On my network, which is called *zeitgeist.com,* I have a subdomain for my cluster called, logically enough, *cluster.zeitgeist.com.* This allows me to have have a separate name and IP address space reserved for the cluster—any changes I make to the larger network, or the cluster's network, will not affect the other.

7. Next, we will enter the IP address of a host that will act as a Domain Name Server (DNS) for the cluster. Enter the IP address 10.0.2.1—this is the IP address of the master node itself. If your company has other domain name servers, you can enter these addresses after the address of the master node—this will enable the master node to find other nodes outside of the cluster.

8. Once you have entered this information, click on the "save" button, and then the "quit" button; this will write the information to the appropriate configuration files and exit the *netcfg* program.

This process of setting hostnames needs to be done only for the master node, when we get to setting up a the slave nodes, this step will be handled automatically. The installation process on the slave/compute node will ask the master node for the domain name, name servers, and the IP address/hostname of the system, but since this is the setup of the master node, we have to set up this information by hand.

Master Node Clustering Software Installation

The installation of the Linux operating system on the master node was just the start of the process of transforming a plain, vanilla computer into a cluster. In order for your machine to be the master node, you will need to install on it packages that let it configure, build, and control the slave/compute nodes.

Once the software packages are in place on your master node, you will also configure the processes that will allow you to automatically configure and install all of the slave/compute nodes of your cluster.

Package Installation

Goal

To install all of the clustering software, utilities, and tool packages on the master node so that they will be available for use by the KickStart system when slave/compute nodes are being built.

A Few Words About IP Addresses

The base for our IP addresses will be using a special address class, known as *Net 10*. Net 10 is a private Class A network.

We will use Net 10 because it allows you to allocate addresses to suit your cluster design needs. Some simple cluster designs can share a common network segment. Others require multiple interconnections with subnetworks in order to function.

Since private networks like Net 10 are unregistered, anyone using Net 10 addresses is strongly advised to put a firewall or other network address translation device between their network and any internal systems that use these addresses.

Using the Net 10 addresses is a safe bet in most organizations. I recommend using these addresses for all of the nodes in your cluster, and if necessary, you can add either an additional NIC card to your master node, or just use virtual addressing (a way of having more than one IP address per network interface) to allow your master node to be visible to the rest of your network.

Prerequisites

In order to start this phase of the installation, you must first successfully complete the installation of Linux onto the master node. You should also have access to the Linux Clusters CD-ROM (which is probably still in the CD-ROM drive of the master node, unless you removed it).

Overview

You will mount the Linux Clusters CD-ROM on the standard mount point for CD-ROMs and begin the process of installing software from the CD-ROM onto the master node.

Task steps

1. If you have not done so already, log in to the master node by typing the username **root** and the password **mr.linux** at the login prompt. Note that both the username and password are lowercase, and that the password will not be echoed back to you as you type. The password **mr.linux** was set up by the master node boot disk as part of the KickStart process. For example:

```
Red Hat Linux release 6.0 (cluster)
Kernel 2.2.12 on an i686
login: root
Password: mr.linux
```

This is the default installation password for both the master node and all slave/compute nodes.

2. If you have removed the CD-ROM from the CD-ROM drive, place the CD-ROM in the CD-ROM drive and close the drive. Otherwise, type:

```
mount -r /dev/cdrom /mnt/cdrom
```

This will tell Linux to read the CD-ROM and to attach the CD-ROM as a filesystem to the mount point */mnt/cdrom*. If you type the command *df*, you should see a listing very much like the following:

```
cluster% df
Filesystem      1024-blocks     Used   Available   Capacity    Mounted on
/dev/sda1            16484       4000       12484        25%       /boot
/dev/sda3           248847      23518      212479        10%       /
/dev/sda7          5747036         20     5449414         0%       /home
/dev/sda8           248847         18      235979         0%       /tmp
/dev/sda6          1018298     126435      839252        13%       /usr
/dev/sda5          1189050         32     1127571         0%       /usr/local
/dev/scd0           499012     499012           0       100%       /mnt/cdrom
```

The actual filesystem sizes may vary slightly depending upon the type of hard disk you have installed on your master node and whether or not you have modified the default partition sizes to meet the needs of your individual disks. All of the filesystems listed here, with the exception of */mnt/cdrom* (which we just attached with the *mount* command), were created by the installation process described in the previous section.

3. In order to begin the installation of the clustering software, you will need to change directory to the CD-ROM's *ClusterTools* directory. This is done by executing the command:

```
# cd /mnt/cdrom/ClusterTools
```

4. This directory contains an installation script to automatically install the software for you. Invoke it by executing the command:

```
# /bin/sh Install.sh
```

This will force the bash shell to execute the commands contained in the script, which invokes the Red Hat *RPM* command to install the tools that will allow your master node to be the head-end of the cluster.

Testing the results

Unless there is a shortage of disk space, this software should install without any errors. The testing will occur when you run some parallel software on your cluster during the system testing phase.

Review

This phase of our cluster installation involves setting up the master node to have all of the clustering software that in fact makes it a master node. This includes message passing libraries, queue management, and administrative tools that will help you manage your cluster.

Building a Boot Server

The next step is vital. You'll set up configuration files that will allow your master node to provide information to slave/compute nodes and automatically initialize them.

Building a boot server involves configuring several important subsystems, including the Domain Name Server and the Dynamic Host Configuration Protocol configuration file. After these elements are configured, the rest of the installation process can be completely automated with the boot disk(s) you created previously for the slave/compute nodes.

DHCP Configuration

The Dynamic Host Configuration Protocol (DHCP) allows an administrator to set up a mechanism for configuring client computers at boot time, without having to keep configuration information on a local disk drive. DHCP allows the boot protocol (*bootp*) to pass a variety of information along to a client, such as its hostname, boot files, and DNS information, which are then used to bootstrap the client system.

Goal

To build the *dchpd.conf* file to include the names and MAC addresses of slave/compute nodes so that they may be initialized and marked as part of the Linux cluster.

Prerequisites

In order to create the *dhcpd.conf* file, you will first need to collect all of the hardware addresses from the nodes in the cluster. When you build or purchase the systems for your cluster, you should make note of the hardware addresses listed on the network interface cards (NICs) that are part of your system. Hardware addresses (for Ethernet adapters) are numbers that are in the format of *aa:bb:cc:dd:ee:ff*—for example, *00:50:56:94:00:00*.

Make a list of the other important system information (such as disk type, number of processors, processor speeds, etc.), along with the Ethernet address, on a sheet of paper so that you will have it available as you are editing the DHCP configuration file.

Finally, you should be familiar with a Unix editor of some kind. Installed by default on the master node are the editors *ed*, *ex*, *vi*, and *Emacs*. Most of the other steps in this and succeeding chapters will require that you have some basic facility with a text editor in order to be able to complete various tasks.

Overview

In this part of the cluster installation, you will take information about the network addresses and hostnames of the systems to be added to your cluster and add it into a configuration file that will provide information to the installation process.

Once that information has been entered, you will start up the DHCP daemon process. If there are errors in the file, as indicated by messages from the daemon process, they will need to be fixed. If there are no errors reported in the configuration file, then you can test the DHCP process by attempting to install a node.

Task steps

1. Make sure you have collected and recorded the Ethernet addresses of all the nodes in your cluster. If you have designed your cluster to use multiple network adapters (for example, if your cluster's network topology is a cube of some sort), you will need to choose an interface to be the primary or "eth0" interface.

2. Choose a slave node that you will designate to be "node1" of your cluster. On a piece of paper, start a table that will record the hostname of your slave nodes, starting with the node name "node1," that node's Ethernet address, and finally, an IP address. We will start with IP address *10.0.2.2*. Table 5-1 provides an example of such a table.

Table 5-1. Node Address Table

Node Name	Ethernet Address	IP Address
node1	aa:bb:cc:dd:ee:ff	10.0.2.2
node2	gg:hh:ii:jj:kk:ll	10.0.2.3
node3	mm:nn:oo:pp:qq:rr	1.0.2.4

You should complete this table before moving on to the next step, as you will need to input all of the information to a file on the master node.*

3. Log on to the master node as **root**. Once you are logged in, make sure that the Linux Clusters CD-ROM is mounted at the standard mount point (*/mnt/cdrom*),

---

* Purists will note that the whole point of DHCP is the "dynamic" configuration of computers at boot-time—*dhcp* can automatically allocate IP addresses (and other resources) to client machines. As your experience with cluster-building grows, you will probably want to have *dhcp* do this work for you. All of *dhcp*'s feature are specified in its manual pages. Unless you are a *dhcp* expert, for your first cluster or two it's a better idea to understand exactly how everything is put together than depend upon the *deus ex machina* where the master node would do everything behind your back.

and change directory to the *Templates* directory on the CD-ROM with the command:

```
# cd /mnt/cdrom/Templates
```

4. Copy the *dhcpd.conf* file in this directory to the */etc* directory. This is a template file that you will modify in order to set the DHCP functionality on your master node.

5. Move to the */etc* directory, and edit the file */etc/dhcpd.conf* with an editor of your choice.

When you open the file, you will notice that this file has a section at the top that describes the network for which this file is configured. This section tells the DHCP daemon about the network being serviced by this process and what ranges of addresses may be given out to client machines.

Any line that starts with the # character is a comment, and all text in a line *after* such a character is treated as a comment and ignored. Most of the entries are designed to be self-explanatory.

6. The first thing you want to edit is the domain name option line. As delivered on the Linux Clusters CD-ROM, the domain name option line looks like this:

```
option  domain-name "cluster.zeitgeist.com";
```

zeitgeist.com is the name of my domain,[*] which is certainly not what you want in *your* DHCP configuration file. Change this to the domain name you entered during the Linux installation on the master node. Make sure that you keep the "cluster" in the domain name; this will allow you to keep your cluster logically separate from the rest of your network.

7. For each of your compute nodes, enter the information you collected about your nodes. Enter the information in the following format, as shown in the examples in the configuration file:

```
host node2 {
            hardware ethernet 00:E0:29:1C:CC:77;
            fixed-address node2.cluster.zeitgeist.com;
            option host-name "node2";
            filename "/mnt/cdrom/";
    }
```

Start by modifying the templates in the file, adding more entries as appropriate. Make sure that you increment the node number as you add nodes. There are three places where the node number appears in each entry. Most importantly, make sure that you enter the nodes' Ethernet addresses completely. Each entry should

---

[*] Just because people always ask about it, *zeitgeist* is the Yiddish (and German) word that means "spirit of the times," and may be pronounced either "ZEET-guyst" or "Zight-guyst" (rhymes with "right price"). I figured it was a domain name that would never go out of style.

have a unique Ethernet address; make sure that there are no duplicates. Duplicate entries will cause the DHCP daemon to report errors and will prevent the compute node from booting.

Once you have created entries for all of the nodes that will be in your cluster, save the file and exit the editor.

8. Finally, you need to edit the */etc/hosts* file to add IP address entries for all of the compute nodes you added into the */etc/dhcpd.conf* file.

    Next, you must add your cluster nodes to the *hosts* file. To do this, edit the file */etc/hosts* with an editor of your choice. The address information is stored in the format of *<ipaddress><tab><hostname>*, such as:

```
#hosts file for a cluster
#
#  $Author: sarahjs $
#  $Date: 2000/07/03 22:52:52 $
#  $Header: /work/linux/clusters/RCS/ch05 1.11 2000/03/24 17:50:23 jstewart Exp jstewart
$
127.0.0.1localhost loghost
10.0.2.1master node1
10.0.2.2node2
10.0.2.3node3
10.0.2.4node4
10.0.2.5node5
10.0.2.6node6
10.0.2.7node7
         :
         :
```

The # character is a comment symbol; anything after a comment symbol is ignored.

Notice that the first host entry is called localhost. This is the hostname for the loop-back address of the computer's network interface. The first actual computer is called cluster, which is your master node and the first IP address in the series on network 10.0.2.x.

As with the *dhcpd* configuration file, you will need to add as many entries as you have compute nodes. The first five have been entered for you already; you should continue the IP addresses in sequence.

Testing the results

To test your work, you will need to start up the DHCP daemon. To do this, execute the following command:

/etc/rc.d/init.d/dhcpd start

If everything is working properly, you should see the following messages on the screen:

```
[root@cluster /etc]# /etc/rc.d/init.d/dhcpd start
Starting dhcpd: dhcpd Internet Software Consortium DHCPD $Name: $
Copyright 1995, 1996, 1997, 1998 The Internet Software Consortium.
All rights reserved.
Listening on Socket/eth0/LOCAL-NET
Sending on    Socket/eth0/LOCAL-NET

[root@cluster /etc]#
```

Normally, DHCP is started at system boot time, and startup messages from the DHCP daemon will also be recorded in the system log file. To view the system log file, you can use the *tail* command, like this:

 # tail /var/log/messages

This will show the last screenful of entries. If you wish to see more lines, you can supply an argument to *tail* such as `tail -50 /var/log/messages` and see fifty lines of output. You should see output from the DHCP daemon that looks very much like this:

```
[root@cluster /tmp]# tail /var/log/messages
Apr 25 13:03:12 cluster dhcpd: Internet Software Consortium DHCPD $Name:  $
Apr 25 13:03:12 cluster dhcpd: Copyright 1995, 1996, 1997, 1998 The Internet Software
Consortium.
Apr 25 13:03:12 cluster dhcpd: All rights reserved.
Apr 25 13:03:12 cluster dhcpd: Listening on Socket/eth0/LOCAL-NET
Apr 25 13:03:12 cluster dhcpd: Sending on    Socket/eth0/LOCAL-NET
[root@cluster /tmp]#
```

Review

In this section you have copied the templates for the */etc/hosts* file and the */etc/dhcpd. conf* file into place. Then, you edited the *dhcp* configuration file to customize it for your compute nodes and their unique Ethernet addresses. Lastly, you tested your work by starting the DHCP daemon to enable the process that will allow you to install your slave/compute nodes.

Slave/Compute Node Installation

Goal

Now that we have installed all of the basic software on our master node, we'll take advantage of the automatic installation features we have configured and use the compute node boot disks to set up the remaining nodes.

Prerequisites

Before attempting to install client machines, you must make sure that all of the compute nodes you are going to configure are connected to a network—the same network as the master node—or you'll be stopped dead in your tracks before you even get going.

If you are building a simple Network of Workstations (NoW) cluster, make sure that the network interface cards on each node in your cluster, including the master node, are connected to a network hub or a network switch.

If your network is more complicated—say, a hypercube or some other form of network mesh—you must make sure that the primary network card of each node (whose interface would be "eth0"), including the master node, is connected to a network hub or a network switch.

Make sure to set up either a console switch, or at least two keyboards and monitors so that you can simultaneously watch the output from the system messages file on the master node, as well as the screen displays on whatever slave/compute node you are building.

Finally, make sure that the Linux Clusters CD-ROM is mounted at the */mnt/cdrom* mount point on the master node. The installation process cannot proceed without it, as the compute nodes will get their software from the CD-ROM during the installation.

Building Slave/Compute Nodes

Unlike the master node that we built, the slave node spends all of its time in usermode, executing user jobs. The only administrative overhead that these nodes should perform is accounting for time spent in user processes.

Goal

The goal here is to get compute nodes up and running by means of the automatic installation system running on the master node.

Prerequisites

In order to complete this step, you will need to have the compute nodes connected to the same network that the master node is connected to, and you will need to have a slave/compute node boot disk. If you wish to boot multiple compute nodes simultaneously, you will need to have one boot disk for each node.

Overview

This is the simplest task that you will perform in any section of this book. All you have to do is put a floppy in the slave/compute node's disk drive and power on the system.

Task steps

1. On the master node, you should log in as **root**, and execute the command:

   # **tail -f /var/log/messages**

   This will allow you to watch the messages from the DHCP daemon, which can give you indications of how the installation is progressing or let you know if there is a problem with the node that is attempting to bootstrap itself. When you have seen enough, you can press Ctrl-C to stop the *tail* program and return to the shell prompt.

2. For each slave/compute node, for which you have created a slave/compute node boot disk, place the disk into the floppy disk drive, and power on the node.

   If you are using a console switch that allows you to switch between a number of hosts that are all sharing a monitor and keyboard, I suggest trying one node for starters. If that goes well, then you can fire up multiple simultaneous installations.

3. The compute node will start itself up, and after loading *vmlinux* and the initial RAM disk (*initrd*), it should very quickly flash a message on the screen about sending a DHCP request. The DHCP request is the "boot packet" the compute node sends, asking the master node to tell it what hostname and IP address to use. This is the data that you entered into the */etc/dhcpd.conf* file. Unless there is a problem with your network, or a typographical error in the DHCP configuration file, the compute node should quickly start flashing dialogs onto the screen indicating that a lot of software is being installed.

4. Once the installation is complete, you will see the "Congratulations" dialog on the screen. You should remove the boot disk from the floppy disk drive and press ENTER to reboot the system.

5. Repeat these steps for each of the compute nodes in your cluster. Once you have completed all of the nodes, you may configure the cluster and make it ready for use.

Screen shots/output

It is impossible to grab screen shots of a KickStart installation because everything happens so quickly.

On the master node, you should see output from the DHCP daemon that looks very much like this for each computer node installation you start:

```
Apr 25 16:11:26 cluster dhcpd: DHCPDISCOVER from 00:e0:29:1c:cc:84 via eth0
Apr 25 16:11:26 cluster dhcpd: DHCPOFFER on 10.0.2.3 to 00:e0:29:1c:cc:84 via eth0
Apr 25 16:11:26 cluster dhcpd: DHCPREQUEST for 10.0.2.3 from 00:e0:29:1c:cc:84 via eth0
Apr 25 16:13:29 cluster dhcpd: DHCPDISCOVER from 00:e0:29:1c:cc:84 via eth0
Apr 25 16:13:29 cluster dhcpd: DHCPOFFER on 10.0.2.3 to 00:e0:29:1c:cc:84 via eth0
Apr 25 16:13:29 cluster dhcpd: DHCPREQUEST for 10.0.2.3 from 00:e0:29:1c:cc:84 via eth0
Apr 25 16:13:29 cluster dhcpd: DHCPACK on 10.0.2.3 to 00:e0:29:1c:cc:84 via eth0
```

```
Apr 25 16:13:30 cluster mountd[293]: NFS mount of /mnt/cdrom attempted from 10.0.2.3
Apr 25 16:13:30 cluster mountd[293]: /mnt/cdrom has been mounted by 10.0.2.3
```

Of course, your output will have different Ethernet addresses (and timestamps), but the general gist will be the same.

What is happening here is that the DHCP daemon is responding to a *bootp* (boot packet) request from a machine with the Ethernet address *00:e0:29:1c:cc:84* that was heard on its "eth0" interface. The DHCP daemon then looks up that hardware address in the *dhcpd.conf* file that you edited to include all of your compute nodes. The daemon looks up the Ethernet address and finds out the name and IP address that it should send out in response.

The DHCP daemon sends out the name and IP address, along with other information in the record for that host, in the form of a "DHCP offer packet." The compute node accepts the name and IP address and then attempts to mount the CD-ROM that is mounted at the */mnt/cdrom* mount point on the master node.

Once the CD-ROM is successfully mounted, the KickStart program installs all of the required Linux packages, and finally installs the clustering software and toolkits.

Testing the results

The proof is, as they say, in the pudding. You now have a master node and a collection of compute nodes; the best way to test them will be to continue on to Chapter 6, *Managing Clusters*, to begin the process of getting your cluster ready to do some real work!

CHAPTER SIX

MANAGING CLUSTERS

Now that we've designed a cluster and installed the operating system and the basic programs we need, the really interesting work can begin.

In order to be able to actually use this collection of machines like a supercomputer, you have to be able to manage it in such a way that you (or your users, if you're using this system in the context of a business) can concentrate on using its computing power and tools and not on the minutiae of managing all of the systems that make up the cluster.

This chapter will present concepts, software, and tools for handling the most critical aspects of cluster management, from basic maintenance such as creation and removal of cluster nodes, through account creation, accounting, and batch system management.

Most of this chapter deals with a cluster management system developed specifically for this book, which is based on a PostgreSQL database and a collection of Perl–CGI scripts.

The last sections of this chapter cover a number of command-line tools and facilities that were installed as part of the installation from the Linux Clusters CD-ROM that will also be helpful to you as you manage your cluster.

It would be nice if there were a single unified collection of tools that were available to manage Unix systems. Unfortunately, such a system doesn't exist. Most commercial efforts to make the management of large systems collections have met with limited success. Although most systems hardware vendors make good packages for running their own equipment, these proprietary systems don't work when used on collections of systems from multiple vendors. It makes sense if you think about it—if you make one machine just as easy to use as any other, where's the competitive advantage? Efforts by consortia composed of multiple vendors aimed to develop a unified management system (such as the Distributed Computing Environment, or DCE, from the

Open Software Foundation) have also missed the mark because they require a lot of operating system modifications on the part of vendors, are expensive to implement, and the services themselves add considerable overhead to the operation of a system.

The state of the world for high performance clustered systems is, sadly, even worse. There are very few commercial cluster systems, and those that exist are from big companies such as Sun Microsystems and Sequent whose management interfaces work well on their own systems, but cannot be used with the kinds of Beowulf-like clusters that are presented in this book.

There are several ongoing projects in the Open Source community to make management environments for distributed systems. Unfortunately, this is fundamentally a difficult problem, since any Linux-based solution would have to run on a large number of hardware platforms and support an almost unlimited variety of devices and peripherals. With this last point in mind, it's no wonder efforts like DCE have met with limited success.

One of the most promising of the Open Source efforts is *LinuxConf,** led by Jacques Gélinas. LinuxConf is an attempt to make a comprehensive graphical interface to administer every subsystem on a Linux system. It is a system daemon process that takes control of subsystem activation very early in the boot process and shepherds the initialization of programs by keeping track of what programs should be started and what configuration files should be used. All of this information is kept in a set of databases that are used to write the actual configuration files used by programs such as sendmail, the FTP daemon, and any other service you can think of.

Its design goals include cluster management, but as of this writing, LinuxConf is not yet ready to run in a production clustered environment. LinuxConf is installed by default on all of the cluster nodes on your system since it comes as a part of the basic RedHat installation, but it is not activated.

Part of my mission in writing this book was not only to explain clusters and help you build one of these systems, but also to make it possible to run a cluster in a way that resembles a "production environment" as closely as possible. To that end, I have provided a system to manage all of the information about major parts of the cluster from a central point, which then propagates complete configuration files to other nodes in the cluster.

This process is accomplished using a database system that stores the vital information about the cluster's configuration and users in a series of tables. This information includes users that are authorized to use the cluster, descriptions of the cluster's hardware and software packages, performance and accounting, and even configuration of batch queues. With this system, you can even break your cluster into subclusters if, for

---

* LinuxConf information may be found at *http://www.solucorp.qc.ca/linuxconf.*

example, you wanted to dedicate a set of processing elements to a given project or run test versions of software.

This chapter presumes that you have built a cluster using the CD-ROM that comes with this book. The KickStart system and the post-installation scripts will have installed all of the components needed to set up the cluster management system. If you are building a cluster based on some other architecture, such as Sun SPARC or the Compaq Alpha, you can still use the management system and tools described in this chapter, but you will have to install the tools manually.

This chapter will work through the most important problems of cluster management first, such as setting up the administration system itself, and then move on to complex topics including scheduling and queueing systems, network management, and accounting.

The majority of this chapter deals with software that has been installed on the cluster during the installation process, much of which is managed through a web interface and is accessible via the version of Netscape Navigator that is included with the Linux Clusters CD-ROM. The rest details third party tools that are included on the Linux Clusters CD-ROM that may be helpful to you as you work with your cluster.

Basic Tools

Before we get into the details of the cluster management system, we should spend a short amount of time on some of the basic tools that are installed on your cluster that the management system works with.

NIS

The Network Information System,* or NIS, is a mechanism designed by Sun Microsystems that allows various small databases to be shared over a network. These small databases can hold anything, but most often are used for publishing host tables, services listings (as in the */etc/services* file), username/password files, and maps that allow filesystems to be remotely mounted from file servers.

In the clustered environment, NIS is very useful for allowing programs that are running on compute nodes to have access to applications and other data in a coherent way without having to copy these items manually from the master server to each of the compute nodes.

---

* NIS was originally named "Yellow Pages," an homage to the familiar phone book, but a British company owns the trademark (in the UK) on the term so the package was renamed the "Network Information System" in the late 1980s.

NIS is also used to distribute username and password files so that login information can be shared by all nodes of the cluster. Normally, cluster users will not log in to compute notes directly; rather, they will log in to the master mode to edit, compile, link, and launch their applications.

Each compute node should know that the user is valid and has an account. Having login info available to all of the compute nodes ensures that these user programs can run without having to manually push password files around the network. NIS takes care of setting up the data that is pulled down periodically by all of the compute nodes.

cfengine

The Configuration Engine (*cfengine*) is a tool that was developed at the University of Oslo in Norway by Mark Burgess. *cfengine* is a scripting tool that is designed to allow system administrators to update packages, edit scripts, and perform a variety of maintenance tasks on networked hosts from a centralized server.

The cluster management system uses *cfengine* to help make the package distribution process more streamlined. Once packages are delivered to compute nodes, the standard Redhat tool, the RedHat Package Manager (RPM), is used to perform the final installation.

Along with a number of *cron* jobs and other scripts, these packages are the major underpinnings of the cluster management system. But there are a lot of ways to effectively implement systems management policies on any collection of distributed systems, including Linux clusters. The methods presented here work well for moderately sized (4–32 node) clusters. As your clusters grow, or if you are going to be running your cluster as part of a much larger infrastructure network, you may want to expand upon them.

You can find good models for comprehensive systems management principles (i.e., methods that work on large diverse networks that have more than just a few workstations and a cluster) in environments where downtime can cost a lot of money. A good paper that discusses a very complete view of infrastructure systems deployment is by Steve Traugott of Sterling Software and NASA Ames Research Center and Joel Huddleston of Level 3 Communications entitled "Bootstrapping an Infrastructure," which was presented at the 1998 LISA conference in Boston, MA.* This paper takes the long-term development view of systems administration and management. A lot of what this paper has to offer will require commitment on the part of both management and implementation, but like all well thought out processes, the ideas it presents can be "grown into" and do not have to be implemented all at once.

---

* This paper is available at the USENIX Association online library, which is available to USENIX members. USENIX may be reached at *http://www.usenix.com*.

The Cluster Management System

In order to be able to use a cluster as a holistic system, you need the ability to treat it as a single computer, rather than a collection of machines tied together by a network. This means that users of your cluster should be able to log in to a single machine, usually the master node of the cluster, and have access to all of the system's facilities, from editing programs to compiling and debugging them to entering jobs into batch queues for cluster-wide execution.

As the manager of the cluster, you need facilities that will allow you to manage and maintain the cluster. Your tasks will include adding nodes as your computing needs grow, removing nodes for maintenance, as well as adding, updating, or removing software from the cluster. Another key function of a cluster management system is managing users, groups, and projects. These functions are part of everyday systems management in single-user workstation environments, but take on added significance in the cluster environment since these tasks must be applied to a larger number of machines simultaneously.

What Can You Do with It?

This cluster management system is based on the Open Source PostgreSQL database, and can be used to manage a large variety of aspects of cluster operation, including:

Nodes
> The node management module allows you to keep track of all of the nodes in the cluster. Among other things, you can define subclusters of machines that can be dedicated to specific projects, users, or group codes, or even test clusters that are running different packages from other cluster nodes.

Groups
> The group management module allows you to create groups into which cluster users can be placed for billing purposes.

Projects
> The project management module allows you to create distinct projects under the auspices of groups and to assign these projects quotas and resource limits that will apply to users assigned to those projects. This is especially useful if you are running your cluster in an environment where you need to account for resource usage.

Users
> The user management module allows you to add, delete, activate, or suspend access to users of your cluster.

Packages
> The package management module allows you to add, remove, or update software packages on your cluster.

Accounting

The accounting module allows you to set up charge-back rates for users and groups. This module also allows you to grant access to group administrators who have the capability to look at and generate reports on account usage in their group.

Queues

The queue management module allows you to manage batch queues on the master node and the compute nodes of the cluster. Batch queues are at the heart of the ability to run long-term, non-interactive jobs on parallel clusters. This module will allow you to create batch queues that feed into the compute nodes of the cluster and help balance the computational load of jobs across the cluster.

Security

The security module allows you to define security for the cluster in terms of who can connect to the cluster, to monitor alerts from subsystems, and so on.

Installing the Cluster Management System

Installing the cluster management system is a two-stage process. Part one involves signing on to the cluster as root and adding the required administrative accounts. Part two requires using the newly created ClusterAdmin account to load the administrative database and then to populate it with information about the cluster, people, and projects.

Creating the Required Accounts

When you installed the Linux Clusters CD-ROM software on your machines, a lot of software was installed. In addition to the Linux operating system and about 240 other supporting packages, several accounts were added to enable the cluster to be administered.

The root account

The most important of these accounts is the *root* account. The root, or *superuser*, account is the de facto owner of all files, packages, and processes on the system. Your users may have unique user and group IDs, but at the end of the day, the root account controls everything and can execute any command or access any file.

You will use the root account to create utility accounts that will allow you to install and configure the cluster management system.

You should use the root account only when you are installing core system components, such as upgrades to the Linux operating system itself, or, as we are about to do, when you are installing the cluster management system. All other management of the cluster should be done through the cluster management system.

Logging in to the root account

In order to start the installation of the cluster management system, you will need to log in to the root account on the master node of the cluster. This step should be done from the console of the master node, preferably with the X Windows system running. Having the window system up and running will make it easier to have multiple shell windows available, should you need to look up manual pages or see the output of multiple programs.

The root account has been given a default password on the master node and on each of the slave/compute nodes listed in Chapter 5. Log in as root. If this is the first time you have logged in as root, it may take several moments as the system copies initialization files and sets up the GNOME window manager.

Once you have logged in, you will see a standard desktop with a number of applications opened, such as the one shown in Figure 6-1. You may see a dialog box warning you that running as root is extremely dangerous since you can destroy your system—acknowledge this dialog by clicking on its "Okay" button. The whole point of this exercise will be to set things up so you *don't* have to use such a powerful account to run your cluster.

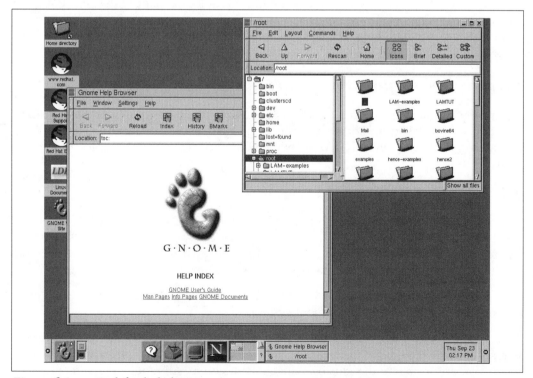

Figure 6-1. root's default desktop

The applications running by default are the GNOME help system and a file browser. Both of these may be closed or minimized if you would like to get them out of the way.

You will need to bring up an X terminal so that you can type commands to the system. To launch an X terminal, click once on the "terminal" icon in the tool bar—it's the one between the toolbox icon and the "N" (Netscape) icon on the GNOME toolbar. After a moment, you should have a new window with a root shell prompt (#).

From this point, you have complete control over the master node of the cluster, and you can start the process of installing the management system.

Mounting the CD-ROM

In order to install the cluster management system, you will need to mount the Linux Clusters CD-ROM.

With the CD in the CD-ROM drive, execute the following command, which will mount the CD-ROM and make it available to the system:

```
[root@master /root]# mount -r /dev/cdrom /mnt/cdrom
```

You can check to see if the CD-ROM is correctly mounted by using the *df* command. The actual sizes of the partitions listed may be different than what is shown here, but should look something like this:

Filesystem	1k-blocks	Used	Available	Use%	Mounted on
/dev/sda1	248847	47711	188286	20%	/
/dev/sda5	5050844	11271	4778117	0%	/home
/dev/sda9	248847	431	235566	0%	/tmp
/dev/sda6	1018298	650548	315139	67%	/usr
/dev/sda7	995115	76970	866739	8%	/usr/local
/dev/sda8	893986	33052	814749	4%	/var
/dev/scd0	589998	589998	0	100%	/mnt/cdrom

The important part of this listing is the last line where we can see that the CD-ROM is indeed mounted and online.

Creating the clusteradmin User

The *clusteradmin* account will be the owner of all of the data about the cluster and will also be the central point of control for all aspects of the operation of the cluster.

In order to create this account, you will need to use the X terminal window. At the prompt, type the following commands:

```
[root@master /root]# /usr/sbin/groupadd -g 502 clusteradmin
[root@master /root]# /usr/sbin/useradd -n -g clusteradmin -G root clusteradmin
```

```
[root@master /root]# chfn -f "Cluster Administrator" clusteradmin
Changing finger information for clusteradmin.
Finger information changed.
```

These commands perform the following functions:

1. Adds a new group to the system for cluster administrators called "clusteradmin"; this will allow you to add subadministrators if you want to divide up the work of running the cluster. The −g flag sets the group number (GID) to 502, which is an unused number in the */etc/group* file.

2. Creates a new user, *clusteradmin*, who will own all of the cluster administrative databases. This user is, by default, a member of the *clusteradmin* group, and is additionally a member of the *root* group. This allows the *clusteradmin* user to execute some commands that would normally be reserved for the superuser.

3. Lastly, sets the name of the *clusteradmin* user to "Cluster Administrator" in the systems password file and makes this name visible to anyone looking up who is logged into the system.

Unless there is an error, these commands should return no output. Make sure that the username *clusteradmin* is spelled correctly. If you make a mistake, delete the account by using the command:

```
/usr/sbin/userdel name
```

where **name** is the misspelled version of the name. This is a command that should be used with great care—*userdel* doesn't prompt you to ask if you're sure about what you are doing. It is possible to delete any user with it, including root. Deleting root would, of course, render the master node (or any other node) unusable and cause you to have to reload the system from scratch.

Once you have created the *clusteradmin* account, check to see that the account is in the system by entering the following command:

```
[root@master /root]# finger clusteradmin
```

The *finger* command will return all of the information about the account:

```
Login: clusteradmin               Name: Cluster Administrator
Directory: /home/clusteradmin     Shell: /bin/bash
Never logged in.
No mail.
No Plan.
[root@master /root]#
```

If the information you get back from *finger* looks like the example, you are all set.

Giving clusteradmin Database Access

Once you have set up the *clusteradmin* user, you will need to insert this user into the PostgreSQL database system so that the *clusteradmin* account can be used to create and manage databases.

Checking PostgreSQL

Before you can add *clusteradmin* as a PostgreSQL database user, you should ensure that the PostgreSQL database processes are up and running. These processes are normally started at boot time, but it's a good idea to check anyway. The command:

```
[root@master /root]# /etc/rc.d/init.d/postgresql status
```

should return:

```
postmaster (pid 613) is running...
```

(The number in parentheses may be different from what is shown here)

If you see the response:

```
postmaster is stopped
```

then Postgres is not running. If this is the case, you should start it with the command:

```
[root@master /root]# /etc/rc.d/init.d/postgresql start
```

which should return the message:

```
Starting postgresql service: postmaster [5157]
```

The number in square brackets will most likely be different. This is the process ID of the Postgres control process, known as "postmaster." It's not important that you know this number; it is given in case you need to manipulate the PostgreSQL processes directly, which should never be done except in an emergency. Starting and stopping PostgreSQL should be done with its control script as above.

Logged in as root, you can use the *su* command to become another user. In this case, you'll want to become the Postgres user by entering the command:

```
[root@master /root]# su - postgres
```

Make sure that you put spaces around the dash (-). Not doing so will cause the system to try to run any startup scripts that may be installed in the Postgres directory, which could have unintended side effects.

Once this command has executed, you will notice that you no longer see the same shell prompt. The prompt has changed to that of the Postgres user, as shown here:

```
[postgres@master pgsql]$
```

To add the *clusteradmin* user to Postgres, you will execute the PostgreSQL *createuser* command at the prompt:

```
[postgres@master pgsql]$ createuser clusteradmin
```

Postgres will then prompt you for information regarding the new user of the database. For the question about the Unix user ID, just press RETURN to accept the default answer, and answer "y" to the other questions, as in this example:

```
Enter user's postgres ID or RETURN to use unix user ID: 500 -> return
Is user "clusteradmin" allowed to create databases (y/n) y
Is user "clusteradmin" allowed to add users? (y/n) y
createuser: clusteradmin was successfully added
```

The user ID number presented may differ from what is shown above.

This will allow the cluster administrator to create the cluster administration databases, and to create more cluster administrators.

This completes the setup of the clusteradmin user account. You should log out of the *postgres* owner account by typing the command *exit* at the shell prompt.

You should now be back at the root prompt. The last task we have to complete before we can log in as the cluster administrator is to set the password on the account. To do this, use the *passwd* command, giving the account name as the argument to the program:

```
[root@master /root]# passwd clusteradmin
Changing password for user clusteradmin
New UNIX password: <somepassword>
Retype new UNIX password: <somepassword>
passwd: all authentication tokens updated successfully
```

The system will prompt you for a password, which, unlike our example *<somepassword>*, will not be displayed on the screen. Make sure that you choose a good password that you can remember. Adding symbols, punctuation, and numbers will make passwords much harder to guess. The Linux password checker will not allow your password to be based on common phrases or words found in most dictionaries.

You can now log out of the *root* account. This is accomplished by clicking on the footprint icon in the toolbar (the left-most icon in Figure 6-1) and selecting "log out" from the bottom of the menu (or by typing "logout" if you are not logged in via the window manager).

Using the clusteradmin Account

Now that the clusteradmin account has been set up, we can get to the heart of the matter: setting up the cluster management system and getting the cluster environment ready to run applications.

Again, you will need to log in to the system. This time, however, you will be using the newly minted *clusteradmin* account that you created in the last section.

At the login panel, enter the username *clusteradmin,* press ENTER, and then type the password you selected for this account. Much like the superuser account, once you log in, you should see a default desktop with a few applications that are started automatically.

As in the previous section, you will need to start an X terminal so that you can enter commands that are required to initialize the cluster administration database.

Initializing the Cluster Administration Database

The cluster administration database is a collection of large tables that have been designed to allow you to keep track of a large number of features of your Linux cluster. In order to enter data into this system, we must first create an empty database, and then tell the PostgreSQL system how we want to handle data entered into that database. In database parlance, this process is called "initializing a database" and "creating tables."

To create the database, we will call use the PostgreSQL *createdb* command:

```
[clusteradmin@master clusteradmin]$ /usr/bin/createdb clusteradmin
```

Unless there was a problem, there should be no output from this command.

If you receive an error message from this command, make sure that the database is running; refer back to "Checking PostgreSQL."

Now that the database has been created, we can set up the tables that will drive the heart of the system. The scripts for creating the tables, and other information you will need in this section, are stored on the CD-ROM in the *ClusterAdmin* directory. We could make reference to the copies on the CD-ROM, but that is a lot of extra typing, so it is a good idea to copy these files to the clusteradmin account home directory. To copy these files, execute the following command:

```
[clusteradmin@master clusteradmin]$ cp -Rp /mnt/cdrom/ClusterTools/AdminDB .
```

This will copy all of the files and subdirectories from the CD-ROM into the current directory.

Note

Please note the "." at the end of the command above. There should be a space between it and the word "AdminDB". The "." is a standard Unix shorthand mechanism meaning "this directory." It functions exactly as if we had typed the full destination directory in the command `cp  -Rp  /mnt.cdrom/ ClusterTools/AdminDB/home/clusteradmin/AdminDB`. The shortcut is just a convenience that saves a little time.

Next, change directory into the *AdminDB* directory with the command:

```
[clusteradmin@master clusteradmin]$ cd AdminDB
```

Finally, create the tables in the database by executing the command:

```
[clusteradmin@master clusteradmin]$ psql -f create_tables.sql clusteradmin
```

This command will tell the PostgreSQL database system to create a series of tables, contained in the file *create_tables.sql* in the database *clusteradmin.*

Postgres will echo the commands in the file to standard output as it executes them:

```
/*********************************************/
/** Tables for describing the cluster      **/
/*********************************************/
create table node
(node_id int,
 name char(32),
 mac_addresss char(32),
 ip_address char(30),
 hardware_type  char(15),
 processor_speed int,
 memory int,
 total_disk_space int,
 master int
);
CREATE

create table node_packages
( node_id int,
  package char(64)
);
CREATE
:
:
```

After several moments, the command will complete and all of the tables will have been instantiated into the database.

The net effect of all of these commands, which are just long strings of Structured Query Language or SQL (pronounced "sequel") commands, has been to create a database that can keep track of information relevant to a clustered environment.

If you want to see the results of your work, you can ask Postgres to show you the contents of the newly created clusteradmin database by executing the command:

```
[clusteradmin@master clusteradmin]$ psql clusteradmin
```

The PostgreSQL database will then return a prompt that shows you what database you are connected to and give you a few tips on how to get help, execute a command, or leave the interactive PostgreSQL monitor. Typing \? at the command prompt will give you complete help on using the system, if you want to see all that the monitor can do. For our purposes, the \d command will print out a listing of the tables created in the last section:

```
Welcome to the POSTGRESQL interactive sql monitor:
 Please read the file COPYRIGHT for copyright terms of POSTGRESQL

    type \? for help on slash commands
    type \q to quit
    type \g or terminate with semicolon to execute query
 You are currently connected to the database: clusteradmin

clusteradmin=> \d

Database    = clusteradmin
+--------------------------+------------------------------+----------+
| Ownee                    | Relation                     | Type     |
+--------------------------+------------------------------+----------+
| clusteradmin             | admin_users                  | table    |
| clusteradmin             | cluster_info                 | table    |
| clusteradmin             | group_info                   | table    |
| clusteradmin             | node                         | table    |
| clusteradmin             | node_cluster                 | table    |
| clusteradmin             | node_packages                | table    |
| clusteradmin             | project                      | table    |
| clusteradmin             | sys_usage                    | table    |
| clusteradmin             | user_group                   | table    |
| clusteradmin             | user_info                    | table    |
| clusteradmin             | user_project                 | table    |
+--------------------------+------------------------------+----------+
clusteradmin=>
```

This listing reports that there are eleven tables in the clusteradmin database. As you can see from their names, they cover a large number of areas.

The SQL monitor can be used to dig even deeper into the tables in the database. For example, to look at the structure of the *group_info* table, where information about resource allocations and costs are kept, you could dump out the structure of that table:

```
clusteradmin=> \d group_info

Table    = group_info
```

Field	Type	Length
gid	int4	4
group_name	char()	20
group_admin	char()	20
group_description	char()	80
disk_quota	int4	4
disk_used	int4	4
disk_cost	float4	4
io_quota	int4	4
io_used	int4	4
io_cost	float4	4
cpu_quota	int4	4
cpu_used	int4	4
cpu_cost	float4	4
connect_quota	int4	4
connect_used	int4	4
connect_cost	float4	4
last_update	timestamp	4

As you can see, the structure of database tables is much like any other programming system for data manipulation. There are a number of fundamental types such as bytes, floating point numbers, integers, and even higher-order data classes such as time-stamps.

Finally, to exit the SQL monitor, you would type:

clusteradmin=>\q

which will return you to the clusteradmin account's shell prompt.

The format, structures, and query methods used in the clusteradmin database are covered completely in Appendix D, *The Cluster Administration Database*.

The cluster administration database is now ready to be used. But, before we start exploring the different modules, we should briefly explore the database itself and how it can be used to implement a system that I hinted previously was unachievable by some very well-funded corporations.

Department of Redundancy Department

Any system that is going to allow a system administrator to maintain the state of a large number of systems is going to need a database. That database is going to contain, for better or worse, a lot of information that seems to be redundant. Unix systems usually have a large number of places where information about users and groups is kept. The standard places are the */etc/passwd* and */etc/group* files for the main user and group information; newer systems have shadow password files to keep encrypted passwords away from prying eyes, as well as files that contain disk quota information. Linux systems add additional files that keep information about password and account expiration dates.

Unfortunately, unlike systems such as Digital's OpenVMS and IBM's OS/390, there are no finely grained administrative resource controls under Linux. This means that beyond simple resource controls, like disk quotas, there is no direct way to control other resources used by a user in a systematic way. At the process level, a user can control how much time a program uses by setting a number of shell variables that can control CPU time limits, but this is not very useful to a cluster administrator.

For example, on an OpenVMS system, it is possible to specify resource controls so precisely that you can control a process's activities at runtime down to the level of how many I/O calls are made. These kinds of controls allow for finely grained accounting and charge-back capabilities. Unfortunately, such real-time controls do not yet exist under Linux.

The cluster administration database is a database that will allow you to create users and apply resource controls in a non-real-time fashion. With this system, you can have allocations for system resources such as aggregate CPU time on a group, project, or user basis. This database is used in conjunction with process accounting that is run on all nodes in the cluster to enforce these limitations.

Figure 6-2 shows the basic schema of the cluster administration database. A more complete description of the database and its components can be found in Appendix D.

The database is designed to have a large amount of system resource and usage information, not all of which is presently implemented. Basic functionality is there, but there are hooks in place so that the database can be extended by administrators or other Open Source developers.

Structure of the Management System

As shown in Figure 6-3, the cluster management system operates at two levels. The first level is geared toward the cluster administrator as the "owner" of all of the resources of the cluster. The cluster owner owns the tasks of cluster building, node setup, account creation/maintenance, and all of the other tasks that are done by a

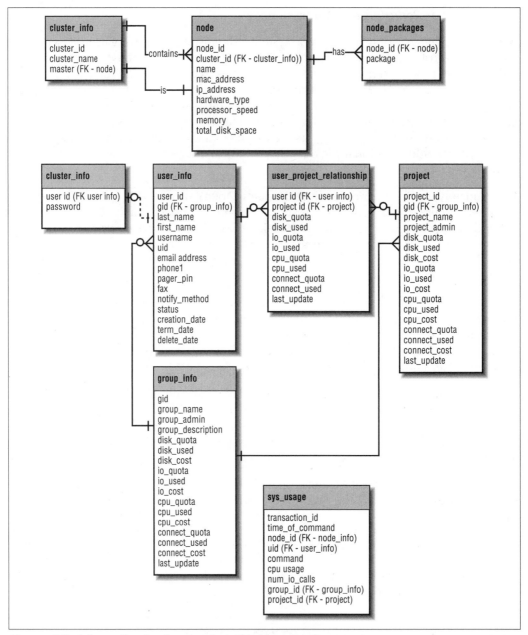

Figure 6-2. Schema for the cluster administration database

typical Unix sysadmin. The only difference here is that instead of supporting a general computing environment where users might be using a variety of commercial applications, the cluster administrator usually is working in a very rigidly structured environment. In this environment, the goal is to squeeze every last computational cycle out of every node in the cluster, and the users typically are high-powered programmers writing seriously "moby,"* intense pieces of numerical code, not folks running word processors and mine-sweeper.

The second level of operation, shown on the right-hand side in Figure 6-3, is for the group administrator who needs to allocate resources in terms of projects, disk quotas, CPU time limits, and other billable resources that must be shared by members of a group using the cluster. These group administrators have the responsibility to ensure that cluster users and their groups/projects have the funding to run their jobs on the cluster (in terms of either real funds, or the budgetary "funny money" that often is attached to project budgets).

Using the Management System

The cluster management system is accessible through the Netscape Navigator browser. To launch the browser, click on the Netscape icon (the graphic "N" in the GNOME toolbar). After a few moments, the browser will open to the start-up page for the cluster online management system. The installation scripts will set up a default set of preferences for Netscape when run as the root user on the cluster's master node, but should you need to access the cluster management system from another machine, the URL will be *http://master*. The management system is also accessible via a link on the cluster's home page. The home page will look like the screen shown in Figure 6-4.†

From this start-up page, you can access either the Linux cluster's documentation set, which has reference material for all of the software tools on the cluster such as MPI, PVI, and a number of other tools and is accessible to all cluster users, or the cluster management system, which is a password-protected set of web pages that control cluster operations.

I believe in a hands-on approach to doing new things, so click on the link for *Cluster Management*, and we'll start using the system to set up some features of your cluster.

The Cluster Management Page

The cluster management page will allow you to access and manipulate the cluster administration database through a web browser. Data manipulated via the browser will then trigger events in the database that will cause changes to occur in subsystems on the master node and on each of the slave nodes.

---

* Moby is defined in *The New Hacker's Dictionary* as "large, immense, complex, and impressive." The kinds of computational problems that are run on clusters (and other supercomputers) by definition are moby. Otherwise why waste the effort? Even though I have avoided using too many hackerisms, *The New Hacker's Dictionary* is really a fun read. It's edited by Eric Raymond, a guru of the Open Source movement, and published by MIT Press.

† In case you're wondering about that cape-wearing fellow on the cluster home page, his name is "UberTux." He's based on the original Linux penguin ("Tux") by Larry Ewing. Ubertux is the mascot of my company, Really Fast Systems, LLC, which sells Linux-based clusters and associated services.

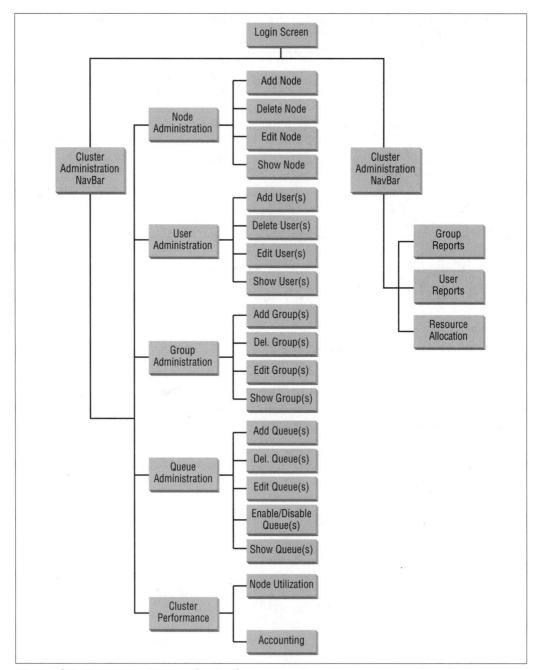

Figure 6-3. Management screen hierarchy

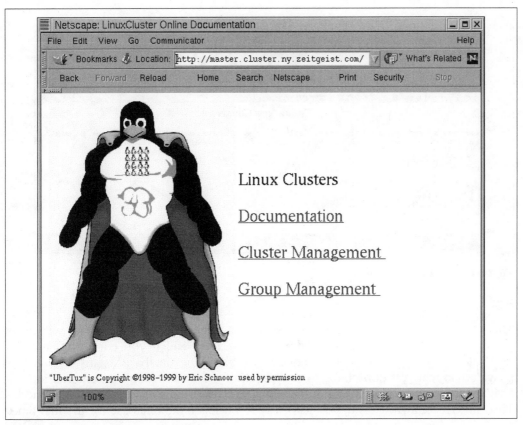

Figure 6-4. *Linux cluster's home page*

Naming Clusters

Our first stop on the cluster management trail will be to add the cluster itself into the cluster management system. Unless you will be breaking a large cluster into subclusters, this is a process that is usually done only once. From the cluster management toolbar, click on the "Add Cluster" icon. This will bring up a very simple window, shown in Figure 6-5, that will let you create a new cluster definition in the cluster administration database.

Once a cluster has been created, you can move on to adding the nodes you have created into the database.

Node Management

The goal of the node management components of the cluster management system is to be able to keep track of the systems in the cluster and to set up a basis by which we can use this system to allocate resources, keep track of packages installed on the cluster, and so on.

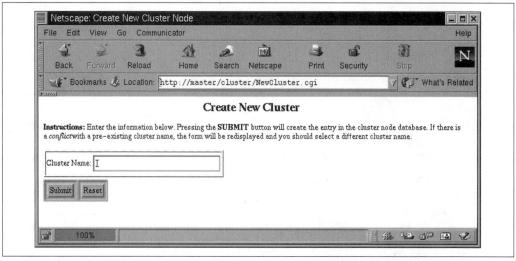

Figure 6-5. Cluster creation screen

Adding nodes

There are two ways to perform the initial database population The first way is by using a Perl script that is in the AdminDB directory, which you copied off the CD-ROM along with the instructions required to create the database itself. This script is provided so that you don't have to re-type all of the information you entered into the DHCP configuration file when you installed the clustering software on all your nodes. This is the recommended (and easiest) way to populate the database for the first time.

The second way—the one that you will make use of when adding nodes to an existing cluster—will be by using the browser interface to the cluster administration database.

Using the Perl script

To run the Perl script, execute the following commands:

```
[clusteradmin@master clusteradmin]$ cd ~clusteradmin/AdminDB
[clusteradmin@master clusteradmin]$ /usr/bin/perl parse-dhcp.pl < /etc/dhcpd.conf
```

The script will read the DHCP configuration file, break down the entries, and insert the data, node by node, into the cluster administration database. Its output will look very much like the following example, except for the hardware addresses, the information specific to your DNS domain name, and of course, the cluster name:

```
Looking for host information...
Cluster name: mycluster.
Domain Name: cluster.ny.zeitgeist.com
Special Case: Inserting master node info... Done!
```

```
Found "node2"....
      Ethernet address is "00:E0:81:10:34:C1"
      IP address is "10.0.2.2"
Inserting node2 into node database... Done!

Found "node3"....
      Ethernet address is "00:E0:81:10:34:5D"
      IP address is "10.0.2.3"
Inserting node3 into node database... Done!

Found "node4"....
      Ethernet address is "00:E0:81:10:32:32"
      IP address is "10.0.2.4"
Inserting node4 into node database... Done!
      :
      :
Reached the end of the file.  Bye!
```

Once this Perl script completes all of the nodes that you had entered into the DHCP system when you started, the software installation will be in the cluster administration database.

You may notice that the third line of the output makes reference to a "Special Case." In fact this script does a little sleight of hand: it puts information about the master node of the cluster into the node database before it starts working on the slave/compute nodes. This is done because the master node, by definition, isn't in the DHCP configuration file—it doesn't have to be since the master node is the DHCP server itself. However, the master node does have to be in the node database. The script takes care of adding the master node for you, and sets the master node's database flag indicating it is the master node of the cluster.

Adding nodes using the browser

Once you have your cluster set up and have initialized the node database using the Perl script above, the next step is to add nodes via the browser interface into the cluster administration database. To activate the node create screen, click on the "Add Node" icon in the toolbar.

As shown in Figure 6-6, the node creation screen asks for a variety of information that will be stored in cluster management system's node database. This database is used to create a variety of access files and system configuration files, including the DHCP configuration file that is used to bootstrap new cluster nodes.

Once a node is added into the database, the management system will add the relevant information from the node's database record into the system-level files that will be needed when the node is bootstrapped with the boot floppy you made back in Chapter 5, *Software Installation and Configuration*.

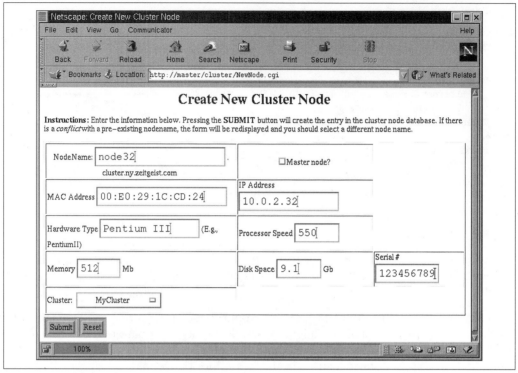

Figure 6-6. Creating a new cluster node

You should also note that there is a menu in this form that allows you to assign a node to a cluster. The cluster selected by default will be the name of the first cluster you created (presumably the one you created at the beginning of this section).

If you want to assign this node to a different cluster, such as a subcluster you are using for testing or dedicating nodes to a specific group of users, this is the place to do it.

Deleting nodes

Deleting a node is even easier than creating one. Clicking on the "Delete Node" icon on the toolbar will bring up a form that asks you for a node name to delete. A confirmation dialog will ask if you are sure you want to delete the node.

This feature should be used with caution—removing a node will delete it from the node database, remove it from all defined clusters, and stop all jobs running on that node. Needless to say, this can upset your users.

Showing nodes

To get a listing of all of the nodes in the cluster administration database, select the "Show Nodes" icon from the tool bar. Entering a node name or an asterisk (*) will display the information about the specific node you have inquired about or all of the nodes in the database, respectively, as shown in Figure 6-7.

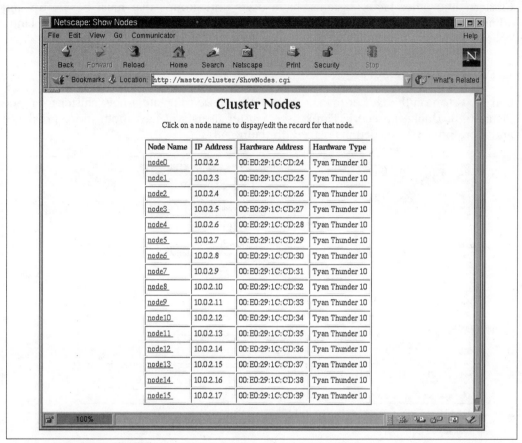

Figure 6-7. Showing cluster nodes

Editing nodes

Editing nodes is something that you may want to do if you upgrade the components that make up a node or a collection of nodes. To edit a node, there are two choices you can make: you can either click on the "Edit Node" icon from the management toolbar and then enter the node name that you wish to edit, or you can have the management system show you all of the nodes in the cluster, and then you can select a node from that list. The node editing screen looks exactly like the Create New Cluster Node screen shown in Figure 6-6, except that all of the information (except the node name) will be editable by you.

User Administration

Clusters, like other Linux systems, have users and groups that must be set up and administered. Cluster users have more specialized functions than on a general Linux system.

Creating New Users

Our next stop on the cluster management trail will be to create a new cluster user (see Figure 6-8). Unlike a generic Linux user, cluster users will have both more privileges and more potential restrictions placed on them.

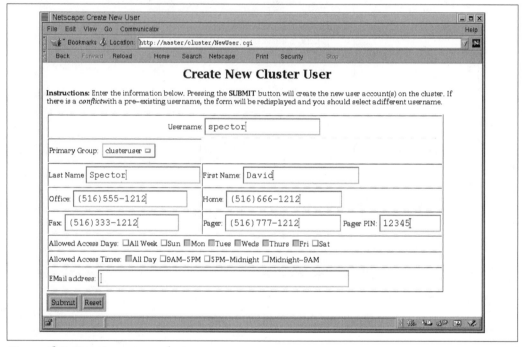

Figure 6-8. Creating a new cluster user

Displaying Users

Once you have created a user or two, you might want to check up on them and see if they were entered into the database.

Entering a username into the form shown in Figure 6-9 will show the database record for that user. Entering an asterisk will show all of the users in the database.

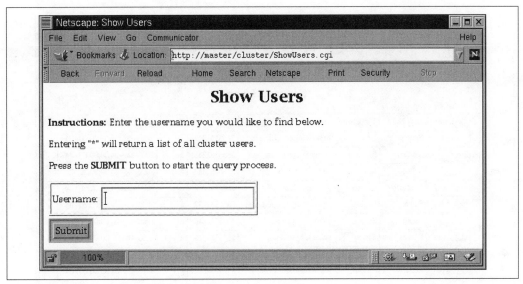

Figure 6-9. Entry screen for displaying user records

Individual usernames are displayed in the results as hypertext links, as shown in Figure 6-10. Selecting an individual username will bring up the complete records for that user.

Group Administration

The group administration forms allow the cluster administrator to break down the users into specific communities with common interests. Groups in the cluster management system are exactly the same as groups under Linux. In fact, when a new group is created, the system is queried for the first unused group number, and a new group is created in the */etc/group* file.

How do you assign a user to a group that doesn't exist yet? Unlike regular Unix systems administration where you could just go and edit the */etc/group* file, one of the rules that has been designed into the cluster management system is that every cluster user must be a member of at least one cluster group. In order to get around this recursive restriction, there is a default group created during the initialization of the database, the *clusterusers* group. This group is the default group for all cluster users and allows you to create users who can be reassigned to other groups as you create new groups and group administrators.

Creating New Groups

To create a new group, click on the "New Group" icon in the toolbar. The form, as shown in Figure 6-11, will require various pieces of information about the new group

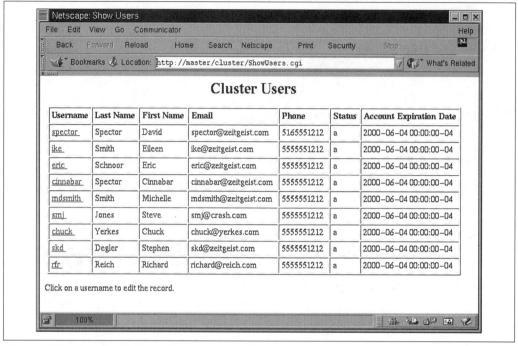

Figure 6-10. Results of displaying user records

including the allocations of CPU, disk space, and other resources that are available to the group and how much this new group will be billed for the use of these resources.

Most importantly, you will have to provide the username of an *existing user* who will be the maintainer of the group. The person you select for this role will have the authority to create projects that are part of the new group and will be able to dole out parts of the group's allocation of CPU time and other resources.

The "billing rates" are used by the accounting portion of the cluster administration database to generate reports that can be used for accounting charge-backs if your organization needs to actually account for time and resources used on your cluster.

If you don't need or want to account for these resources, you can fill in any of the quota items with "−1." This will tell the cluster management system that this group can use an "infinite" amount of these resources. If you should decide to do this, you should also fill in the rate areas with zeros; this will disable the accounting functions for the group so that group accounting reports will not be generated.

Remember that no activity takes place in a group all by itself. A group is an administrative placeholder for users and the projects that users work on. When each group is created, there is a special default project called the "general project" that is created along with it to hold all the users of the group that are not assigned to other projects. The group administrator can then create projects and assign users to them. The group's resources are then used by this general project or by specialized projects created by group administrators.

This system is designed to mirror the real world of business where companies have hierarchies that are in the general form of:

Company → Group → Project → Individual

This allows for tight control over the resources used by the members of the group.

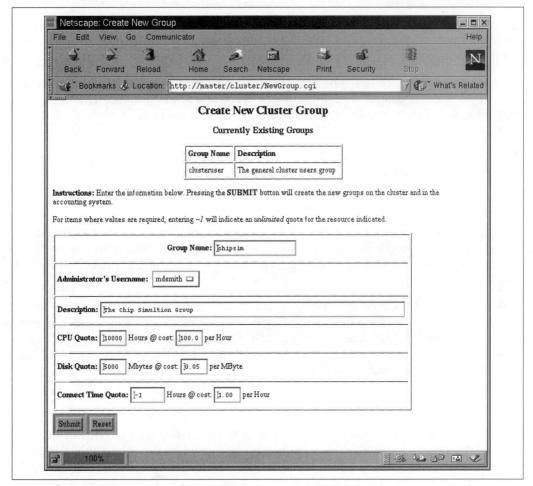

Figure 6-11. Creating a new cluster group

Editing Groups

Once groups have been created, there is very little reason to change any of their settings. Most of what happens inside the group is in the realm of project creation, termination, and resource allocation.

One of the reasons that a group may need to be edited is to add to its budgetary allocations for resources. If you are billing for CPU time, connect time, disk space, and other resources, it is entirely possible that a group (because of the activities of its subprojects) may exhaust some or all of its quotas.

With the group editing facility, you can update these allocations, change the billing rates for the group, or even change the designated group administrator.

Deleting Groups

Deleting groups is, hopefully, a rarity and should be done with *extreme* caution. Removal of a group has far-reaching ramifications not only for the group as an administrative entity, but also for every user and project that is contained by that group.

If a user is a member of only one group, for the purposes of this example the one that is being deleted, it will mean that the user's account will be disabled. This is a necessity since the cluster management system requires that users be members of at least one group.

One group can never be deleted: the *clusterusers* group that was created when the cluster administration database was initialized. *clusterusers* is a special group that contains the clusteradmin user and other system-level users. Its removal would damage the cluster administration database itself.

All users in a group that is going to be deleted should be removed or moved to another group beforehand, as the cluster administration database will not allow a group to be removed that still has users associated with it; having projects still extant in the group is okay.

To delete a group, click on the "Delete Group" icon in the toolbar. You will be shown a list of groups that are eligible for deletion. You can then select the group (or groups), and press the "Delete" button. You will be asked to confirm your decision and then, as long as the groups contain no active users, the groups and all of their subordinate projects will be purged from the system.

Deactivating Groups

A less extreme method for turning off a group is *group deactivation*. Group deactivation allows cluster administrators to turn off a group without permanently destroying it. This can be handy when a group has run out of funding and shouldn't be using the cluster but may be back in action soon.

Deactivating a group has the effect of suspending the accounts of users whose primary group is the focus of the deactivation. In other words, if there is a user named "jim" who has the primary group membership of "physics" and is also a member of the groups "chemistry" and "graphics," his account will be suspended when the group activation takes effect even though he is a member of other groups that may still be active.

Therefore, you should change the primary group membership of such users before deactivating groups. The group deactivation command will warn you about such users before asking you to confirm your group deactivation decision.

To deactivate a group, select the "Deactivate Group" icon from the toolbar; you will be presented with a list of available groups to deactivate. When you make your selection(s) and press the "Deactivate" button, you will be warned if your deactivation will suspend any users who are members of more than one group. You will have the chance to cancel the operation and reassign primary group memberships for these users.

Project Administration

Until this point in our exploration of the cluster administration database, we have been working with cluster administration commands that required the privileges of the cluster administrator, *clusteradmin.* This was because all of the commands being executed could affect the entire cluster administration database and could even cause system-level commands to be involved that could be quite dangerous if used improperly.

The project administration part of the cluster administration database allows semi-privileged users—group administrators—to work on a more narrowly focussed portion of the database where they can affect only users in their own groups and their sub-projects.

The project management forms allow group administrators to create and manage projects in the groups that they are responsible for. This allows group administrators to set up quotas and other billing resources out of their group's master quotas according to a number of different schemes.

In order to administer a project, a user must be logged in as the *clusteradmin* user, or as a user who has been designated as the group administrator for a given group.

Project Concepts

Projects in the cluster administration database map very nicely to projects in the real world. Typically, a development project is composed of a team of people, and the project is given a budget that comes out of resources assigned to a larger group. The same principles apply in the cluster management system.

All projects exist in the context of a larger group that has a pool of resources, and these resources are divided up in some fashion and given to projects in the group. In the real world, these resources are usually money in the form of a budget that can be spent on materials needed to complete the assigned project; in the cluster context, the resources are disk space, CPU time, and connect time on the Linux cluster.

For example, suppose we have a group called *simulation* that has a master allocation of 10,000 CPU hours, 12GB of disk space, and an "owning user" whose username is *alice*. Presume also that there are five cluster users, *bob, celia, donna, edward,* and *francis,* all of whom have group *simulation* as their primary group membership. Next suppose that there are three projects in the simulation group, called *CPU, memory,* and *disk.* These are charged with simulating new CPU, memory, and disk products respectively. Bob and Francis are assigned to the CPU project, Ceila is on the memory project, while Donna and Edward are responsible for the disk project.

Just like the real world, there are a number of ways that these group allocations can be subdivided among these projects, each with its own benefits and pitfalls.

The "lazy" allocation model would allow any user of any project to use as much of the available pool of resources as they wanted up to the limit of the available resources that have been allocated to the parent group. This means that any member of any of the three projects could use all 10,000 hours of CPU time or all of the disk space, leaving the other members of the group unable to do any work because there would be no quota left for them to work with.

Surprisingly, this is the method that is employed by most systems managers of large-scale systems, even though it usually results in some small number of users monopolizing most of the resources (especially disk space) on a system.

The next allocation strategy is called "fair share." In a fair share allocation, available resources are divided equally among all projects in the group. In our example group, under such an allocation method, each project would be allocated 2,000 hours of CPU time and 2.4GB of disk space. This strategy works well if all of the projects can be expected to use cluster resources evenly, but it can become a problem if you expect your project to grow or shrink. Then you will have to reallocate resources to ensure that everyone retains their fair share of the available (and remaining) resources. It also locks out key users who may need to use more CPU time or disk space than other members of the project and hinders projects that need more resources than others.

The final allocation method is called "explicit allocation." Explicit allocation is the most common method used by system administrators for allocating resources on non-Unix systems (such as IBM mainframes and DEC VMS systems). Unix systems have traditionally had fewer tools to enforce these resource constraints, so system managers often employ the "lazy allocation" method and then, when they run out of a resource such as disk space, cajole users with the largest disk usage to pare down their holdings.

In an explicit allocation scheme, each project is given an explicit amount of CPU time and disk space. This scheme ensures that everyone gets access to resources and that users that need more of a given resource can get it without monopolizing the total resources of the project or of the group.

The project administration tools will allow you to set up resource allocations at the project level using any of these three schemes.

Creating New Projects

A new project is created by first accessing the group administration page from the cluster administration navigation bar. If this is the first time the page is being accessed during a login session, you will need to authenticate yourself to the system by entering your password at the login panel.

Once you have entered the group administration page, you can access the new project form by clicking on the "New Project" icon, which will display the form shown in Figure 6-12.

Assigning Resources

The new project form has a number of fields that allow the group administrators to allocate resources to the project and to name and describe the new project.

As a first step, the project should be given a name and a description. Case is not important, but the name must be unique; the form will return an error message if the name is already in use when you press the "submit" button.

Next, decide how much of the group's resources should be allocated to this project. Part of this decision is deciding whether to apply any kind of resource control to the project. If there is only one project in the group or if accounting for resources is not an issue, you should select the "lazy allocation" scheme.

If you need to track resource usage, you will need to select one of the other allocation schemes, depending upon whether your users are likely to use cluster resources in a fairly evenhanded way (the "fair share" method), or if it is likely that this project will use so much of the group's quota that you will have to ensure that something is left for everyone else (the "explicit allocation" method).

Finally, you will need to move users into the project. You will notice that the only users available in the group members box are users that were explicitly designated as members of the group at the time their user IDs were created. These are the only users that can be added as project members. If you need to add other users to the project, you will need to add the usernames into the group you are working with before they can be added to the project.

You may perform this function after you set up the project by adding new members to the parent group and then editing the project to add new members.

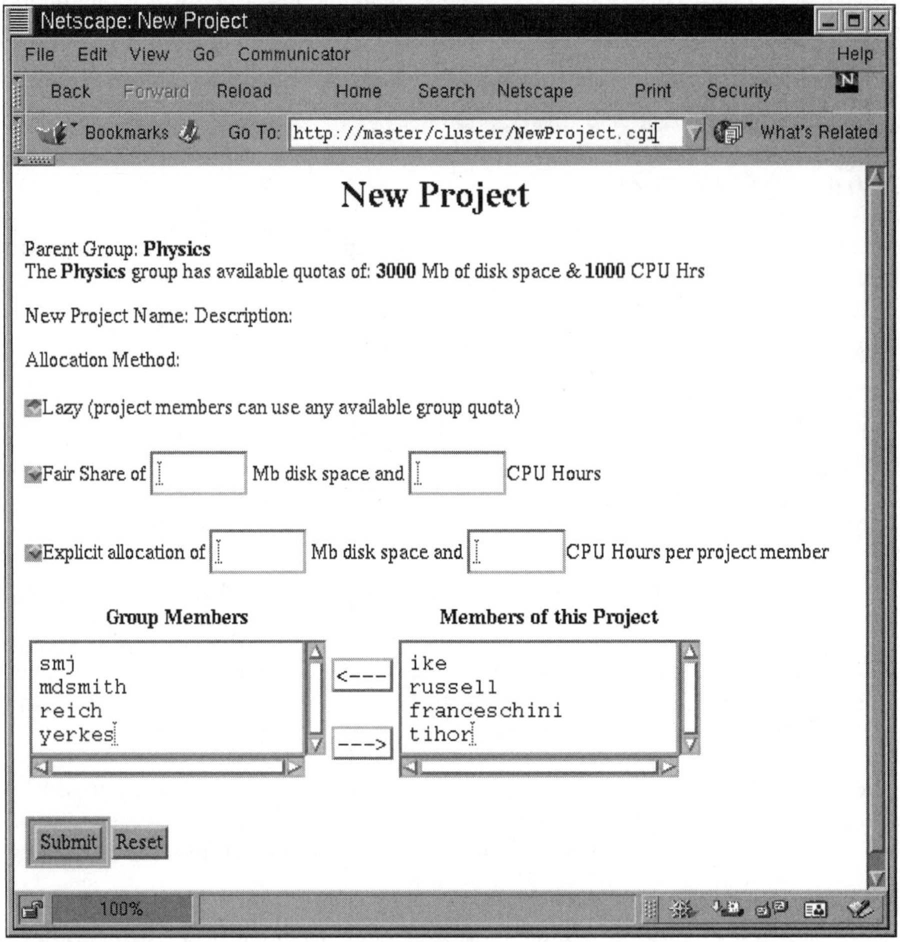

Figure 6-12. New project form

When everything is set up correctly, press the "submit" button and the data will be entered into the cluster administration database.

Editing a Project

Occasionally, people leave a group to do something else, or new members join a team to work on a project. When this happens, the group administrator will need to edit the project details to take these changes into account.

A more common occurrence is the need to add resources to projects that are under-way to ensure that they have enough computational resources to get their jobs done.

To edit a group, select the "Edit Project" icon from the group administration toolbar.

As before, if you have not yet authenticated with the cluster administration database, you will have to enter your username and password in order to access the project information.

The project editing form is just like the project creation form except that the project name and description are not editable.

Deleting a Project

Deleting a project is as serious an affair as deleting a group. It should be done only when all of the project's work is done, or if the project needs to be deconstructed.

To delete a project, click on the "Delete Project" icon in the group administration toolbar, select the name of the project that is to be deleted, and press the "Delete" button. A confirmation dialog will ask you to confirm that the project is to be deleted. If the deletion is confirmed, the project will be removed from the database. Any reserved, unused quota will be returned to the quota pool of the parent group.

Deactivating a Project

Another way to stop a project without removing it from the database is to deactivate it. Deactivating a project will suspend activity by project users. To disable a project, click on the "Disable Project" icon in the group administration toolbar, select the name of the project that is to be disabled, and press the "Disable" button. A confirmation dialog will ask you to confirm that the project is to be disabled.

Batch Queues

Users can, of course, log in at a console and run interactive programs. A cluster doesn't differ from any other Linux system in this respect, though clusters do differ in the type of programs typically run. It would not be unusual for a parallel program to take days or even weeks to run. In these cases, you'll want to use some sort of batch processing.

A *batch queue* is an administrative facility that allows users to place a program on a list to be run at a specified time and for a specified amount of CPU time. Batch systems are almost as old as computing itself. They have been used for close to fifty years as a way to carve up access to computing systems so that a program (or "job") can be run non-interactively and in such a way that its resource usage can be strictly controlled.

Batch queues can be set up to limit CPU time used by a program, to allow programs to run at non-peak hours, or to control access to special devices such as tape libraries, film recorders, etc.

On mainframe systems and commercial supercomputers, system administrators often set up large number of these queues, as shown in Figure 6-13, to meet various computing needs. For example, they can set up queues for "fast" jobs that will run to completion in a few hours, "medium" jobs that might run for up to a day, and "slow" queues that are reserved for jobs that might need days or even weeks to run.

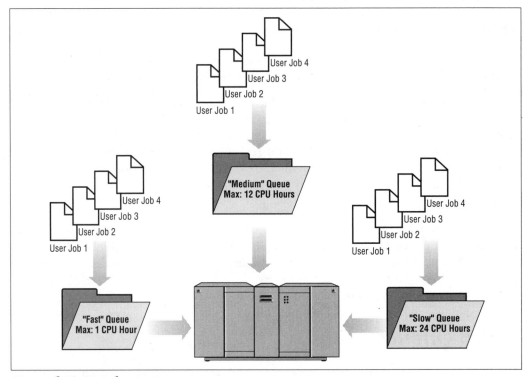

Figure 6-13. Mainframe queues

On Linux clusters, batch queues are interesting because Linux clusters are composed of groups of systems. Unlike mainframe systems, there is no one place that these programs run. Clustered programs are designed to be run on a collection of processors that are physically distinct; therefore, the batch systems that are created for Linux clusters must be "aware" of this reality and know how to take advantage of these distinct systems.

Batch systems under clusters are designed to balance the jobs that need to be run across these multiple systems in such a way that no one system is overwhelmed with work while other systems are idle or lightly utilized. This is a process called "load balancing."

As shown in Figure 6-14, cluster queues are set up on the master node so that jobs can be distributed to compute nodes. This example shows a single queue called "fast" into which users have submitted programs to be run into a "fast" queue on the master node. Individual jobs are then distributed from the master node's queue to available compute nodes. A typical Linux cluster master node might have any number of queues available for use by the groups and projects that make use of the cluster.

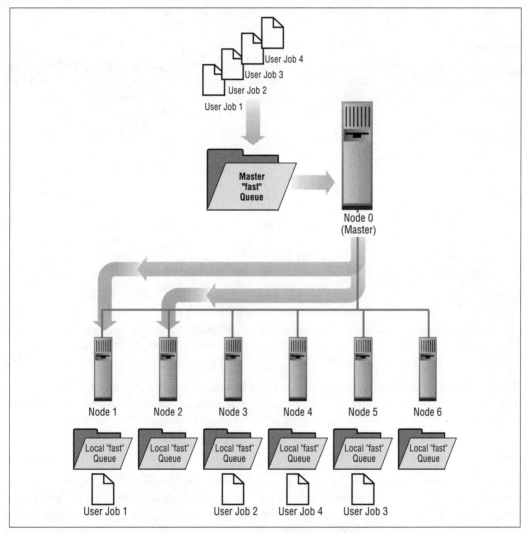

Figure 6-14. Cluster queues submitted through a master node

Generic NQS

The batch system used by the Linux clusters that are built with the software that accompanies this book is called the Generic Network Queueing System or "GNQS."

GNQS was originally developed for NASA and is now an Open Source project maintained by Stuart Herbert,[*] a director of an independent consulting firm in Great Britain.

GNQS and other similar queueing systems allow administrators to set up queues that can have a variety of attributes, including:

Queue length
Queue length is the number of jobs that may be outstanding in the queue at a given point in time.

Run limit
A run limit describes the number of jobs that are in the queue that may actually be running at any given time. If there are more jobs in the queue than are allowed to run, then the first ones in get to run first. The others must wait until jobs that are running are finished or are stopped/aborted for some other reason.

CPU limit
A queue's CPU limit is the amount of CPU time a job in the queue may use for the duration of its existence in the queue. A job that exceeds the CPU time limit imposed by the queue is stopped.

Environmental limits
Environmental limits can include the amount of memory a batch job is allowed to use, what command shell is used to execute commands that carry out the job's instructions, and how the user that started the jobs is to be notified when the job starts, ends, or is stopped due to an error or exceeding a resource constraint.

Pipe attributes
Some queues are designed to run on the machine where the queue has been created, while other queues serve only as placeholders for queues that actually run on other machines. The pipe attributes of a queue specify whether or not the queue is local or remote.

These attributes are just the tip of the iceberg in terms of all of the kinds of things that can be done with batch queues. The queue management portion of the cluster management system will allow you to create and manage these queues across a cluster.

Queue Management

Managing queues on a large system is a balancing act. A cluster administrator must create enough facilities to meet the needs of the majority of the users while not swamping all of the compute nodes so that no one's job is ever complete. There are no hard and fast rules for how to achieve this goal. The right number of queues and the priorities these queues support is something that must be determined by

---

[*] The GNQS project, managed by Stuart Herbert, may be found at *http://www.gnqs.org*. You can find papers, software distributions, and other information related to the ongoing development of GNQS there.

experimentation and trial and error, based on the kinds of jobs that will be running on the cluster.

The cluster management tools will give you a way to experiment with these facilities more easily than by using the command-line tools that come with the GNQS package.

In order to access the queue management tools, you will need to authenticate yourself to the cluster administration database as the clusteradmin user. From the toolbar, select the "Queue Management" icon.

Creating queues

Creating batch queues with NQS's command-line tools can require an almost bewildering array of options and flags. Creating queues on a cluster is even more complex because the queue set up on the master node must be complemented by queues on all of the slave/compute nodes, all of which must be set up with the appropriate load-balancing directives.

The browser-based tools in the cluster management system reduce some of this complexity by presenting the most common and important options needed to create a batch queue.

The queue creation tool shown in Figure 6-15 will create a batch queue on a whole cluster or on just a subset of one.

You will need the following information in order to create the new queue:

- Name of the queue
- Number of jobs that may be in the queue on the master node simultaneously
- Number of jobs that may be running in the queues on the slave nodes simultaneously
- Amount of CPU time any one job is allowed to use

In the example shown in Figure 6-15, the queue is called "physics-fast." It allows ten jobs on the master node's queue at any one moment. On each of the slave/compute nodes, two jobs may run simultaneously. Another important parameter is how much CPU time any one job is allowed to use, which is set here to 15 CPU hours, after which the jobs would be stopped.

The last thing to note in this example is that this "fast" queue is being created for an explicit group, not as a general-purpose queue that can be used by any cluster user. In this case, the group is "physics." In order to submit jobs into this queue, a user's primary group at the time of the submit command would have to be "physics." Otherwise, they would receive an error message telling them that the use of the queue was restricted to that group.

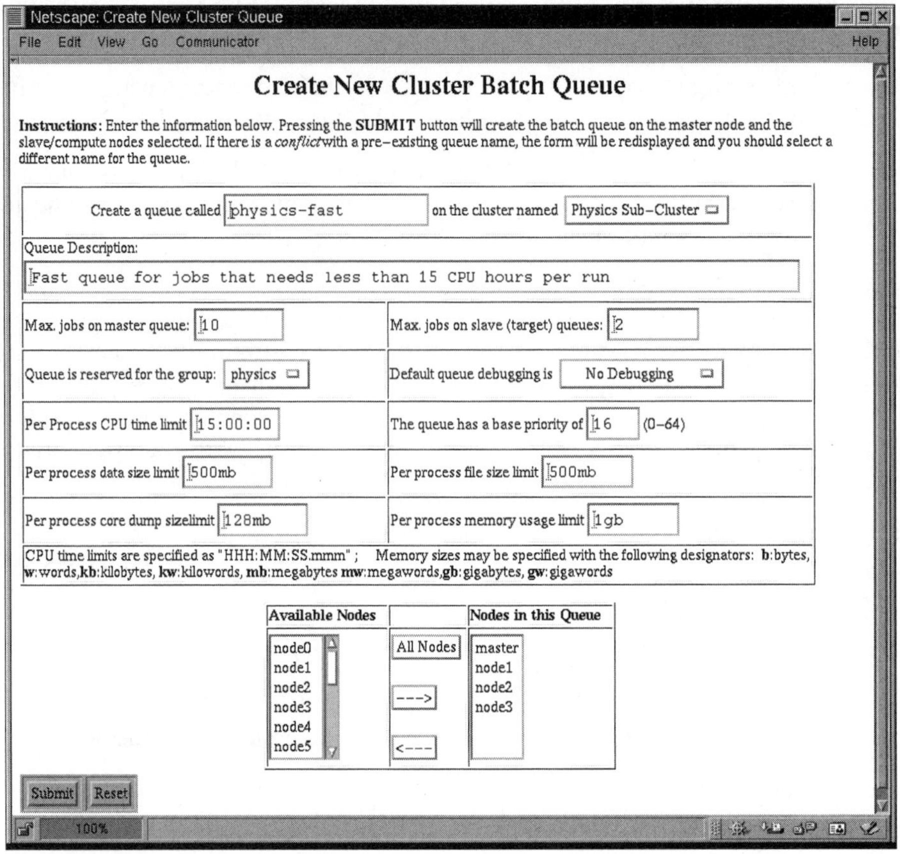

Figure 6-15. Creating new batch queues

Once the parameters are set on the form and the "Submit" button is pressed, a large amount of activity happens behind the scenes. In order to make a cluster-wide queue, there are actually several queues created to handle the scheduling and distribution of jobs across the nodes selected for the queue.

On the master node, the base queue would be created called "fast." This is the queue where users would actually submit the control files that would run their programs. Next, a scheduling queue would be created, in this case called "fast-sched," which would receive jobs from the base queue. This scheduling queue would have as its target a list of queues on compute nodes that were specified when the queue was created. In our "fast" queue, the target compute nodes are *node1, node2,* and *node3.* On each of the compute nodes, a queue is created to actually run end-user jobs, which run queues that all have the same name (which is not a problem since there is only one of them on each slave node), in this case "fast-in."

As you have probably noticed, the queue management software that is part of the cluster management system uses a set of stylized names to create and manage queues, as shown in Figure 6-16. These are not a part of the GNQS software, but are rules that have been built into the administration software to make the queue creations process a little more understandable. The hierarchy of cluster-wide queues works as follows.

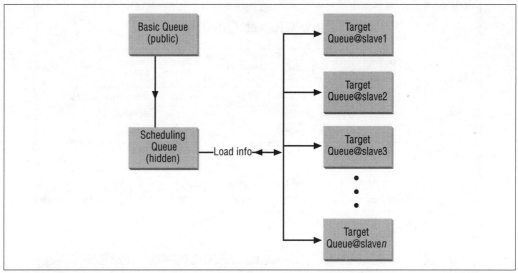

Figure 6-16. Cluster queue hierarchy

A base queue ("fast," in the queue creation example) feeds into a private scheduling queue ("fast-sched"). The scheduling queue then submits jobs to execution queues ("fast-in") on individual cluster compute nodes. The scheduler queue makes its decisions about what queue to send a job to based on load information returned from all of the slave queues. This information includes data such as the system load average, the current length of the queue, and how many jobs are currently executing. If all of the target queues are at capacity, the job is retained in the queue until resources are available to execute the job.

Showing queue activity

Activity in queues can be examined by selecting the "Show Queue" form, as shown in Figure 6-17.

This form will display a list of queues; selecting the name of a queue will show an in-depth display of the queue activity, as shown in Figure 6-18, on the master node of the cluster as well as the target queues on the slave/compute nodes.

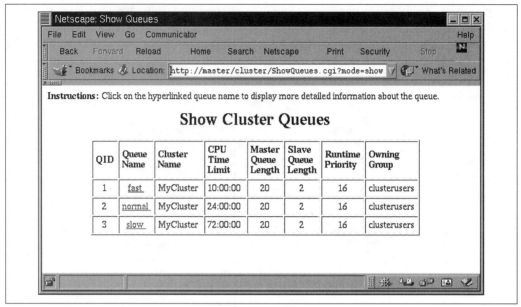

Figure 6-17. Showing queues

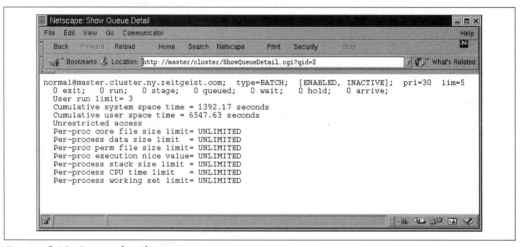

Figure 6-18. Queue details

Editing queues

Once a queue is set up, you may change its settings in order to tune queue parameters to meet new requirements. For example, as you add nodes to your cluster, you will probably want to add these new nodes to the existing collection of queues, or you may need to adjust the amount of CPU time a process can use, and so on.

To edit a queue, select the "Edit Queues" icon from the queue management toolbar, and a form will be displayed (which looks remarkably like the "Show Queues" display—a CGI variable controls which mode the form is in). As shown in Figure 6-19, the form lists all of the queues that are known to the management system.

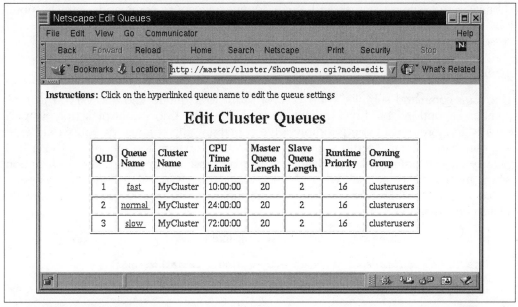

Figure 6-19. Edit queue listing

The queue name will be underlined. This is an HTML hyperlink that will invoke the queue editing form when selected. Editing a queue is very much like creating one. The form looks exactly like the one that creates queues and will allow changes to all of the queue parameters, with the exception of the queue's name and the cluster the queue runs on.

Warning

Use great care when editing queues! If you change the amount of CPU time a queue supports, the next job that is scheduled to run may terminate prematurely. Other parameter changes can also confuse users. Even more importantly, if you delete a node from a cluster-wide queue, any jobs already in that queue on that node will be terminated, and jobs waiting to run on that node will be thrown away!

Using the command-line interface

Using the browser-based queue management tools is a lot easier than using the command-line interface for complex tasks such as queue creation. These tasks can involve upwards of fifty individual commands to create a single distributed queue. There are many instances when using the naked GNQS command-line interface is simply more convenient, such as when you're at a command shell and don't want to bother with a browser.

The most important commands for everyday use of cluster queues are the *qsub* (queue submit), *qstat* (queue status) and *qmgr* (queue manager) commands, which submit jobs to a queue, show the state of the queue, and control the underlying queue processes, respectively.

qsub

The *qsub* command submits a job control script to a queue and allows you to set a number of options for how the job should be run. A job control script, as we'll explore in more detail later, is simply a file containing the commands you would enter at a command prompt to run your job; the job's options are too numerous to list here (they're in the online manual pages). The two most common are the *-mb* option, which means "Send me mail when this job starts actually running," and the *-q* option, which is always followed by a queue name indicating to which queue you want the jobs to be submitted.

A typical job submission command would look like this:

```
[spector@master /home/spectort]%qsub -mb -q slow    setiathome.nqs
Request 11.master.cluster.ny.zeitgeist.com submitted to queue: slow.
[spector@master /home/spectort]%
```

The filename *setiathome.nqs* isn't special, but it does indicate to me that the program being run is most likely the *SETI@Home* client and the *.nqs* extension will keep me from confusing it with a shell script.

The response from the GNQS system tells me that the job has been submitted. When the job actually starts, I will get an email message from the batch system letting me know when and on what target node the job is executing at, such as:

```
Message 1/2  From root                                       Aug 13, 99
03:02:09 PM -0400


Return-Path: <root@node4.cluster.ny.zeitgeist.com>
Date: Fri, 13 Aug 1999 15:02:09 -0400
To: spector@master.cluster.ny.zeitgeist.com

Subject: NQS request: 11.master.cluster.ny.zeitgeist.com beginning.

Request name:    setiathome.nqs
Request owner:   spector
Mail sent at:    Fri Aug 13 15:02:09 EDT 1999
```

qstat

qstat allows you to look into a queue to see what is happening. If we apply this to the "slow" queue based on the previous job we submitted with *qsub*, we would see something like this:

```
[spector@master /home/spectort]% qstat -l slow
slow@master.cluster.ny.zeitgeist.com;  type=PIPE;  [ENABLED, RUNNING];  pri=16  lim=1
   0 depart;   1 route;   0 queued;   0 wait;   0 hold;   0 arrive;

   Rank    1: Name=setiathome.ngs
   REQUEST: 11.master     Owner=spector  Priority=31  State: ROUTING  Pgrp=24509
   Created at Fri Aug 13 15:09:15 EDT 1999
   Mail = [BEGIN, END]
   Mail address = spector@master.cluster.ny.zeitgeist.com
   Owner user name at originating machine = spector
   Request is notrestartable, notrecoverable.
   Broadcast = [NONE]
   Per-proc. CPU time limit = UNSPECIFIED
   Per-req. CPU time limit = UNSPECIFIED
   Per-req. tape drives limit = UNSPECIFIED
   Per-proc. core file size limit = UNSPECIFIED
   Per-proc. data size limit = UNSPECIFIED
   Per-proc. perm file size limit = UNSPECIFIED
   Per-req. perm file space limit = UNSPECIFIED
   Per-proc. memory size limit = UNSPECIFIED
   Per-req. memory size limit = UNSPECIFIED
   Per-req. # of cpus limit = UNSPECIFIED
   Per-proc. quick file size limit = UNSPECIFIED
   Per-req. quick file space limit = UNSPECIFIED
   Per-proc. stack size limit = UNSPECIFIED
   Per-proc. temp file size limit = UNSPECIFIED
   Per-req. temp file space limit = UNSPECIFIED
   Per-proc. working set limit = UNSPECIFIED
   Per-proc. execution nice pri. = UNSPECIFIED
   Standard-error access mode = SPOOL
   Standard-error name = master.cluster.ny.zeitgeist.com:/home/spector/setiathome.ngs.e11
   Standard-output access mode = SPOOL
   Standard-output name = master.cluster.ny.zeitgeist.com:/home/spector/setiathome.ngs.o11
   Shell = DEFAULT
   Umask =    2
```

It's clear that there's a lot going on in this queue on the behalf of my little *SETI@Home**
job. Most of the information relates to options that either have (or mostly in this case
have not) been specified that would affect the running of this batch job.

---

* *SETI@Home* is a subproject of the Search for Extra-Terrestrial Intelligence (SETI) that uses spare computing cycles
to analyze portions of the electromagnetic spectrum for intelligent signals from other civilizations. More information about SETI and the *SETI@Home* project can be found at *http://setiathome.ssl.berkeley.edu*.

The most interesting lines are actually at the top of the listing where the queueing system reports the state of the job including, in this case, "ROUTING"—the process of moving from the scheduling queue into an execution queue on a slave/compute node.

Almost all of the other parameters listed in the queue entry can be user-specified and are available to users to set up jobs to run in the most efficient manner.

You may have noticed that the one function that is not covered by the forms interface provided to GNQS is stopping and starting queues. This is because there is no programmatic way in the current version of GNQS to pull information about which queues or queue complexes are in what state (started, stopped, paused, etc.). The best way to run these commands is to use the GNQS manager command shell directly.

qmgr

The *qmgr* program is the core of the GNQS system. It is the underlying program that is called by all of the queue management forms presented in the previous sections and is used to do everything from creating queues and setting queue parameters to starting and stopping queues. The background processes that create cluster queues will enable the queues to be used, but if you need to stop or restart them for any reason, you will need to do this from the command-line interface. Because of the power of this command to create queues and affect system-level facilities on a whole network of machines, *qmgr* must be executed by root.

qmgr has an interface that is very much like *lpc*, the line printer control program under Linux. *qmgr* is a command shell that supports all of the commands needed to manage GNQS. To use it to start a queue, use the *qmgr* program as a command shell:

```
[root@master /root]# /usr/local/bin/qmgr
Mgr:
```

Like *lpc*, qmgr has extensive online help:

```
Mgr: help
```

The available commands are:

```
ABort      ADd        Create     DElete     DIsable    ENable
EXit       HElp       HOld       Lock       MEmdump    MODify
MOVe       Purge      Quit       RELease    REMove     SEt
SHOw       SHUtdown   SNap       STArt      STOp       Unlock
```

To obtain more information about a command, type:

```
Help <command-name>
```

Each command keyword will always be shown as a sequence of upper- and lower-case letters. The uppercase prefix at the beginning of each keyword shows the smallest abbreviation acceptable for the command keyword.

Lengthy commands can be broken across line boundaries by placing a backslash character (\ ) at the end of a partial command line. For example:

```
help st\
op
```

is equivalent to the command:

```
help stop

Mgr:
```

In order to start (or stop) a queue, simply use the start or stop command followed by the name of the queue at the prompt:

```
Mgr: start queue slow
```

The GNQS queue manager will respond with a message indicating the result of the command:

```
NQS manager[TCML_COMPLETE  ]:  Transaction complete at local host
```

A complete listing of the available GNQS commands can be found on your cluster by typing man 1 nqs at any command prompt.

Accounting

The accounting system under Linux (and other Unixes) keeps track of who did what, when, and for how long. The accounting system keeps track of all CPU usage, the number of I/O calls, and the duration of logins for users.

On a cluster, accounting is important for a couple of reasons. First, it allows projects and programs to be accounted for in terms of a budgetary process. If your cluster must pay for itself, accurately reporting activity will be important. Secondly, process accounting can be used as a rough application performance reporting tool. Since all activity generated by a process is recorded in the accounting, the accounting reports can show where a program is spending time in terms of I/O and other high-level system calls.

Processing the Accounting

Once you have all of the nodes in your system busily gathering accounting information, you will want to have the data processed on a regular basis. If the data is not processed on a regular basis, it will eventually fill up the disk that the *pacct* (process accounting) file resides on and will cause problems for other processes on the cluster.

Fortunately, as installed from the Linux Clusters CD-ROM, the accounting is done via a *cron* job so you don't have to take care of it manually. Additionally, the accounting for all nodes in the cluster is brought together under the master node, and the results are updated nightly and published on a set of internal web pages that are accessible on the master node of the cluster. The URL is dependent on the name of your cluster, but if your master node is called "master," the URL would be *http://master/acct*.

The accounting page gives a number of different ways the data can be viewed, as show in Figure 6-20.

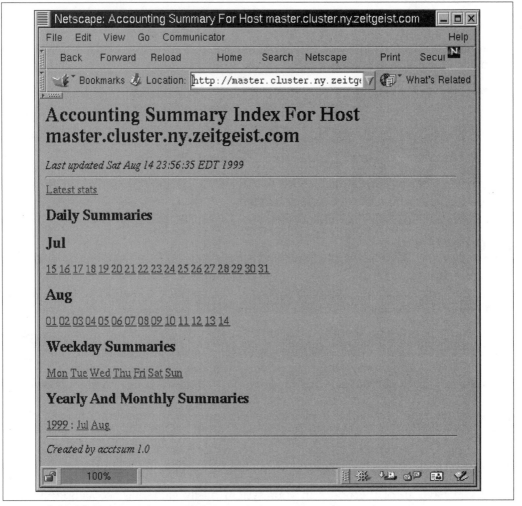

Figure 6-20. The process accounting page

Cluster Maintenance

Just when you thought you had finished doing everything and could just run a lot of cool fast simulations, you find there's more to do. For better or worse, running a large cluster is just like any other large project—it's a never-ending series of little sub-projects. Clusters are never quite finished; there is always something more to do. This section deals with the day-to-day things that have to be done to keep your parallel Linux cluster in tip-top shape. Most of these day-to-day cluster operations (like system accounting, covered earlier) can be set up so that they take are of themselves via *cron* jobs or the batch processing system. However, some things will need your personal attention, as we'll discuss in the next three sections.

Kernel Patches

Running a production system requires keeping all of the nodes that your users depend upon up, running, and as stable as possible. All of the value of a cluster is lost if jobs don't get to run to completion because the underlying systems are in a state of flux.

Of course, if the underlying systems are unreliable, it may be that a kernel patch (or an entire new kernel version) will fix things. Kernel patches and kernel revisions should be installed only to fix problems you have identified.

The best place to learn about Linux kernel changes is the Linux kernel mailing list. This mailing list is a very high-volume forum where very deep technical discussions on the current and future development of the kernel are hashed out by the folks who are actually creating the future of Linux. It is also a good place to ask informed questions about problems that you may be experiencing with your particular kernel version.

The Linux kernel mailing list may be subscribed to by sending an email message to *majordomo@vger.rutgers.edu*.

Putting one of the following lines in the body of the message will subscribe you to a specific version of the mailing list:

subscribe linux-kernel
> Using this subscribe command will sign up for a message-by-message rendition of the list traffic. In other words, every time someone sends email to the list or some-one responds to such an email (where the list address is somewhere in the reply line), you will receive the message. This can amount to hundreds of email messages per day. This is not for the faint of heart or those with little free disk space.

subscribe linux-kernel-digest
> Using this subscribe command will sign up for a "digested" version of the list. A digested list is a newsletter format where email messages are collected until they reach some defined number or size (such as 32 kilobytes). Then the messages are

bundled together with an index listing the subject line of each message and sent to the subscribers of the digest.

Either way, you will receive the same amount of information, but many people find list digests easier to cope with since there is not a steady flood of individual messages.

There are also a number of web sites where is it possible to browse/search messages posted to the Linux kernel mailing list. Among these is Red Hat's corporate web site, *www.redhat.com.*

Speaking of Red Hat, another excellent place to get updates to the kernel is from Red Hat's FTP site. The Linux distribution included on the CD-ROM that accompanies this book is based on Red Hat Linux version 6.0, so one of the most effective ways to get new kernels is to download them from *http://updates.redhat.com.* You can be sure with the Red Hat site that the kernels have been compiled correctly and will work with your cluster.

Lastly, updating the kernel yourself is an option if you want to have a much tighter rein on exactly what is loaded into your system and how memory is used. Out of necessity, the kernel that is loaded by this book's CD-ROM kit is pretty big—it has to be to be able to work with all of the varieties of hardware that you might have that I would have no way of knowing about. This means that there are device drivers on the system for hardware devices that might not even be in the same country as your systems.

In order to allow you complete control over the customization of your systems, the Linux kernel sources are loaded on the master node of your cluster in the directory */usr/src/linux.*

It is possible, following the instructions in the *documentation* directory (located in the Linux source tree), to build a completely customized kernel and module set that exactly reflects the hardware attributes and devices connected to your machines. If your systems are homogeneous, it is also possible for you to simple copy new kernels directly to compute nodes in order to update them.

I strongly recommend keeping old kernels around on each machine as kind of an emergency escape measure in case something goes wrong, especially on the master node. Slave nodes are meant to have as little on them as possible, and if you get into a bind with a bad kernel you can always just re-initialize the whole node from scratch with a slave boot floppy.

Disk Space

Pay special attention to disk space used on clusters. Quotas are enabled by default not only on the master node, but on all slave/compute nodes. Even with quotas, you may find that users or packages have consumed all your disk space, and it will be up to the cluster administrator to exercise Solomon-like judgement to keep order on the cluster. Of course, you could just add more disk space, but that could be seen by some as "coddling" the users.

Clustering Tools

There are three major packages installed from the Linux Clusters CD-ROM: MPI, LAM, and PVM. At the time the CD-ROM was created, the versions of these packages were up-to-date in terms of being the latest production versions of these packages. Like Linux itself, these tools are in constant motion; but unlike Linux, when they're in a testing phase, they are a lot less stable. It is not recommended that unfinished versions of any of these packages be installed unless you are very sure of what you are doing. You will not harm your cluster, but you may become very frustrated because debugging a clustered program in a buggy clustering package is nearly impossible, since you will not know where the potential error is—in your code or in your message passing libraries such as PVM, LAM, or MPI:

MPI

The Message Passing Interface is an industry standard that is published by the MPI consortium. The portable reference implementation, known as MPICH, may be found at Aragonne National Labs at *http://www-unix.mcs.anl.gov/mpi/mpich/index. html.*

PVM

The Parallel Virtual Machine was developed at Oak Ridge National Labs, which still maintains and enhances this software on a regular basis. The most recent, as well as test versions, of the software may be found at *http://www.epm.ornl.gov/ pvm.*

LAM

The Local Area Multicomputer project is located at Notre Dame University. Current version of the LAM software may be found at *http://www.mpi.nd.edu/lam.*

Other Management Interfaces

There have been a number of other projects in the commercial world, in academia, and in the Open Source community geared toward making the management of large networks of workstations, like Linux clusters, easier.

The cluster management system supplied on the Linux Clusters CD-ROM is just one attempt at solving parts of this problem. If you are so inclined, there are other avenues to explore for management tools for Linux systems; some are commercial and others are based on older academic projects.

Commercial

Commercial software vendors have finally started to notice Linux and have begun porting their management applications to the platform. Two of the widely used and better-known packages include:

UniCenter™

UniCenter from Computer Associates is perhaps the best-known of all large scale system-management packages for Unix systems. In the spring of 1999, Computer Associates announced that they would port UniCenter to the Linux operating system. This is a very large and comprehensive package with agents to control almost every aspect of the operation of a Linux machine. It also requires a lot of modifications to out-of-the-box Linux systems in order to function, since it is capable of being integrated into so many aspects of the system. Information on UniCenter can be found on Computer Associates web site at *http://www.cai.com/unicenter*.

HP OpenView™

OpenView is a comprehensive set of system tools from system monitors though management workstation tools that is the product of Hewlett-Packard. HP is a leader in everything, including electronic test and measurement systems, and makes some of the fastest Unix boxes around, based on their PA-RISC architecture. Information on OpenView may be found on the HP web site at *http://www.hp.com/openview*.

Academia

University computer science programs are usually the source for most innovations that eventually make their way into commercial mainstream software. Often these packages are years ahead of commercial packages simply because the university environment includes a wide variety of hardware and software that is given as grants to these institutions. Two of the most popular are:

MIT Project Athena

The originator of most modern consolidated system-management/services system is the Athena Project from the Massachusetts Institute of Technology. The Athena Project, initially sponsored by IBM and Digital Equipment Corporation, developed tools and technology that allowed for great economies of scale in the number of systems a single systems manager could handle. This was done by making systems interchangeable regardless of their underlying architecture.

Although not in widespread use today by themselves, the protocols and services developed by Athena are the basis for the Open Software Foundation's Distributed Computing Environment (DCE).

Most of the Athena components have been ported to Linux and are available from large Linux software archives.

CMU's Andrew Project

The Andrew project is the peer of MIT's Athena. It's a complete systems environment that gives its users a unified view of their files, email, and other resources that is independent of the platform that the user is operating on. Included in Andrew are many systems-management tools and high-level services such as the Andrew File System (AFS), which has become a major component of the OSF's Distributed Computing Environment (DCE).

Other Useful Tools

The remainder of tools and packages described in this chapter are third-party packages that are installed on the clusters built with the CD-ROM that accompanies this book. They are not integrated into the cluster management system, but are standalone tools that may be useful in various areas of the administration or management of your cluster.

Some of these tools may need in-depth configuration; this will be indicated in the descriptions for individual packages.

bWatch

bWatch (short for "Beowulf Watch") is a Tcl/Tk tool that gives a view of system-load and memory information across a cluster. It was designed for use on Topcat,* which is a Beowulf class supercomputer at the University of Southern Queensland in Australia.

It is a standalone tool that is not integrated into the cluster administration database, but it is useful for both administrators and end-users to get a quick snapshot view of nodes in the cluster. bWatch is installed on the cluster; to start it, simply type the command:

```
[spector@master /home/spectort]% /usr/local/bin//bWatch &
```

As shown in Figure 6-21, bWatch will start up and show the load on the master and slave nodes of the cluster and create a local preferences file called *.bWatchrc.tcl*. To show the entire cluster, it is necessary to edit this file to list the hosts to be watched.

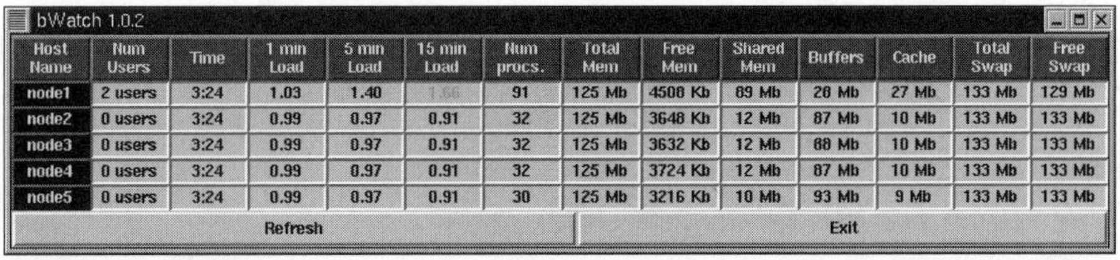

Host Name	Num Users	Time	1 min Load	5 min Load	15 min Load	Num procs.	Total Mem	Free Mem	Shared Mem	Buffers	Cache	Total Swap	Free Swap
node1	2 users	3:24	1.03	1.40		91	125 Mb	4500 Kb	89 Mb	20 Mb	27 Mb	133 Mb	129 Mb
node2	0 users	3:24	0.99	0.97	0.91	32	125 Mb	3648 Kb	12 Mb	87 Mb	10 Mb	133 Mb	133 Mb
node3	0 users	3:24	0.99	0.97	0.91	32	125 Mb	3632 Kb	12 Mb	68 Mb	10 Mb	133 Mb	133 Mb
node4	0 users	3:24	0.99	0.97	0.91	32	125 Mb	3724 Kb	12 Mb	87 Mb	10 Mb	133 Mb	133 Mb
node5	0 users	3:24	0.99	0.97	0.91	30	125 Mb	3216 Kb	10 Mb	93 Mb	9 Mb	133 Mb	133 Mb

Figure 6-21. bWatch

---

* Topcat information can be found at *http://www.sci.usq.edu.au/staff/jacek/topcat*.

bWatch also requires that each user have *.rhosts* access to every node to be watched; this configuration must be done on a per-user basis.

Cheops

Cheops is a network mapping and analysis tool written by Mark Spencer that can be useful for visualizing a network. Cheops is capable of automatically mapping a network (such as a cluster) and determining what kind of operating systems the hosts it discovers are running.

As shown in Figure 6-22, Cheops can be a useful tool for mapping the network your cluster is on to determine what network connections are possible between the cluster and other machines that may be connecting to it. Cheops can also perform rudimentary scanning of hosts to determine what services are running on a host of interest.

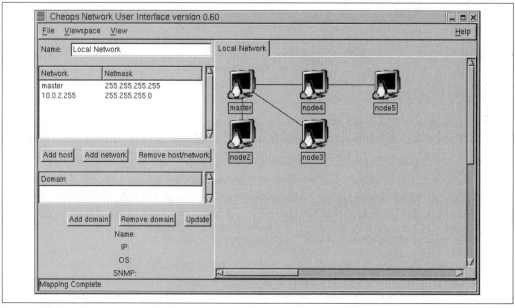

Figure 6-22. Cheops network view

Cheops can be run by any user since it does not require special privileges. But its use can result in a lot of network traffic, which could degrade the performance of your network and reduce the communication capabilities of the cluster.

Multi-Router Traffic Grapher

The Multi-Router Traffic Grapher, or MRTG as it's commonly known, is an exceptionally powerful and cleverly designed utility designed by Tobias Oetiker that can be used to generate HTML pages that contain graphs of almost any kind of network statistic.

MRTG uses Perl scripts and the Perl SNMP library to query SNMP variables on routers or other systems to gather statistics on aspects of system performance. As shown in Figure 6-23, these values are then plotted and presented as web pages. MRTG can be used to keep track of performance and utilization over varying periods (from minutes to years), and since all the data can be viewed in a browser, it is a good way to keep a record of system activity in a way that anyone can make sense of it.

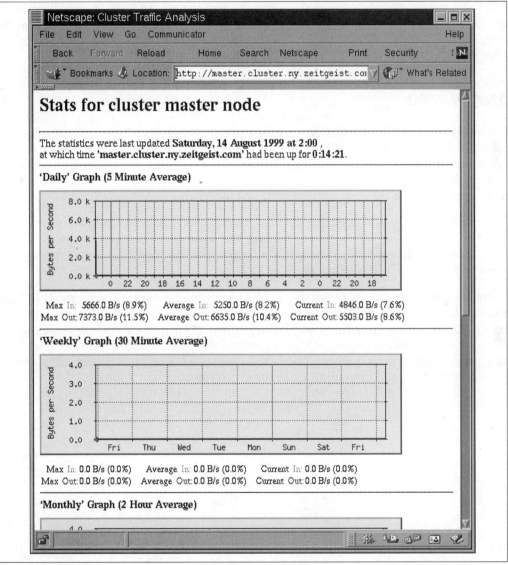

Figure 6-23. Typical MRTG graph

MRTG is a very popular tool that has been extended by contributors all over the Internet to allow it to plot non-SNMP values such as login frequencies, performance of the domain name service (DNS), and dozens of other statistics. Many of these extensions are in the *contrib* directory that comes with the MRTG sources, which can be found in */usr/local/mrtg* on your cluster.

Since MRTG is so dependent upon the configuration of the systems it will be monitoring, the package is not configured to actually run out of the box. You will need to configure it yourself. The configuration instructions may be found in */usr/local/mrtg/ doc.* More information on additional extensions may be found at the MRTG home page at *http://ee-staff.ethz.ch/~oetiker/webtools/mrtg/mrtg.html.*

Summary

Obviously there is a lot to do when managing a cluster. The fact that a cluster is composed of distinct systems is a source of its strength in that it can be easily built and enhanced to provide more computational performance. But it is also an area of weakness in that it does take a lot more work to manage a collection of cooperating systems than would be the case with a traditional monolithic supercomputer.

The cluster management system supplied with Linux Clusters CD-ROM provides a basic interface that will allow you to manage the most critical aspects of cluster operations, from the definition of cluster nodes and cluster groups to the management of users and resources such as batch queues.

Lastly, the software supplied with this book is just the beginning. There are also Open Source and commercial tools than can be used to add to these capabilities, including smaller Open Source packages such a *cheops* and *MRTG* that allow cluster administrators to visualize various network characteristics and performance parameters, as well as comprehensive tools such as Computer Associates' UniCenter™ and HP's Open-View™ at the high end of systems-management systems.

PART II

CLUSTER PROGRAMMING AND APPLICATIONS

This section focuses on the programming environment on a Linux cluster. This part aims at readers who have just built or have access to a Linux cluster and want to start harnessing its power. These chapters will cover a variety of programming areas such as the selection of programming language for cluster programming, publicly available programming libraries, and tools that are specifically oriented to clusters. They will also show some complete but non-trivial examples of complete applications that can be used as the basis for larger systems.

CHAPTER SEVEN

TOOLS AND LIBRARIES FOR PARALLEL PROGRAMMING

Programming any kind of parallel computer, from a traditional supercomputer to a Beowulf-style cluster, requires development environments and tools.

This chapter will present some of the most popular and readily available tools for working in a clustered environment. These tools include entire development systems such as PADE (the Parallel Applications Development Environment) and XPVM, as well as code profiling tools such as *TAU*.

The systems that help ease the tasks of parallel programming fall into three kinds of packages: development environments, parallel libraries, and profiling tools.

Development Tools

The user environment comes with a complete collection of GNU tools required to build and run both sequential and parallel programs, including:

GNU Emacs
> GNU Emacs is known as the kitchen sink of editors because it not only edits files, but also can be used as an integrated development environment in its own right. All of the GNU tools can be run from inside GNU Emacs, and their output is used by Emacs to help aid in the development process.

GCC
> GCC is the best known and most widely used C/C++ compiler in the world. It can deliver highly optimized code.

G77
> G77 is a development version of the FORTRAN front-end to the GNU compiler suite. It is a highly functional system usable for most clustered applications. However, since G77 is both 1) not a finished package and 2) not a FORTRAN90/95 compliant compiler, you might want to investigate one of the commercially

available compilers if your cluster work will require an industrial-strength FOR-TRAN compiler.

GDB

GDB is the GNU debugger, one of the most powerful debuggers in the world, that can be connected to GUI-based front-ends such as the Data Display Debugger (DDD), which can be used to trace programs written in almost any known computer language including scripting languages such as Perl.

Parallel Development Environments

In the PC world, development environments are usually self-contained systems that include a compiler, an editing system, and various utilities that work with these tools to create applications. Microsoft's VisualC++ is an example of such a development system. On parallel machines like Beowulf clusters (and Unix machines in general), the toolsets are not as tightly integrated; all of the components are separate pieces of software that operate as independent tools.

Without a unified development environment, each tool is a standalone entity, making it difficult* to create a single set of development tools that all have a common look and feel.

On the other hand, the Unix model of development allows you to pick and choose the best tools for a given task. Since most tools operate in a command-line mode (unlike their Windows counterparts), it is quite easy to make highly specialized and precisely targeted development environments that can be reconfigured and rearranged on the fly to meet new requirements.

Examples of this can be seen in the exceptionally vibrant Unix marketplace where compilers, libraries, and utilities from almost any vendor can be used together. It's *The Cathedral & the Bazaar*† writ small.

Under Linux (and other Unixes), a GUI can be constructed that "knows" about the commands used to invoke these individual tools and allows the user to customize their interactions. Good examples of Open Source IDEs are Code Crusader and gIDE. These tools act as a GUI shell that ties together tools like GCC and other members of the GNU software development tool-chain as well as an arbitrary collection of other packages.

---

* Difficult, but not impossible. Metrowerks has ported their popular Codewarrior to Linux. Cygnus Solutions, a pioneer in Unix IDEs, has released their CodeFusion IDE for Linux as well.

† *The Cathedral & the Bazaar* (O'Reilly & Associates, 1999) is Eric Raymond's seminal work exploring the success of the Open Source software model and how it works to meet the needs of developers/users better then closed, proprietary methods of software development.

For building programs that run on parallel computers, the choices are even more eso-teric. Since parallel computing has been a very specialized domain, there are few integrated development environments of any kind available. Usually parallel program-ming tools are supplied by the hardware vendor and supplemented with third-party packages that implement some desired feature.

Fortunately for cluster users, several groups of parallel programmers at various organi-zations have come up with tools that help put together a lot of the parallel program-ming puzzle and make the program building and testing jobs easier. Two of these environments, PADE and XPVM, are included on the Linux Clusters CD-ROM (in the *ProgrammingLibs* directory) and are discussed here.

PADE

PADE, the Parallel Applications Development Environment, is a set of tools devel-oped at the United States National Institutes of Standards and Technologies (NIST). PADE presents a management console that allows a programmer to control most aspects of the development of a parallel program from a single location, even if the actual program is going to execute on a machine that may consist of many—even hundreds of—nodes using the PVM or Parallel Virtual Machine software developed at Oak Ridge National Labs.

Key features of PADE

PADE allows the developer to control the edit–transfer–link–execute cycle of parallel program development.

During the development cycle of a non-parallel program, programmers usually keep all the files related to a program's development in some directory on a disk. They may apply a source-code control system to keep track of changes and allow for multiple developers, but in essence it is possible just to throw together code, compile it, and run it.

Parallel programs on clusters are a bit different. Often there is not a single program that needs to be built, but several. Some are "master" programs that control things on the master node of the cluster, and some are "worker" programs that are strictly com-putational and feed their intermediate results back to only the master program. More importantly, if the cluster is heterogeneous, made up of different computing plat-forms, versions of the same program will have to be built for different hardware archi-tecture that may have very different characteristics and capabilities, including word size, byte order, and even precision of their number formats. This means that there may be large variations in the source files that are compiled to run on different com-puting elements in the cluster.

If the cluster is homogeneous, the software maintenance issues are lessened since there is only one set of sources to keep track of.

PADE takes care of two major aspects of the management of parallel programs. First, it helps the developer by keeping track of which bits of the source code must be compiled on which hosts. As mentioned previously, on heterogeneous clusters, different nodes may have different capabilities, so there will probably be different source files (or at least source code that is conditionally compiled) for each kind of node. There also may be different compilers/libraries and other tools on the different nodes as well.

The second way PADE assists in the development process is by actually sending the appropriate files to the appropriate host where they can be compiled.

PVM's major functionality, as described in Chapter 2, *Basic Concepts*, is to create a virtual machine out of a collection of computers. All of the nodes look like one big computer to a PVM process using the system. The virtual machine software takes care of routing messages from node to node regardless of the underlying hardware architecture.

Interestingly, PADE itself is a PVM application. It uses PVM as the transport mechanism to send files and instructions from the PADE console to the nodes in the virtual machine. As shown in Figure 7-1, PADE provides a visual workspace in which all of the cluster nodes are displayed, and the output from tools is collected.

What it can do

PADE is a mutifaceted application. It can:

Set up a parallel virtual machine
> PADE has menus and dialogs that allow you to define nodes that will be controlled by the PVMd process (the daemon that coordinates the activities across a virtual machine). Once nodes are defined, you can have PADE start up the virtual machine for you; this prepares the system for use for building or running parallel applications.

Automatically distribute files
> One of the nice things about this application is that given a definition of a program to build, PADE can use the parallel virtual machine itself to distribute files that need to be compiled to different nodes in the cluster. This is very useful during program development as PADE will keep track of the source files and distribute them as needed. This is especially useful on heterogeneous clusters. Without this feature, a developer would have to keep track of this information by hand and take care of getting changed files to the appropriate target nodes in the PVM.

Build parallel applications
> PADE makes use of another NIST tool supplied with PADE, called PVMMake, to run parallel builds. The building process is controlled by a configuration file that can be built from inside the application and that contains directives and

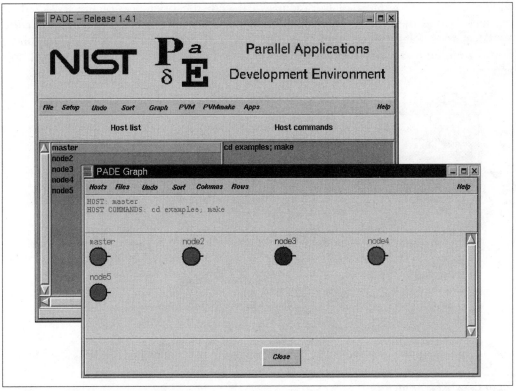

Figure 7-1. The PADE windows

commands that specify how the parallel build process should be spread across the nodes defined in the parallel virtual machine.

Run or trace parallel applications

PADE has tools to allow you to launch parallel applications. It can monitor their activities in the context of a tracing system that uses external applications such as XPVM to display program activities.

XPVM

XPVM is another front-end to the Parallel Virtual Machine (PVM), written by the developers of PVM at Oak Ridge National Labs. Unlike PADE, its function is limited to the execution and monitoring of PVM applications. It isn't very useful unless you have already built a PVM application and want to watch it run.

XPVM provides a graphical front-end to PVM that can be used to start up a parallel virtual machine and control the execution of programs that run across nodes in the cluster.

There are a number of menus that control what XPVM displays and how it affects the parallel virtual machine it is managing, as shown in the portion of the XPVM window shown in Figure 7-2. Most of the menus deal with the operation of the PVM virtual machine, while the "Views" and "Options" menus control what is displayed in the XPVM window itself. These options can be changed as required while a PVM application is running to show whatever display is most useful in analyzing the application's activity.

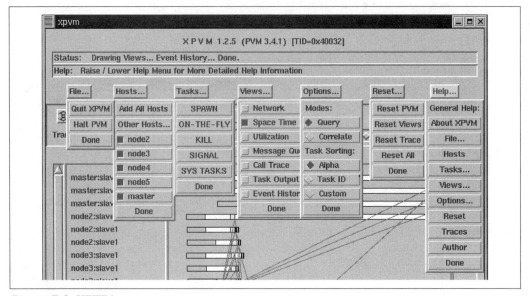

Figure 7-2. XPWM menus

At startup, as seen in Figure 7-3, the XPVM console contains several panels, the most notable of which shows a graphic representation of the virtual machine itself. The virtual machine shown is a five-node cluster composed of Linux machines. Since PVM was designed to assist in the clustering of *heterogeneous* machines, this panel would display other machine icons if the parallel virtual machine it was monitoring was composed of different kinds of processors.

The rest of the default main window of XPVM is concerned with the capture of the effects of a running PVM application. The middle section is used to control the recording and playback of event records that are generated as a PVM application executes. The recording of events is a "freebie" that comes with PVM, and nothing special has to be done to allow PVM applications to be traced.

The graphs available in the "Views" menu are displayed in the main XPVM window and replace the "Cluster" and the "Playback" panes with other graphics that can be used to display graphs and traces that can be helpful in visualizing the interactions between PVM tasks.

The graph displayed in Figure 7-4 shows the relationship of tasks in the parallel virtual machine over the runtime of the application. The task names are listed along the

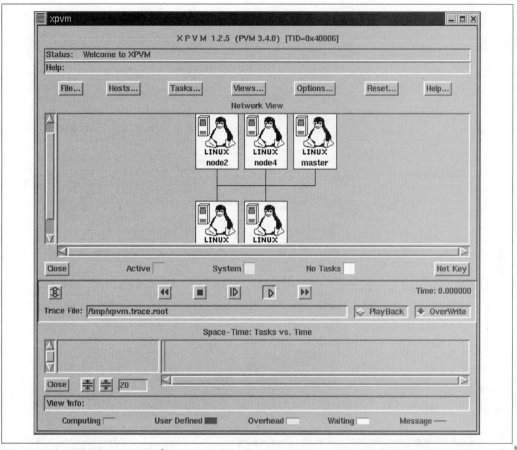

Figure 7-3. XPVM user interface

left side of the window, and the lines linking the tasks represent communication over time between tasks. This shows the "Space time" selection in the "Views" menu.

There are a number of other tools in XPVM like the call trace, shown in Figure 7-5, that is useful for profiling parallel applications. This display can show you exactly what parts of your parallel program are executing and on which nodes in the cluster.

One of the most useful tools is the event output display, which can be used to watch PVM events as they occur in a running application, as shown in Figure 7-6. All of this information, like the communication graph shown previously, are features that are built into PVM applications. No extra code has to be written to take advantage of them.

Lastly, the task output screen is useful for watching other debugging statements that could be put into your PVM applications or for reviewing results of work printed out by the program.

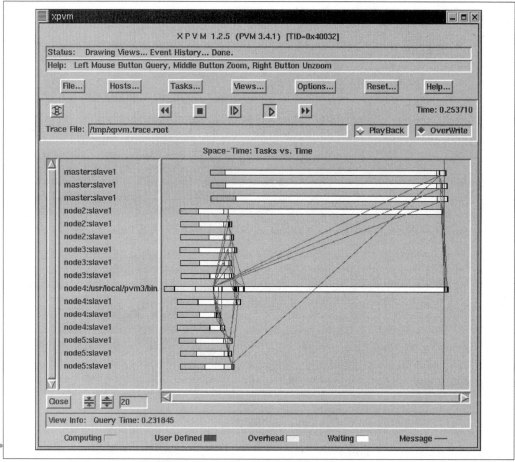

Figure 7-4. XPVM tasks versus time

XPVM is a very useful tool for parallel applications, but it is just one of several options available to the parallel application developer. Complete information on XPVM can be found in the XPVM manual pages, which are accessible by typing *man xpvm* at any shell prompt. The sources for XPVM and several other visualization tools for use with PVM can be found on the Linux Clusters CD-ROM in the *ClusterTools* directory.

LAM

The Local Area Multicomputer (LAM) package was originally developed at the Ohio Supercomputer Center, and is currently being maintained at Notre Dame University. LAM is a programming environment that uses MPICH as the basis for its parallel processing capabilities but presents a complete program execution environment for MPI-based programs.

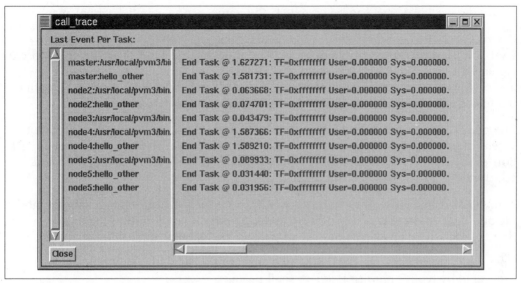

Figure 7-5. XPVM call trace

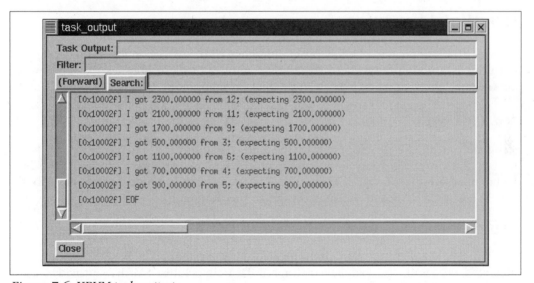

Figure 7-6. XPVM task output

The MPI standard is a message passing standard that defines a collection of APIs and libraries that implement the APIs that define how messages and data are passed among cooperating parallel processing systems.

LAM extends MPI by providing a complete execution environment that sits on top of the MPI libraries and allows a complete processing environment to be defined simply by installing the LAM software on a collection of nodes and then naming the nodes to be used as a collective computer, much the same way a parallel virtual machine is defined in PVM.

LAM is intrinsically a user-centered tool. The number and kind of nodes used to create an MPI virtual machine are defined by the user and not at the system level. When a user wishes to run a parallel application under LAM, two files need to be defined: the first is called a *nodes file*, and the second is an *application schema file*.

The nodes file is a list of hostnames that have the LAM software installed and that list where the user has an account that may be accessed over the network. The application schema file is a description of the components that need to be executed and which nodes they should be run on.

Using LAM commands, you can instruct LAM to start a virtual machine using the nodes file and then start the actual programs running with the application schema file, which directs LAM where to run the individual parts of the parallel application.

Complete information on LAM can be found in the LAM manual pages, which are accessible by typing *man LAM* at any shell prompt.

Parallel Libraries

Libraries that can make parallel programming easier are becoming more common. Since this is a young field, there are a large number of these libraries that address all sorts of specialized areas of interest in parallel programming.

ACL Libraries

Fortunately, with the development of message passing standards like MPI and PVM, most of these packages are complementary rather than conflicting. Some of the best documented are the Advanced Computing Lab tools from Los Alamos National Laboratory. These tools cover the whole spectrum of programming.

SMARTS

SMARTS (Shared Memory Asynchronuous Runtime System) is a library that supports integrated task and data parallelism for MIMD architectures. SMARTS provides user-level threads that allow an application developer to create lightweight virtual processors natural to the algorithm being implemented. It supports a subset of the Pthreads API, which is the standard threads library shipped with Linux systems.

SILOON

SILOON (Scripting Interface Languages for Object-Oriented Numerics) is an interface to parallel programming libraries that allows programmers to use scripting languages such as Perl, Tcl, and Python. Using scripting languages can allow for the rapid proto-typing of applications that would normally take a long time to write and test.

SILOON provides toolkits and runtime support for building easy-to-use external inter-faces to existing numerical codes. This enables application programmers to easily access existing object-oriented scientific frameworks and numerical libraries written in C, C++, and Fortran.

SILOON generates "glue code" to link external library interfaces and provide runtime support and a computational server that is controllable under the scripting languages of choice. SILOON relies on the PDT toolkit (described later in the chapter) for infor-mation about applications and libraries.

PAWS

PAWS (Parallel Application WorkSpace) is a framework for lining parallel applications using parallel communication channels. These applications can be run on different machines, and the data structures in each component can have different parallel distri-butions. PAWS is able to carry out the communication without resorting to global gather/scatter operations. Instead, point-to-point transfers are performed in which each node sends data to remote nodes directly and in parallel.

POOMA

POOMA (Parallel Object-Oriented Methods and Applications) is an object-oriented framework for applications that require high-performance parallel computers. It is a library of C++ classes designed to represent common abstractions in these applica-tions. POOMA allows programmers to create multithreaded applications on shared-memory multiprocessors using the SMARTS runtime system. Additionally, multi-threaded POOMA programs can be profiled using the TAU library described later in this chapter.

Math Libraries

Other tools that may be helpful in the development of your applications are math libraries, which work on parallel computers and can be used in combination with other parallel application development tools.

PETSc

PETSc is a large suite of data structures and routines for both uni- and parallel-proces-sor scientific computing. Intended especially for the numerical solution of large-scale problems modeled by partial differential equations, PETSc provides a rich environ-ment for modeling scientific applications as well as for rapid algorithm design and prototyping. PETSc includes scalable parallel preconditioners and Krylov subspace methods for solving sparse linear systems, as well as parallel nonlinear equation solvers and parallel ODE solvers. The high-level PETScView tool provides profiling and visualization of PETSc programs.

PLAPACK

PLAPACK is an MPI-based Parallel Linear Algebra Package that provides an infrastructure for building parallel dense linear algebra libraries. PLAPACK provides three unique features: 1) a matrix distribution that is a step towards one that is driven by the natural distribution of an application (physically based matrix distribution), 2) an application interface for filling and querying matrices and vectors, which provides communication using MPI-1.1 implementation, and 3) a programming interface that allows the code to be written in a way that closely resembles the way algorithms are naturally explained, using object-based programming.

ScaLAPACK

ScaLAPACK is a library of high-performance linear algebra routines for distributed memory MIMD computers. It contains routines for solving systems of linear equations, least-squares problems, and eigenvalue problems. Most machine dependencies are limited to two standard libraries called the PBLAS, or Parallel Basic Linear Algebra Subroutines, and the BLACS, or Basic Linear Algebra Communication Subroutines. LAPACK and ScaLAPACK will run on any machine where the PBLAS and the BLACS are available.

These packages are not installed by default on clusters built with this book's accompanying CD-ROM. Complete sources to these packages are available in the *ProgrammingLibs* directory.

Debugging/Profiling Tools

One of the hardest parts of developing parallel programming is figuring out if the programs you've written are spending their computational time where you think they are, or if your programs are as efficient as they could be.

The easiest way to figure out what's going on in your programs is to use the standard Unix profiling tools that can take advantage of profiling information inserted by your compiler. This works well for serial programs running on a single processor, but becomes unmanageable on a parallel system because of all the complex interactions that are possible and the difficulties inherent in wading through the profiling output generated on all of the individual nodes of a cluster.

A more effective way is to use a profiling system designed to work in a parallel environment. Two tools described here, TAU and PCL, can make this aspect of parallel programming a lot easier.

TAU

TAU is the acronym for Tuning and Analysis Utilities. It was developed at the University of Oregon and the Los Alamos National Lab. TAU is a library that will help profile parallel applications and write out detailed performance traces that can be used to visualize where a program is spending its time.

The TAU *pprof* command will read the generated profile files and produce a text listing that describes the activity of the program being profiled. For example:

```
Reading Profile files in profile.*
NODE 0;CONTEXT 0;THREAD 0:
```

%Time	Exclusive msec	Inclusive total msec	#Call	#Subrs	Inclusive usec/call	Name
100.0	5,012	5,012	1	0	5012920	main() int (int, char **)

```
USER EVENTS Profile :NODE 0, CONTEXT 0, THREAD 0
```

NumSamples	MaxValue	MinValue	MeanValue	Std. Dev.	Event Name
1	2048	2048	2048	0	Memory allocated by arrays
1	1	1	1	0	Number of Iterates

```
NODE 0;CONTEXT 0;THREAD 1:
```

%Time	Exclusive msec	Inclusive total msec	#Call	#Subrs	Inclusive usec/call	Name
100.0	0.022	5,010	1	1	5010298	threaded_func() int ()
100.0	5,010	5,010	1	1	5010276	work() int ()
0.0	0.064	0.159	1	1	159	first() int ()
0.0	0.037	0.095	1	1	95	second() int ()
0.0	0.038	0.058	1	1	58	third() int ()
0.0	0.02	0.02	1	0	20	fourth() int ()

```
USER EVENTS Profile :NODE 0, CONTEXT 0, THREAD 1
```

NumSamples	MaxValue	MinValue	MeanValue	Std. Dev.	Event Name
3	1.638E+04	1024	7168	6636	Memory allocated by arrays
6	1	1	1	0	Number of Iterates

```
FUNCTION SUMMARY (total):
```

%Time	Exclusive msec	Inclusive total msec	#Call	#Subrs	Inclusive usec/call	Name
50.0	5,012	5,012	1	0	5012920	main() int (int, char **)
50.0	0.022	5,010	1	1	5010298	threaded_func() int ()

50.0	5,010	5,010	1	1	5010276 work() int ()
0.0	0.064	0.159	1	1	159 first() int ()
0.0	0.037	0.095	1	1	95 second() int ()
0.0	0.038	0.058	1	1	58 third() int ()
0.0	0.02	0.02	1	0	20 fourth() int ()

FUNCTION SUMMARY (mean):

%Time	Exclusive msec	Inclusive total msec	#Call	#Subrs	Inclusive usec/call	Name

----

50.0	2,506	2,506	0.5	0	5012920	main() int (int, char **)
50.0	0.011	2,505	0.5	0.5	5010298	threaded_func() int ()
50.0	2,505	2,505	0.5	0.5	5010276	work() int ()
0.0	0.032	0.0795	0.5	0.5	159	first() int ()
0.0	0.0185	0.0475	0.5	0.5		

Racy

Racy is a utility that is part of the TAU toolkit and presents the profiling information generated by TAU in graphical format. Racy makes it easier to understand the results of the profiling information generated because it shows the runtime statistics in a set of bar-graphs as shown in Figure 7-7.

TAU can also be used in conjunction with the other tools described in this section, including PCL, to generate even more detailed reports and analyses.

PCL

PCL stands for Performance Counter Library. Written by Rudolf Berrendorf and Heinz Ziegler at the Central Institute for Applied Mathematics in Juelich, Germany, PCL works on a variety of CPUs from DEC Alphas through the Intel Pentium II/IIIs, and takes advantage of counters in the CPU to track program performance.

The information tracked by PCL is very specific to the CPUs that it is compiled against. It can track very esoteric information about what the CPU has done on a number of different fronts, ranging from instruction counts to data on how the functional units of the CPU (FPU, integer unit, instruction loader, etc.) are performing to data on how often the instruction and data caches are being utilized, including:

Instruction counts
   Cycles spent in process/thread
   Elapsed cycles
   Number of completed integer (or logical) instructions
   Number of completed floating-point instructions
   Number of completed load instructions
   Number of completed store instructions
   Number of completed load or store instructions

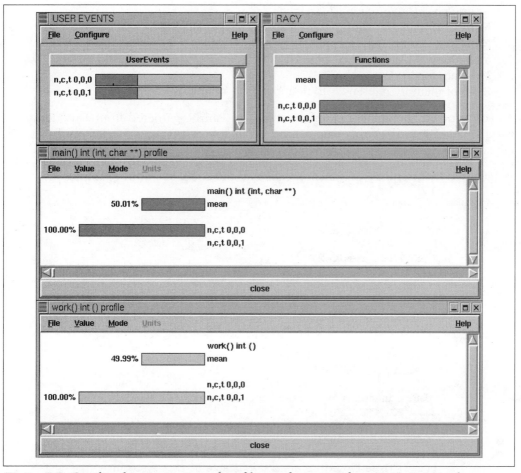

Figure 7-7. Graphical interpretation of profiling information from TAU's Racy tool

Sum of all completed instructions
Number of correctly predicted branches
Number of mispredicted branches
Sum of all branches
Number of successful atomic instructions
Number of unsuccessful atomic instructions
Sum of all instructions concerning atomic operations

Functional unit counts
Number of cycles the integer/logical unit is stalled
Number of cycles the floating-point unit is stalled
Number of cycles the branch unit is stalled
Number of cycles the load unit is stalled
Number of cycles the store unit is stalled (write buffer)
Sum of all cycles a unit is stalled

Ratios and counts relating to CPU caches
    Number of million floating-point instructions per second
    Number of completed instructions per cycle
    Miss rate of L1 data cache
    Miss rate for L2 data cache
    Ratio of memory references to floating point operations

As you can see, the amount of information that can be garnered from a modern CPU is quite extensive. All of this data can be invaluable in tuning a parallel application to take advantage of specific CPU characteristics.

PCL is used by inserting PCL function calls into the code, as in this example:

```
#include < pcl.h>
      int
      main(int argc, char **argv)
      {
        PCL_CNT_TYPE i_result[2];
        PCL_FP_CNT_TYPE fp_result[2];
        int counter_list[2], res;
        unsigned int flags;

        /* define events to be measured     (Floating point instructions and cycles)

        counter_list[0] = PCL_FP_INSTR;
        counter_list[1] = PCL_CYCLES;

        /* define in what mode to count (only user mode) */
        flags = PCL_MODE_USER;

        /* query for functionality */
        if ((res = PCLquery(counter_list, 2, flags)) != PCL_SUCCESS)
          printf("these two events are not available on this system\n");
        else
          {
            /* start counting */
            if ((res = PCLstart(counter_list, 2, flags)) != PCL_SUCCESS)
             {
                printf("problem with starting two events\n");
                exit(1);
             }
            /* do work -- you should include here your piece of code to measure */
            /* stop counting */
            if ((res = PCLstop(i_result, fp_result, 2)) != PCL_SUCCESS)
              printf("problem with stopping two events\n");
            else
              printf("%15.0f FP-instructions in %15.0f cycles\n",
                     (double) i_result[0], (double) fp_result[1]);
          }
        return 0;
      }
```

PCL in and of itself is useful for gaining insight into what a program is doing at the microcosm level of the insides of the CPU. But it is even more useful when used in conjunction with the TAU package, which can be configured to use the PCL counter information to generate even more precise program timing information as a whole.

PDT

Lastly, there is PDT, the Program Database Toolkit. PDT is a collection of source code analysis tools that look at C and C++ source codes and make the information about these sources available to other applications such as TAU and SMARTS.

PDT is an exceptionally useful tool in that it can be used in conjunction with TAU to automatically instrument a given set of sources for profiling.

Online Documentation

The online documentation system that is installed with the clustering software provided with this book provides an online reference to all of the major tools installed on the cluster, as shown in Figure 7-8.

The documentation system is provided in HTML format that can be viewed with a web browser so that it can be available to you while you are editing or debugging your programs.

The packages covered in the online documentation system include:

PVM

The documentation for the Parallel Virtual Machine include the programmatic interface, the PVM libraries, as well as the commands that exist in the PVM shell that is used to launch and control PVM applications.

MPI

The MPI documentation includes all of the programmatic interfaces to version 1.1.2 of the Message Passing Interface.

LAM

The LAM documentation includes all of the programmatic interfaces to version 6.2-pl13 of the Local Area Multicomputer package. This documentation overlaps to some degree with the MPI documentation set since LAM implements a superset of the MPI protocol, adding some MPI version 2 extensions.

PADE

The Parallel Applications Development Environment (PADE) documentation contains instructions on all aspects of the use of the application to build and test parallel applications. These documents also contain links to other NIST parallel computing projects that are available on NIST's web site.

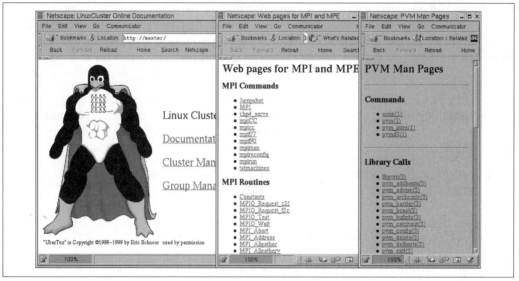

Figure 7-8. The Linux Clusters documentation system

Since the documentation is provided in HTML, you can add additional documentation packages to your cluster as required when you add new capabilities to your system.

System Extensions

All of the cluster configurations that have been covered in this book are generic Beowulf-style clusters. There are no kernel modifications that need to be made to the Linux kernel to make them work. They are actually just the beginning when it comes to making clusters more like monolithic supercomputers.

There are ways to more tightly integrate systems into clusters to allow the master node to have access to very specific information about activities on the slave/compute nodes.

Tighter integration of the master and slave nodes could mean a mechanism that puts all of the process information relating to slave nodes into a space that is readable by the master node. Then the master node can start a client process on any node in the cluster, which would free the user from having to specify nodes for their programs to run on (as is currently the case with PVM and MPI).

Another way to achieve a closer coupling of cluster nodes is a facility that allows processes to actually circulate around the cluster, moving processes from more heavily loaded nodes onto nodes that are lightly loaded, as system conditions warrant.

Two facilities that make such integration possible are BPROC and MOSIX.

BPROC

BRPOC, or Beowulf-distributed process space, is a kernel enhancement from the creators of Beowulf clusters, NASA's CESDIS project.

BPROC creates a unified process ID (PID) space on a Beowulf-style cluster. The unified process space allows a node to run a process that appears to be local when it's actually running on another cluster node.

The key to making such a process work is reserving a block of process IDs on a cluster of workstations for migratory processes. That way, process IDs are unique across all systems participating in the cluster and providing a set of tools that allow processes to be moved from machine to machine.

One node is assigned to be the master of the process space (i.e., the master node of the cluster), and other nodes are slaves that receive work from the master in the form of processes. This is accomplished via several non-trivial modifications to the Linux kernel and a set of daemon processes that keep track of the comings and goings of processes on each node.

On the master node, the master daemon keeps track of all configuration information about remote machines and processes. This daemon also acts as a message router that can deliver data to remote processes and slave daemons on remote nodes.

On the slave nodes, the slave daemon takes care of the creation of all new processes at the request of the master daemon. It also performs as a message router, passing information back to the master daemon about process states of the processes under its care, as well as handing data bound for the processes themselves. The slave daemon keeps track only of the processes in its own space (i.e., on the local machine) and has no knowledge of where other processes may be in the cluster.

The big benefit to BPROC is that it allows the programmer to see something resembling a "single system image." A single system image is the concept that the cluster is really just one big machine like a big symmetric multiprocessor with as many CPUs as there are nodes in the cluster. On massively parallel computers such as the Cray T3E and the Sun Enterprise-10000, this is actually how the computer looks to a process— all the memory CPUs and I/O devices are in one place. This is not true on Networks of Workstations (NoWs) like Linux clusters; normally software such as message passing libraries like PVM and MPI are used to give the illusion of that single image.

Processes started on the master node appear to reside on the master, but they take up almost no system resources such as memory, file descriptors, etc. They do have signal handlers so they can be controlled from the master node and message queues so that data can be sent and received from remote processes. The BPROC daemons on remote nodes keep the master updated on the status of remotely processing jobs. This information is kept up to date in the */proc* file system on the master node which can be read by other programs such as execution monitors or system performance tools like *top*.

Processes running under the control of BPROC pick and choose when they are moved to new processors. In other words, you must code BPROC support into your applications. While BPROC does give you more control over where jobs run, there are some challenges in using it. You must add code into your application to initiate a BPROC move to another node. Your application must also have logic to assess processor load and know when to initiate a move to a less heavily loaded processor.

Another issue that can be problematic with BPROC is that any file descriptors that may be open when a process is moved by BPROC are lost. Programs using BPROC facilities will need to have very carefully crafted check-pointing code to ensure that they don't lose their state during process migration.

Finally, BRPOC has a few scaling problems in that a process ID is needed for every process in the system—for very large clusters, this may exhaust the PID space of the master node.

BPROC is under very active development by CESDIS, and none of the "problems" mentioned should take away from the accomplishments of this project. It is a very elegant and useful way to extend the capabilities of clusters and bring them more in line with traditional supercomputers.

BPROC version 0.2 is included on the Linux Clusters CD-ROM in the *ClusterTools* directory. BPROC is constantly evolving, and it ties very closely to the features of the particular Linux kernel version it runs on. It is always a good idea to check the CESDIS site to ensure that you have the most current version. BPROC can be found at *http://beowulf.gsfc.nasa.gov/software/bproc.html.*

MOSIX

MOSIX is a process migration system developed at the Hebrew University of Jerusalem under the leadership of Professor Amnon Barak.

MOSIX is a kernel-level extension for supporting cluster computing that has been developed seven times for different versions of Unix, including Linux. MOSIX uses kernel-level, adaptive load-balancing, and memory movement algorithms that are geared for high performance and scalability. The algorithms are designed to respond to variations in the resource usage among the nodes by migrating processes from one node to another, preemptively and transparently. The MOSIX software provides some SMP/NUMA features that allow a cluster of PCs to work cooperatively as if they were part of a single system.

MOSIX, like BPROC, is implemented as a set of kernel-level patches. MOSIX is currently only supported for Linux on Intel platforms. This is because in order to make possible the preemptive process migration that MOISX is able to do, the package needs to have very CPU-specific features.

Unlike BPROC, it is the kernel, rather than the user process, that is in complete control of when a process moves from node to node. MOSIX also is decentralized in that there is no master node or slave node. Each system participating in a MOSIX cluster makes its own decisions about when and where to migrate processes based on the scheduling and resource allocation algorithms in the package.

MOSIX version 0.93 is included on the Linux Clusters CD-ROM in the *ClusterTools* directory at the top level of the CD-ROM. It's in the form of a compressed *tar* file that contains the complete set of kernel patches and documentation needed to install the software. The main site for MOSIX is *http://www.mosix.cs.huji.ac.il,* where updates to the software and papers can be downloaded.

Summary

Of course, the tools that are listed in this chapter barely scratch the surface of the number of research and commercial tools that are available to support parallel computing on Unix machines in general and Linux clusters in particular. Two very good resources for finding out what is available in the marketplace are the *Scientific Applications for Linux* web site and the *High Performance Clustered Computing Resources* web site.

The Scientific Applications for Linux site, found at *http://sal.kachinatech.com,* is a searchable directory of scientific applications, both commercial and Open Source. There is a very extensive listing of freely available parallel computing resources that can be downloaded for Linux systems and that will work on a variety of parallel architectures including Beowulf-style clusters.

The High Performance Clustered Computing Resources site, found at *http://www.dgs. monash.edu.au/~rajkumar/cluster/index.html,* is dedicated to sources for parallel and clustered computing topics. The resources at this site range from research papers to software for almost every imaginable esoteric aspect of mathematical computing.

These two sites are good starting points for exploring areas of active research and for finding libraries that may help your parallel program designs.

CHAPTER EIGHT

PROGRAMMING IN A PARALLEL ENVIRONMENT

This chapter explores parallel programming on a Linux cluster by exploring a process that can help with the design of parallel applications. We will discuss this process in terms of a straw-man application that is focussed not on the traditional highly mathematical areas of cluster applications, but on the design of a multi-user game translated to the parallel environment of a Linux cluster. Finally, after we have developed an analysis program, we will look at languages and tools that are amenable to parallel programming on a cluster that could be used to implement parallel programs.

Programming a Clustered System

Parallel programming is fundamentally different from writing sequential (serial) code. Parallel programming is centered on finding ways to decompose (break down) problems in two basic ways:

Functional decomposition
> Breaking the things a program *does* into smaller work units that can be run on multiple processors known as MPMD or Multiple Program Multiple Data oriented programming.

Data decomposition
> Breaking *data* down into reasonable chunks that can be run by different copies of the same program on a large number of processors or by use of a large number of processes known as SPMD or Single Program Multiple Data oriented programming.

After solutions are found for either the smaller work-units or the subsections of the data, depending upon which method is used in the resulting program, the results are then re-integrated into the end result to whatever problem is being solved.

Basic Parallel Program Design

Creating parallel programs is fundamentally different from creating programs that run on sequential processors. This is because, unlike sequentially executed programs, there are multiple possibilities for communication, processing, and data access at almost every possible step of a parallel program's execution. In sequentially executed code, programs progress in a fairly linear fashion, usually not worrying about the problems of concurrent access to variables (with the exception of multi-threaded or recursive applications), or whether or not another part of the program is using a communications channel. The design of such programs is deterministic and relatively straightforward as long as the problem that you are trying to solve is well understood.*

Parallel programs on the other hand require a different starting point for their design. A multitude of decisions must be made before the first line of code is written to determine how to attack programming in a parallel context. Because so much thought must go into these applications, it is interesting to note that many parallel applications are better designed and implemented than their sequential cousins, simply because it is so much harder to just write a "toy application" to test out some ideas and have it turn into a large body of software.

Ian Foster, in his excellent book *Designing and Building Parallel Programs,*† presents a very clear and concise way of thinking about designing parallel systems that he calls "methodical design," which breaks the design process into four distinct stages:

Partitioning
> This is the breakdown of the problem domain into smaller tasks that can be performed in parallel.

Communication
> This is the analysis of where smaller work elements determined in the partitioning of a problem will need to communicate by exchange of information. On parallel processors like clusters, this boils down to examining the number and kind of communication paths that are available on a given cluster and thinking about what kinds of methods might be effective.

Agglomeration
> This process examines results from the first two stages and looks for either processing level or communication optimizations.

Mapping
> This is the process by which tasks that have been divined from the first three stages are mapped into some real-world parallel processing environment such as a

---

* This is not to say that the design of nonparallel programs is somehow less difficult; parallel programs just have a greater degree of interdependent complexities because of the number of nodes/processors.

† This book is available both online, at *http://www-unix.mcs.anl.gov/dbpp,* and in hard copy from Addison-Wesley. Complete details may be found in the bibliography at the end of this book.

cluster that balances out the need to maximize processing capabilities while minimizing communications overhead.

The first two stages address the breakdown tasks and the communication between tasks, while the last two stages focus on the locality of operations and how to meet performance goals given the hardware available to solve the problem being analyzed.

Foster's methodology makes the job of parallel design easier because these four analysis points can be used as an iterative process by which a large problem can be broken down into smaller problems whose interactions and complementary processes are more easily understood. After each iteration, the resulting concepts and designs can be used to develop a parallel application that is more efficient and that will automatically scale to the hardware available to attack the problem.

The rest of Foster's book describes processes for the design of parallel applications that are much more involved than the four basic principles outlined here. These other processes include very in-depth processes for the analysis of messaging models, program structure, performance issues, communication costs, and a lot more. I would highly recommend this text if you are new to parallel computing development or are looking for a good methodology to improve your existing parallel development processes.

Applying Foster's Design Processes

Usually examples of parallel program design are given from the point of view of a large simulation system such as a weather model, a fluid dynamics system like a jet engine simulator, or other larger magnetically oriented process. Ian Foster's book is a great resource for such examples, and they explain the principles he presents very concisely. Most of the examples are given in a mathematical context, so it's a good idea to be comfortable with set theory and some advanced algebra in order to get the most out of his book.

Since this book is about cluster *building* and not cluster *programming*, I'm going in a different direction. Mathematical examples are, overall, the best showcase for parallel analysis. My feeling, however, is that more everyday uses of clusters make parallel processing more concrete because they can be discussed in a more functional and mathematical way.

Let's look at the essence of Foster's method applied to the straw man of a hypothetical parallel processing problem for a totally different kind of clustering project: the porting of a distributed multi-user game such as a MUD or Multi User Domain.[*]

---

[*] The original definition of "MUD" was "Multi User *Dungeon*," but the very mention of that last word conjured up all sorts of untoward images in the minds of teachers, preachers, and certain high-strung political types and sent them into fits, so MUD authors gradually changed it to "Multi User *Domain*" to keep people from hyperventilating.

A Clustered MUD

On the Internet, MUDs were the original "chat rooms." Long before there was an America OnLine, aficionados of "Dungeons & Dragons" style role playing games were getting together online in these virtual spaces to discuss their adventures and even implement them as online games. This section explores the MUD concept and how it might be implemented using a Linux cluster in order to enhance the gaming experience.

What's a MUD?

A MUD is a computer program that presents a text-based virtual reality where people can log in and communicate with one another over a network. This may sound a lot like what we know of as a "chat room," but it is actually much more.

MUDs are not only spaces where people can talk to each other; they are also places that have structure defined by the MUD administrator and the users. This structure can represent rooms, buildings, and whole worlds where users (called "players" or "player characters") build a personae that becomes an integral part of the shared environment, and all of these attributes remain intact after the user logs off. All of the creations and players in a MUD will even be around if there is no one logged in at all. The "world" that makes up the MUD and information about the users are stored in a database. The MUD itself usually has a built-in programming language that allows players to build permanent features of the MUD that can even interact with other players, such as virtual furniture or virtual tools that can be used in the context of the virtual reality.

MUDs are used for a variety of purposes, including as online virtual educational spaces where classes are taught. They can be purely social spaces where people come to participate in chat-type environments that have a bit more structure than a typical chat room. MUDs can even be built into incredibly complicated virtual communities that have online economies with virtual currency, court systems, electoral processes, and so on. Some of these online worlds have been around since the 1980s and are used daily by hundreds and sometimes thousands of users all over the world.[*]

How Do MUDs Work?

MUDs have straightforward programmatic structure. They are composed primarily of:

- A main loop that keeps track of "time" in the MUD. It is the "tick" of the main loop that enables the other tasks that are happening in the MUD to run.

- A database that keeps track of the locations ("rooms") in the MUD and their contents (if any), as well as the locations of the player characters and anything they may own or be holding.

---

[*] Two very good resources on the design and the sociology of MUDs can be found in *High Wired* and *My Tiny Life*; details on both books can be found in the bibliography.

■ A built-in email system that enables email between users and, on some flavors of MUD, connections to the wider world of Internet email.

■ Tools and utilities that allow the MUD to use external protocols such as the Hyper-Text Transport Protocol (HTTP), Telnet, or FTP to bring in information from the Internet for use inside the MUD.

■ A way of processing input from player characters (usually via a network connection) and executing commands (such as movement or programming commands). As part of this processing, whenever a player types something that is not a command, it is shown to any other users who are in the same room; this allows other users to see what a player has "said" when he or she types something. So, processing player input also potentially involves displaying output to other players.

■ A process that allows internal programs written by the MUD administrators or users to run and gives them time to perform whatever tasks they do (kind of like a time-sharing system).

There are many different kinds of MUD server programs, but they all follow this basic pattern as shown in Figure 8-1. One of the most popular flavors of MUD is called a "MOO," which is a MUD server developed by Pavel Curtis at Xerox's Palo Alto Research Center (Xerox PARC). "MOO" stands for "MUD, Object-Oriented." Xerox PARC's own MOO, called "LamdaMOO," which is modeled after a large beach house, has been in continuous operation for over twelve years and has thousands of users.

A typical MOO session looks like this session fragment:

```
[spector@thx1138]% telnet zeitmoo.zeitgeist.com 7777
Connected to zeitmoo.zeitgeist.com
Welcome to ZeitMOO!

ZeitMOO is a MOO that emulates the very quaint town of Northport, Long Island
and includes a lot of the scenery and locales that make the real town a nice place to
live and work. Feel free to
walk around and explore...
connect david mypasswd

Last connected Mon Aug 30 17:20:05 1999 EDT from localhost
Main Street
You are on Main St. in Northport, LI at the corner of Woodbine Avenue.
Off to the northwest is a beautiful harbor with a long pier that sticks out into the
harbor, to the east is the bulk of Main St. and the main shopping district. To the north
is the memorial park, which has lots of benches, chessboards, and a gazebo.
Obvious exits: East to more of Main St., Northwest to the pier, North to memorial park.

michelle is here, distracted.
There is a wind-up duck here.
There is a newspaper here.
say Hi, Michelle!
You say, "Hi, Michelle!"
```

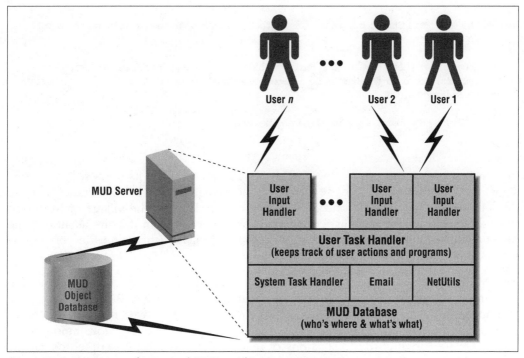

Figure 8-1. Overview of a typical MUD and its constituent processes

michelle kisses david on the cheek
michelle says, "What are you making for dinner?"
say How about McDonalds?
You say, "How about McDonalds?"
michelle says "yucko! You know I'm a vegetarian!"
say I don't suppose you'd like some duck then?
You say, "I don't suppose you'd like some duck then?"
take duck
You pick up the wind-up duck.
wind duck
You wind up the wind-up duck.
drop duck
You drop the wind-up duck. Upon hitting the ground, the wind-up duck rolls around in
circles at your feet.
The wind-up duck says "Quack! Quack! Quack!" as it slowly winds down...
read newspaper
(you pick up the newspaper) It seems to be a recent copy of the Northport Observer. The
cover stories are about the prowess of the local high-school football team and something
about a local author's book about building Linux clusters...
east
Part of Main St.
Looking west from here you can see Northport Harbor, which is home to an impressive array
of sailboats as well as lobster boats, clam boats, and other working craft of all
description. Off in the distance you hear seagulls cry...

> To the east Main Street continues for another 6 blocks with very pretty shops on both
> sides of the street.
>
> Obvious exits: West to Main St., East to Middle of Main St., Southwest to Skipper's
> Restaurant, South to the Harbor Deli, Southeast to the Soup du Jour Bistro, North to the
> North Side of Main St.
>
> The Wizard (SysAdmin) is here, creating new exits.
> :
> :

ZeitMOO models a village on New York's Long Island and lets its users see the virtual sights, walk into shops, and even look at the actual menus of restaurants that are described inside its virtual world. For several of the shops in the village of Northport that are actually on the Internet, connections can be made from the virtual shop in the MOO to the web site of the actual shop in the real village (this comes in very handy for ordering lunch from the Harborside Deli!).

This MOO and hundreds of other MOOs and MUDs that exist out on the Internet are very much self-contained worlds that are created by their users. But unlike old-style text adventure games (such as Infocom's *ZORK* or the old Crowther & Woods *Adventure* game) the environment can change dynamically and the interactions amongst the characters are (usually) the interactions of real people and not pre-scripted characters whose actions and responses are static and unchanging.

MOOcode

Before we look at issues with the MOO that might be solved by a new life on a cluster, we should look for a moment at where to find the opportunities for the parallelism that will make such a move possible.

The MOO server has an internal language that is an object-oriented scripting language system called "MOOcode" (hence the "object-oriented" bit in the name "MOO"). MOOcode is the basis for all of the things that can be done with the MOO from creating users and rooms to developing software robots that can act as pseudo-users that roam the virtual environment acting on behalf of, or interacting with, users. For example, when users are created, they are entered into the server's database by MOOcode routines. When a user enters a room, MOOcode is executed that prints out the room's description. The wind-up duck mentioned in the example above is also written completely in MOOcode.

MOOcode is a language that has a syntax halfway between Pascal and C++. Objects are defined by entering commands to the MOO itself, which then assigns them an "object number" that uniquely identifies them. In fact, everything in the MOO is an object, including rooms, users, and the MOO commands themselves. Once MOOcode object classes are defined, they can, like objects in any other object-oriented language, be used as the basis (the superclass) for other (derived) classes.

For example, a command that creates an object that can be used as the basis for the wind-up duck could be:

@create $thing name Generic Wind-Up Toy, Toy

The MOO will respond with:

```
You now have a Generic Wind-Up Toy  (aka Toy) with object number #12345 and parent
generic thing (#5)
```

This created an object called a "Generic Wind-Up Toy" that has a short alias of "Toy." The object number assigned to the Generic Wind-Up Toy will differ, but the parent ("generic thing") is the base object for a class of MOO entities that are things that can be held by a user (i.e., not a command object, a user object, or a room object). There are many types of objects that are predefined and can be used as the base class for creating new object classes.

Once base classes are created, they can be given properties (which are the same thing as class variables in Java and C++), and methods can be defined to make the toy do whatever it is that virtual toys do. For example:

```
@property  toy.wound   0
@verb  toy:wind this
@verb  toy:wind
         this.wound = this.wound + 2;
         player:tell("You wind up the'", this.name, ".");
         player.location:announce(player.name, " winds up the ", this.name, ".");
```

This set of commands tells the MOO to create a property for the generic toy class called "wound," initially set to zero, which will be used to indicate whether or not the toy has been wound up and then will define verbs that can be applied to the class to make the generic wind-up toy do something. In this case, the "wind" verb is defined that allows a player to wind up the toy.

Once a base object has been defined, higher-level objects may be created using the base object as a parent, as in:

```
@create #12345 named Wind-up Duck, Duck
```

Here the object number of the parent class (the Generic Wind-Up Toy) is used to tell the MOO what to base the duck on. The name "toy" could have been used, but the object number is *absolutely* unambiguous. The MOO will respond with:

```
You now have a Generic Wind-Up Duck  (aka Duck) with object number #12346 and parent
generic thing (#12345)
```

As in all object-oriented languages, since the Wind-Up Duck is based on the Generic Wind-Up Toy, it inherits whatever functionality was defined in its parent class, but it is a new object in its own right with its own unique object number—in this case, the verb "wind."

If we were in a MOO where these classes were defined, we would give the duck a try with the following command:

    wind duck

And the MOO would respond:

    You wind up the Wind-Up Duck.

Everyone else in the same room in the MOO would see:

    David winds up the Wind-Up Duck.

We could then add all sorts of other interesting behaviors to our wind-up duck (such as its action when dropped, as in the example MOO session, above). We could even override inherited behaviors if we so chose.

All of this talk about MOOcode is to show that the MOO is a place where a lot of distinct processes work in parallel. At the same time I am programming my wind-up toys, other users might be talking about some shared interest. The MOO database is keeping track of users and updating/checkpointing itself, while other MOOcode programs are running on behalf of the system or other users, and so on. All of this concurrent activity is a place to start looking for reasonable places to define a "partition"—places where we can discover parallelism that can be exploited on a cluster.

MOOving to a Linux Cluster

One of the problems with the MOO server is that it runs on a single server and becomes bogged down when there are a lot of users connected. The more users that are logged in, the longer it takes for commands and other output to be echoed to a player's terminal. The amount of time between when a player types something and when it is displayed is called "lag" (as in time-lag). On very busy MOOs (and other MUDs), the lag can be in tens of seconds and can really rain on an otherwise fun evening of chat and adventure.

There are also limits on the sizes of the online environment that can be built and the internal programs that can be loaded or run because of the processing constraints imposed by a single system. One of the drawbacks to MOOcode programs is that they can take up a lot of processing time. This slows down the MOO's performance even more than the typing of individual players. So, interesting programs that use a lot of compute time need a very fast CPU. And, like most computing tasks we have discussed, this quickly becomes a never ending cycle.

The addition of multiple processors (as in SMP systems) hasn't added a lot to the performance of these systems because although internally they support a kind of pseudo time-sharing, they are actually single-threaded systems.

An interesting application of cluster design distributes the operation of a MOO over a cluster. A cluster can increase the number of simultaneous users. A MOO database distributed over a cluster will respond more rapidly. In short, a clustered MOO will have increased performance and permit more complex MOO code programs.

If we use the four points of Foster's design methodology and apply them to the six general elements of MOO functionality, we can start to look at ways a MOO server might be rewritten to work on a cluster.

Partitioning

If we start breaking the functionality of a MUD down into sets of tasks, we find a number of different processes at work:

Main loop
> The main loop of the server serves as the shell in which all other activities take place. For the time being, it can be left out of any in-depth analysis. We know that whatever aspects of the MOO are broken down into subtasks for a cluster will have to have some way of synchronizing with the overall flow of events in the clustered MOO.

Database
> The database is a focus of a lot of activity—many other processes that are running continuously as a part of the main loop of the MOO server will enqueue requests to the database component to either retrieve or store information about rooms, users, or MOOcode routines.

> The database is also a trigger-point for MOOcode activities; rooms can contain MOOcode that is executed based on user activities upon entry to or exit from a room, or even based on some other set of events or conditions.

> Overall, the database represents a difficult bottleneck that needs to be addressed if MOO performance is to be increased, since so much activity is centered on it. One solution might be a partitioned data storage system that can be used to design a distributed database, such as PVFS, a parallel file system that will be discussed in Chapter 9, *Application Examples.*

Users
> Users are both entities in the database and, when they are logged in, continuous processes that receive some share of the time made available to all users in order to run whatever programs they may own (such as the Wind-Up Duck). Users also have a quota of bytes they are allowed to use in the database; this quota can be consumed by objects built by the user, including programs and, if they have been authorized by the MOO administrator, rooms in the MOO itself.

> A user and his or her activities look very much like a traditional "process" in the context of an operating system—as mentioned above, users and MOOcode programs operate very much like a time-sharing system that runs inside a program

(the MOO) that runs inside another operating system (Linux). This is valuable abstraction that can be capitalized on later.

MOOcode execution

The internal programs component of a MOO deals with the execution of MOO-code programs written by either a system-level entity such as an administrator, or a player-character (a user). MOOcode programs, like users, have a lot in common with operating system-level processes, but only in the case of MOO system-level tasks or user-level programs that run as MOO background tasks for users. The MOOcode that is executed upon entering a room is more event-driven and could be considered to be more of a database-related activity, like triggers that are executed in a relational database when some condition is met on a row value.

There are a number of issues that must be dealt with for every program that is run:

MOOcode verification

Every program that is run must be checked to ensure it is a syntactically valid program.

Security

Programs must be checked to ensure that they do not do anything obviously harmful before they are executed (e.g., attempt to overwrite the database), and to ensure they don't violate any privileges they aren't entitled to while they are running (such as a play-character's program attempting to use administrator commands).

Quota

Users and programs are granted quotas by MOO administrators. Programs can use only as much CPU time and storage space as their owners have been granted. Programs that exceed either limitation are terminated.

Communication

The crux of a MOO is communication. Everything that happens in a MOO (or any other MUD) is the transmission of a message of some kind from one entity to another. When a user enters a command that takes them from one room to another, a message is sent to the database, which updates itself to reflect the new user position. When a user types to "say" something to another user, a message is sent from that user to the user they are talking to. Unless the message was private (said via a "whisper" command that specifies whom should be whispered to), every user in the room receives messages that display the conversations taking place in the room they are in.

Another area of communication is the messages that pass between MOOcode programs and all other parts of the system.

Lastly, there is the communication between users (through the use of MOOcode) and the world outside the MOO. This can be WWW, Telnet, FTP, or any other kind of protocol that has been programmed into the MOO. The result of these interactions must be delivered to programs, users, or rooms, or stored in the MOO database as appropriate.

Agglomeration

With all of these different kinds of activity and communication, it would seem that there are some processes that naturally fall together into the same category. Agglomeration is the process by which you look at the available opportunities for parallelism and try to find things that fit together (or should be put together). You do this because they are complementary and separating them would incur costs in terms of communications or other overhead that would not be beneficial to the overall development of a parallel system.

Examples of tasks that can be agglomerated in a MOO might include:

MOOcode processing
> Every MOOcode program must go though verification, security, and quota checks as part of its execution. It would not make sense to break these functions up on to different processing nodes. However, it would make sense to give each node on a cluster the ability to execute MOOcode on behalf of a larger system.

Database
> Most of the database functions need to be integral (i.e., they need to function atomically), but redesigning the database to be distributed might yield performance gains if the mechanisms are employed to maintain its integrity in a distributed fashion on a cluster with updates synchronized by the use of a message delivery mechanism.

Users
> Users (players) are clearly entities that do not need to be agglomerated. Since users operate as "free agents" inside the MOO, they can be designed so that they migrate to where the most resources are. Since everything a user does (i.e., "says") in a MOO is a message, the clustered environment is perfect for them. Even user applications can migrate around a cluster and give a performance boost to the MOO since the actions and results of MOOcode programs are delivered by means of messages to either the user or another subsystem of the MOO.

Email
> Email is also a distributed database function. It has the same requirements as the main MOO database that stores MOO's rooms and other objects, so its database and storage functions might be a good fit to be agglomerated with the main database.
>
> Notification of mail delivery falls nicely into the domain of the MOOcode processing and might be handled in the same way that MOOcode is processed, as a distributed service that runs on multiple cluster nodes.

Links to external processes

> The processes that interact with external services such as the web and FTP are pretty much self-contained, but they do interact most often with user processes, so it might make sense to distribute this capability so that they are "close" to where users/players are executing.

Mapping

Mapping processes to cluster nodes requires creating a framework in which database processes are balanced against user interactions. User actions might affect the database directly (such as moving from room to room). User interactions might also affect the database indirectly by triggering a MOOcode program that manipulates the database.

The trick will be to make this a dynamic framework so that the load is distributed dynamically and as evenly as possible over the available compute nodes of the cluster.

Parallel MOO Design

Now that we have identified the core elements of a MOO and what areas would be good targets for parallelization, we can postulate what kind of design might be used to implement the MOO on a Linux cluster as a parallel application.

Since this is a design exercise, we will stick to the abstract notions of what would be required to rewrite the MOO code. The actual code is several hundred pages of C and would require a book of this length to document before we even got into the beginning of our code rewrite.

Let's start by defining some symbols, shown in Figure 8-2, that we can use to represent elements of the MOO that we want to distribute on the cluster.

With these symbols, we can diagram some of the processes that we have identified as part of the MOO and see how they can fit into a parallel system with enough detail to talk in a cogent way about what's going on, without getting too lost in actual implementation details.

A basic MOO parallel infrastructure

The basic MOO infrastructure on a sequential machine is simply a server with some disk space, and a network connection. A cluster implementation will require more hardware, but rather than start out with an unrealistically large cluster for our design, let's keep it simple. A four-node cluster should allow us to design the basic facilities needed by the parallel MOO.

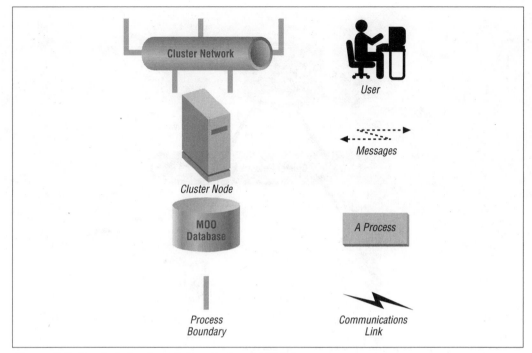

Figure 8-2. Symbols for describing clustered MOO processes

The MOO object database

The logical place to start on the parallelization of the MOO server is the database. As mentioned in the previous section, the database is the central point from which all objects originate and through which all objects are eventually stored.

A simple way to parallelize the database might be to rewrite the appropriate code to work over a shared NFS disk, as shown in Figure 8-3. This would require a basic rewrite of the database to enable some sort of locking for concurrent database transactions but no other changes.

A more aggressive way to parallelize the MOO database component would be to use a facility like a parallel filesystem that would actually distribute the database over the nodes of the cluster.

As shown in Figure 8-4, this would require some portion of the database to be stripped* across the cluster nodes, which would balance out the load on the database. Unlike an NFS implementation of a distributed MOO database, the distributed file-system has the same programmatic semantics as a local one, so there would be no

---

* Stripping is a method of laying out a filesystem so that it is spread out across multiple devices to increase the overall performance of the filesystem. This is the way disk arrays and RAID boxes work.

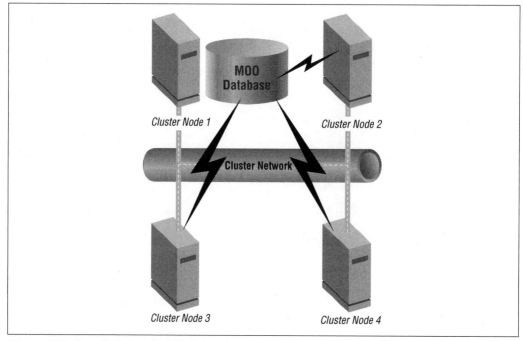

Figure 8-3. Parallelizing the MOO database via NFS

rewriting needed to make this part of the MOO application cluster-friendly, providing the database process was run on a single host. If we wanted to make the database process itself parallel, we would incur the same rewrites that would be needed for the NFS version, above, but we would use the cluster's inherent message passing abilities using PVM or MPI to make database updates more efficient.

The MOOcode execution environment

The next step to enhancing the MOO would be to make the MOOcode execution environment work on a cluster. Everything that exists in a MOO outside of the database is an object of some sort, which means that it is actually some data with a bunch of methods that act on that data. In other words, it's MOOcode.

The clustered execution environment is pretty simple. There would be a MOOcode interpreter that performs all of the verification, security, and quota checks as it is executing the instructions in the code on each node in the cluster.

In order to ensure that MOOcode programs don't step on each other, there will need to be some kind of state table that describes all active MOOcode programs on the cluster. This state table will keep track of what files are open, what user is in what room, etc. This could be implemented as a shared memory construct, using the cluster shared memory mechanisms supported by PVM or MPI, or as a specialized process that is handled by some (yet to be written) message-based white-board protocol

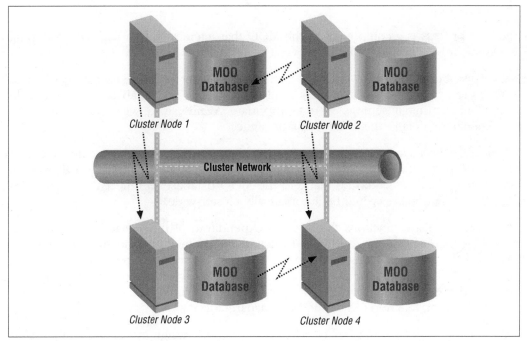

Figure 8-4. Parallelizing the MOO database using a parallel filesystem with message passing

that keeps all of the MOOcode processes informed about the system's state by sending messages around the cluster.

As distributed MOOcode programs run, part of the process will be to request locks on variables and other resources that are in use by other programs or, if necessary, to wait for locks to be freed by other programs.

One thing the MOOcode subsystem would not have to worry about would be access to the database; since the database would exist on all machines, all of the MOOcode accesses would appear to the running program to be "local." Any sleight of hand needed for either an NFS for PVFS implementation to actually get data onto a disk would be handled transparently from the point of view of the program running on the cluster node.

Another nice thing about having a distributed MOOcode execution environment would be that the user process (the thing the user types when he or she says "pick up duck") doesn't have to be on the same node as a MOOcode program executing on their behalf. Subprocesses can be executed on whichever cluster node is the least busy. Since MOOcode is object-oriented, this fits nicely into the general scheme of things in that communication between users and their MOOcode objects can all be done with cluster messaging.

User processes

The user process is a component of the MOO that interacts with a user who is typing at a keyboard connected to the MOO via a network.

With a distributed MOO, it would not matter what cluster node the user/player logged in to, as long as there was a process available to access the database to set them up with whatever initial settings were appropriate Again, since we're not going into implementation details, this is deliberately vague.

Whenever a user executes a simple command (such as a movement command that moves the player to a new location), the command could be handled on their local cluster node, updates could be made to the MOO database to reflect their new location, and these updates would be automatically cluster-wide.

When they perform functions that require expenditure of more elaborate computing resources, their commands could be launched on another node in the cluster if the local node is too busy to handle things. Again, with very small reworkings of code, this could all be done transparently by using cluster messaging. Since we postulated a distributed execution environment in the last step that would take care of locking and resource control, this step too would be transparent to the user.

If we wanted to make things really elaborate, we could design our distributed MOO to work on a cluster that has been enhanced by some form of active process migration such as MOSIX or BPROC (these are covered in Chapter 7, *Tools and Libraries for Parallel Programming*) that allows a running process to be picked up and moved from one cluster node to another to help balance the load across all of the systems on a busy cluster.

Active process migration could allow user processes to circulate around the cluster dynamically as the load varied, but it could also add a great deal of overhead in terms of moving data back and forth across the network. Even though processes in process migration schemes *execute* on remote hosts (other than the ones they started on) they still retain some state on their node of origin. If they perform any kind of I/O, the data in those requests must be forwarded between nodes to keep everything properly synchronized.

Email/messaging system

The email/messaging system is really just another instance of a set of MOOcode programs. The only issues here would concern locking user/player mailboxes so that two or more pieces of email wouldn't collide if they were delivered at the same time. But this would already be handled by both the distributed execution environment for the MOOcode and the distributed aspects of the MOO database where the mail messages are stored (like I said, *everything* in the MOO database is an object—even the email).

Networking utilities

Lastly, the only thing that presents a real challenge in terms of whether or not to attempt some distributed processing is the MOO's networking facilities.

The MOO server supports access to TCP/IP networks on any port defined by the MOO administrator; usually this means access to services such as email, HTTP, FTP, Telnet, and a few others. On many systems, network bandwidth is an issue and most of the protocols listed can consume a lot of available bandwidth if used by a large number of users/players. It may make sense in a distributed MOO to leave facilities that consume external resources active on only one node of a cluster, or at least on some subset of the whole cluster.

Alternatively, the MOO could be configured in such a way that the services are broken up, one to a node, so that no one node can be subsumed by users of that service, or in the case of email, this protocol could run on all cluster nodes. This could make the mail service a lot faster if there is a lot of mail to be processed.

The other issue that comes into play when considering how to distribute network services is process migration. Process migration is probably not a good idea for TCP/IP-based MOO services for the same reason it's a problem with the user processes. Since most TCP services are stream-based (much like a user typing on a keyboard), there are major performance penalties if the cluster has to forward a lot of small packets around to get data from a source socket on an origination node to a socket on a migration (destination) node where that same socket is being fed to a guest (migrated) process.

Overview of the clustered MOO

After we put all of these disparate processes together, we get a distributed system that looks a lot like the diagram shown in Figure 8-5.

The system envisioned by this diagram meets all of parallelization possibilities that were identified in our analysis. This design proposes:

- A distributed database for storing MOO objects

- A distributed MOOcode interpreter to execute code and communicate results via messages to client user processes or client database processes

- A distributed set of network utilities

- A user input handler that allows users to connect to any node in the cluster in order to use the clustered MOO, and uses cluster messaging to use other distributed MOO facilities

A clustered MOO server such as the one described here could allow many thousands of players to be connected simultaneously, compared to the 100–200 that are possible with current servers, even with the fastest CPU clock speeds.

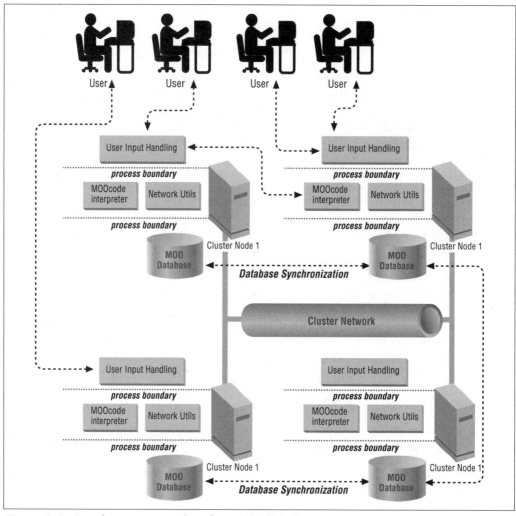

Figure 8-5. Complete process outline for a distributed MOO

With the distributed computing power of a cluster behind it, there are also multimedia extensions that would be possible on such a MOO. At the moment, MOOs and other MUDs are usually purely textual environments. There are some MOOs, such as the one described in the book *HighWired*, by Cynthia Hayes (University of Michigan Press, 1997), that do include built-in web servers or other facilities that enable some graphical content and navigation, but these are fairly crude efforts. There is a trade-off between the amount of work that can be done on a single thread in terms of presentation of enhanced media versus the number of users that can be supported.

With the enhanced network capabilities on a cluster and the availability of a distributed MOO database, it is not hard to envision the addition of a few more distributed processing capabilities that add all sorts of multimedia extensions to our hypothetical clustered MOO. With the power and load-balancing capabilities inherent on a cluster, these additions could be made without impacting the ability to support large numbers of users.

The implementation of this distributed MUD is left as an exercise to the reader. If you want to undertake such a development effort, there are several sources for the Xerox MOO server code (which is free for use under the GNU General Public License). One of the most reliable is *http://www.moo.mud.org,* which is an archive that contains a lot of information and source code for various kinds of MUDs including the Xerox MOO server.

Of course, if you were to undertake such a project, you would want to explore ways to make your development as effective and easy as possible. This means looking at the available candidates in cluster-friendly languages. The original MOO server from Xerox is written in plain old ANSI C. C is a great language for many tasks, but there may be ways to more closely match another language to the abilities of the cluster and the process of parallel programming.

Language Selection

The choice of programming languages is probably the most contentious topic amongst programmers, next to the debate of what window managers or editors are the best. Parallel programming is a very different beast from your run-of-the-mill computer programming assignment, because so much more is happening all at once. The choice of language can make or break a software project, not because one language is intrinsically "better" or "worse" than another, but because there are different levels of experience and maturity that different languages bring to the parallel programming party. Some languages, such as FORTRAN, have the benefit of 30+ years of experience, while Java, although very powerful and easy to use, has less than a decade of development behind it.

The choice of language is very much a matter of individual taste, but it might be a good idea to look at some of the most popular languages that are used for parallel programming projects and see why some get more use than others.

FORTRAN (F77, F90, HPF)

FORTRAN is the granddaddy of all mathematical programming languages. Its name is even a translation of its function—FORMula TRANslator. FORTRAN was developed in the mid-1950s to allow programmers to write complex mathematical programs without having to resort to writing in the machine language that drives computer hardware directly.

FORTRAN is a very simple, minimalistic programming language that provides the basics of flow-control, arrays, and a wide array of mathematical operations. Some have even called it "the BASIC of the scientific world." In its initial release, it did not even include subroutines.

Although FORTRAN was designed to be simple and is not as complex as C++ or Java, it is not a dead language. As the use of FORTRAN for mathematical software has driven the use of high-performance computers, so has the advancement in those computers driven the evolution of FORTRAN.

Over the years, the language has been extended to include more and more features that were found in later, more structured languages such as C and C++. FORTAN90/95, the latest version of the standard, includes parameterized data types, virtual functions, explicit interfaces, and other features that allow FORTRAN to play in the pool with object-oriented languages such as C++.

FORTRAN's biggest benefit from a performance perspective is that since it is simple syntactically, it can be easily optimized. This simplicity and ease of optimization also make FORTRAN a great choice for a parallel programming language. In its latest incarnation, FORTRAN90/95, the language includes explicit features and keywords that can tell a FORTRAN compiler when it needs to generate code that can run on a parallel processor.

C/C++

C was originally designed as a systems programming language. It allows very efficient manipulation of primary data types (bits, bytes, words) and is well-suited to the creation of device drivers and other low-level systems code. Over the years, large numbers of external libraries have been developed to extend its functionality into hundreds of areas including the realm of high-performance computing. But it has never quite reached the momentum and acceptance that FORTRAN has for work on supercomputers.

C++ is a close cousin of C (it has C's syntax and almost all of its keywords). But it is really a totally different programming paradigm. C++, when used as designed, treats the universe quite differently than nonobject languages. In object-oriented languages, the focus is on data and what kind of operations need to be performed on that data. The pieces of data are "objects," and the functions that act upon data are "methods." Object-oriented programs focus on messages sent to objects that cause specific methods to operate on the data and the interactions between classes (which are the named agglomeration of data and methods) in a program.

This extremely modular approach lends itself well to distributed high-performance computing: the kind of work that clusters excel at. C++ has become very popular in the high-performance computing community precisely because the object-oriented methodology maps so well onto the kinds of data and functional decomposition that are required to make high-performance systems work.

The difficulty in using C++ for parallel programming comes from finding libraries that support the kinds of operations that are needed for your application. Fortunately, as shown in Chapter 7, there are a number of well-funded academic groups and a large number of software development shops working on such problems. The other issue with C++ (as well as other object-oriented languages) is the amount of processing overhead, in terms of both CPU time and memory, taken up by the objects themselves. Unlike traditional, non-object programming models, C++ objects take up more storage and have more persistent data than their non-object analogs, and there is also a large amount of processing overhead in the allocation and garbage collection involved in keeping track of C++ objects. Lastly, debugging object-oriented programs can be very confusing since there is so much going on behind the scenes in terms of method and object naming. It takes a good debugger (like GDB or DDD) to present data to a programmer in a clear, uncluttered fashion to make parallel debugging tasks easier.

Java

Java isn't a language strongly associated with parallel processing. Usually Java is seen in web browsers in the form of annoyingly cute applets. However Java supports all of the paradigms that are needed for parallel execution—it just doesn't have them embedded in the language.

Java has a whole set of external classes—called the Remote Method Invocation (RMI) classes —that allow Java executables to be moved transparently from one computing platform, or Java Virtual Machine ("JVM"), to another. The RMI allows programmers to write distributed applications that can be spread out to as many machines as have JVMs. The RMI can be used to implement distributed processing systems and is the basis for Sun's JINI network computing environment.

The only drawback to Java is that Java "executables" are actually run in an interpreter called a Java Virtual Machine or JVM. As of this writing, JVMs and Java byte-codes do not (yet) run as fast as native object codes.

FlotM

"Flavor of the Month" or "FlotM" is the term I use to describe the hundreds of "little languages" that are used by parallel programmers to experiment with new ideas in parallel program/algorithm development.

There are dozens of research languages developed every year by parallel programming researchers in both business and university settings that allow people to test out novel features of both parallel hardware and syntaxes that make the parallel programming process easier or more efficient.

Among these languages are:

Cilk

A multi-threaded parallel programming language developed at MIT's Laboratory for Computer Science that is based on ANSI C. Cilk provides a number of primitives that encapsulate load-balancing, communications, and synchronization and can be used on either a traditional SMP machine or a cluster of workstations.

TkPVM

TkPVM is a hybrid of the TCL/Tk (Tool Command Language plus its visual extension called "Tk") language and PVM that allows parallel programs to be written very quickly.

PyPVM

PyPVM is a Python module that gives Python programmers access to the PVM libraries. Python is a very popular programming language for RAD (Rapid Application Development).

Some might see the "little languages" designation as hostile to these languages. Nothing could be further from the truth; most of these languages are meant to be used as *gedanken* or thought experiments to see how such tools make a difference in the parallel programming process. Some of them are very clever extensions to already powerful languages that allow them to operate in the larger domain of parallel processing without forcing the programmer to learn a completely new language. Also, just because some of these are not mainstream languages like FORTRAN or C++ doesn't mean that they're not worth trying out if they support features that are germane to your applications.

Where to Go from Here

In this chapter we have covered a lot of ground in a relatively small space.

Clearly, clusters have a lot of power to solve problems, but that power can only be harnessed by effective design of parallel applications. Effective application design is not, whether on a parallel system or any other, something that is carved in stone. Rather, it's a process that begins before any code is written and that contemplates effective ways to understand a problem that you want to solve.

The problem domain analysis that needs to be undertaken with the design of parallel applications is the most critical part of making things work on a cluster. The more you understand about a problem, the more easily opportunities for parallelism can be found. These opportunities enable creative solutions in terms of how to partition work across the hardware available in your cluster. The best designed parallel programs usually turn out to be those where the designer has effectively balanced the processing components and the communications components to make a system that is efficient and will scale well as needs change.

Our straw-man application of a clustered MOO presents a pretty well balanced set of ideas on how such a system might be analyzed and scoped out, and it would be an interesting project to actually implement.

However, actually coding up applications like the clustered MOO might not be everyone's idea of how to spend a Friday night. Fortunately, other, ready-to-run examples of clustered applications can be found in the next chapter, which can give you a good idea of just how fast Linux clusters are.

CHAPTER NINE

APPLICATION EXAMPLES

After all this talk about the potential of clusters, and the various ways a cluster can be put together and managed, you probably would like to see some applications in action.

The choice of applications to include here has been difficult. It would have been very easy to include some examples of high-energy physics applications. Molecular modelling code would have made for some large, impressive bits of code. But these examples would not illustrate how easily clusters can be used for down-to-earth applications. Instead, I have chosen to document a few smaller, more interesting applications; one that might be of use to you if you are running your cluster at home, and another that might come in handy in a parallel development setting for developing applications that need to move data more effectively.

The first application is called mp3pvm, written by Brian Guarraci. mp3pvm is an audio application that is useful if you use MP3 audio players on your Linux systems or if you own a hand-held MP3 player such as a Diamond RIO.

The second application is called PVMPOV, a parallel version of the popular ray-tracing application Persistence of Vision (POV). With POV you can generate breathtakingly real images or even render frames for computer-generated animation; with PVMPOV, that process can be sped up by orders of magnitude.

Another interestingl application is PVFS, the Parallel Virtual File System, written by Matthew M. Cettei, Walter B. Ligon III, and Robert B. Ross at the Parallel Architecture Research Lab at Clemson University. PVFS allows you to construct an extremely high-performance filesystem out of a cluster.

mp3pvm

mp3pvm is a tool that will allow you to use a Linux cluster to create MP3 (MPEG Layer 3) files from music CDs that can be played on popular hand-held devices like the Diamond RIO.[*]

MP3[†] is a specification for a very high-quality audio recording format that can rival CDs in its fidelity. MP3 has become the preferred format for small independent artists who typically don't have large recording contracts. It enables them to get their music in front on an increasingly techno-savvy audience. All they have to do is put a file up on a web site, and people download it to play on an MP3-capable device.

It is also possible to take off-the-shelf commercial audio CDs and pull out the individual tracks. They can be on a computer hard disk to be downloaded to devices like the RIO or even used to make a personal "jukebox" where audio tracks are serviced up on demand from a server connected to an MP3 player.

Obviously, neither I nor O'Reilly and Associates condone the use of this program for any unlawful purpose.

Now that we have covered the required legalisms, let's take a look at how you can use a cluster to make your CD collection a little more portable.

How It Works

mp3pvm uses some very simple clustering techniques to speed up the process of MP3 conversion.

First, a music CD is placed in the CD-ROM drive of the master node. A program is invoked that reads the music on the CD as though each song were just a data track (which it is, after all) on a regular CD-ROM. The audio tracks are then stored on a shared (cluster-wide) disk as individual files.

Next, by using a divide-and-conquer method, the individual audio tracks are processed by nodes in the cluster. This is done by another program, called an MP3 encoder, that translates the CD audio format files into the portable MP3 format files. The MP3 then can be put into a database and played on a Linux workstation with an MP3 player or downloaded to MP3 players and enjoyed on-the-go.

Sounds simple, no? It is a pretty straightforward process, and you may be wondering: "why anyone would bother to make this a cluster project?" MP3 conversion is an interesting problem for a cluster because the conversion process is very CPU-intensive.

---

[*] Diamond Multimedia is the creator of the RIO; information on the RIO hand-held music player can be found at *http://www.s3.com/products.htm*.

[†] MP3 information can be found at innumerable places on the Internet, but one of the most popular is *http://www.mp3.com* where MP3 players, music, and other related materials can be found.

Something to Think About

Before we get too far into making music CDs into portable MP3 files, I must point out a few things about this process that are important from a legal point of view. The very existence of devices that can play copyrighted music on devices other than those that were originally intended is, to say the least, an *extremely* contentious issue.

The Recording Industry Association of America (RIAA) has been fighting increased piracy of copyrighted music. This involves people copying music off of audio CDs, converting the tracks to MP3 format, and then making them available over the Internet, often violating copyright laws. RIAA feels that devices such as the Diamond RIO and programs that create MP3 files contribute to this piracy problem and take money away from the artists who create the music.

The use of this tool is meant as a demonstration of how to use a cluster to make a library of recordings of music that you own for playback on an MP3 player. Using this program to illegally copy music is, obviously, against U.S. law and would violate international agreements on copyrights and intellectual property. Having said all of that, U.S. law allows the purchaser of audio CDs and other electronic media to re-record copies of copyrighted works for their own personal use as long as the copies are not distributed to others, whether for free or for profit.

Reading and converting a 72-minute audio CD can take over two hours depending on how dense the data in the individual tracks is (tracks that have more bits of silence are easier to process than tracks that have continuous sound).

Using a distributed process speeds up the conversion from audio to MP3 format by orders of magnitude for every compute node that is added to the process, once the tracks are read off of the CD.

What's Required

In order to use the mp3pvm program, you will need to have the following

- A master node with a CD-ROM drive. No audio card is required since the conversion software will be reading the audio tracks as "data" rather than attempting to play them though an audio card connected to the system.

- A shared disk space across the cluster. This can be accomplished via NFS, or the automounter. (Or, with modifications to the mp3pvm program, it should be possible to actually parcel out the data tracks to slave nodes, but that would consume a lot of network bandwidth.)

- Slave nodes. The more, the better.

- *cdparanoia*—an Open Source program that can read audio CDs and rewrite the audio track as data streams onto another medium such as a file on a hard disk.

- *bladeenc*—an Open Source program that can translate various audio formats into MP3.

Building and Installation

Building this package is pretty easy. All of the software you need has been included on the Linux Clusters CD-ROM.

In order to install mp3pvm, you will need to mount the Linux Clusters CD-ROM; this will need to be done by the superuser (root). You will need to "su" to root, or have the administrator of your cluster complete this step in order to copy the software.

Mounting the CD-ROM

With the CD in the CD-ROM drive, execute the following command, which will mount the CD-ROM and make it available to the system:

```
[root@master /root]# mount -r /dev/cdrom /mnt/cdrom
```

You can check to see if the CD-ROM is correctly mounted by using the *df* command. The actual sizes of the partitions listed may be different than what is shown here, but they should look something like this:

Filesystem	1k-blocks	Used	Available	Use%	Mounted on
/dev/sda1	248847	47711	188286	20%	/
/dev/sda5	5050844	11271	4778117	0%	/home
/dev/sda9	248847	431	235566	0%	/tmp
/dev/sda6	1018298	650548	315139	67%	/usr
/dev/sda7	995115	76970	866739	8%	/usr/local
/dev/sda8	893986	33052	814749	4%	/var
/dev/scd0	589998	589998	0	100%	/mnt/cdrom

The important part of this listing is the last line where we can see that the CD-ROM is indeed mounted and online.

Once the CD-ROM has been mounted, all of the required software can be copied with a single command:

```
[root@master /root]# cp -Rp /mnt/cdrom/ExampleApps/mp3pvm   /tmp/mp3pvm
```

The data will be copied into the temp directory. If you would like to copy the programs to another directory, just change the target directory on the command line. For the purposes of this example, we will assume that the files are in */tmp/mp3pvm*.

The directory contains three gzippedd tar files:

```
-rw-rw-r--   1 root      root       137035  Aug 22 23:17 bladeenc-082-src-stable.tar.gz
-rw-rw-r--   1 root      root       97126   Aug 22 23:18 cdparanoia-III-alpha9.6.src.tgz
-rw-r--r--   1 root      root       4817    Aug 22 23:14 mp3pvm-0.3.tar.gz
```

The first file is the *bladeenc* MP3 encoder that translates the audio files into MP3 format; the second is the *cdparanoia* program that reads the audio tracks off the CD-ROM; and finally, the third is the *mp3pvm* package that will perform the conversion in parallel on the cluster.

Each package should be uncompressed and untar'd with the following command:

```
root@master /root]#  tar zxvf  filename
```

where *filename* is one of the files listed above. Each file should be processed in turn. The *tar* command will print out an in-depth listing of all of the files that are being unpacked from each archive as they are being processed.

At the end of the process, there will be three directories created that can be listed (along with the original gzip'd tar files) as follows:

```
[root@master /root]#  ls -FC
bladeenc-082-src-stable/        cdparanoia-III-alpha9.6/        mp3pvm/
bladeenc-082-src-stable.tar.gz  cdparanoia-III-alpha9.6.src.tgz  mp3pvm-0.3.tar.gz
```

The next step is to build each piece of software and install it in an accessible place on each node of the cluster.

Building bladeenc

The bladeenc encoder comes pre-configured and will compile on any Linux system.

To build the encoder, change to the blade encoder source directory by typing:

```
[root@master /root]#  cd bladeenc-082-src-stable
```

Then, start the build process by typing "make" at the shell prompt:

```
[root@master /root]#  make
gcc -O2 -m486 -malign-jumps=2 -malign-loops=2 -funroll-all-loops -c -o bladesys.o
bladesys.c
gcc -O2 -m486 -malign-jumps=2 -malign-loops=2 -funroll-all-loops -c -o bladtab.o bladtab.
c
           :
gcc -o bladeenc bladesys.o bladtab.o codec.o common.o encode.o formatbitstream2.o
huffman.o l3bitstream.o l3psy.o loop.o main.o mdct.o reservoir.o samplein.o strupr.o
subs.o tables.o -lm
```

The process will complete very quickly; the resulting binary will be called "bladeenc." This binary should be installed in a generally accessible place, such as */usr/local/bin* on the master node as well as any cluster nodes on which you wish to run the *mp3pvm* application.

Building cdparanoia

To build *cdparanoia*, change to the *cdparanoia* directory by typing:

[root@master /root]# **cd .../**

to move back up to the mp3pvm distribution directory which houses the applications, and then type:

[root@master /root]# **cd   cdparanoia-III-alpha9.6**

to enter the *cdparanoia* source directory. Unlike the blade encoder, *cdparanoia* uses the GNU autoconfigure script to set up the build parameters for the package. Part of the autoconfigure process allows the builder to specify where the resulting binary should be installed.

To configure the package, type the command:

[root@master /root]# **./configure --prefix=/usr/local**

The script will print out information about the packages and configuration of the system it is running on, and it will create a *makefile* that can be used to compile the package:

```
bash# ./configure --prefix=/usr/local
loading cache ./config.cache
checking host system type... i686-unknown-linux
checking for ranlib... (cached) ranlib
checking for ar... (cached) ar
checking for install... (cached) install
checking how to run the C preprocessor... (cached) gcc -E
checking for ANSI C header files... (cached) yes
checking size of short... (cached) 2
checking size of int... (cached) 4
checking size of long... (cached) 4
checking size of long long... (cached) 8
checking for linux/sbpcd.h... (cached) no
checking for linux/ucdrom.h... (cached) no
checking whether make sets ${MAKE}... (cached) yes
checking for working const... (cached) yes
creating ./config.status
creating Makefile
creating interface/Makefile
creating paranoia/Makefile
```

When the configure script completes, type *make* at the shell prompt to compile the package:

```
[root@master cdparanoia-III-alpha9.6]# make
make cdda_interface.a CFLAGS="-O -Dsize16='short' -Dsize32='int' "
make[2]: Entering directory `/tmp/mp3pvm/cdparanoia-III-alpha9.6/interface'
gcc -O -Dsize16='short' -Dsize32='int'  -c scan_devices.c
scan_devices.c: In function `cdda_find_a_cdrom':
scan_devices.c:69: warning: passing arg 4 of `idmessage' makes pointer from integer
without a cast
                 :
make[1]: Leaving directory `/tmp/mp3pvm/cdparanoia-III-alpha9.6'
strip cdparanoia
```

Once the build process has completed, all that's left is to install the binary in the directory that was specified in the configure command by typing *make install* at the command prompt:

```
[root@master cdparanoia-III-alpha9.6]# make install
```

The makefile will then install the executable and its manual page:

```
install -m 0755 ./cdparanoia /usr/local/bin
install -m 0644 ./cdparanoia.1 /usr/local/man/man1
```

Depending upon what installation directory was specified to the configure command, you may have to be *root* in order to actually install the files.

Building mp3pvm

To build the mp3pvm parallel application itself, change to the *mp3pvm* directory by typing:

```
[root@master /root]# cd .../
```

to move back up to the mp3pvm distribution directory, which houses the applications, and then:

```
[root@master /root]# cd mp3pvm
```

to change to the mp3pvm source directory.

In order to correctly operate, the *mp3pvm* application needs to know where to put files that it reads off of the audio CD. The information that controls this aspect of the program's operation is in the file *mp3pvm.c* in a line of code near the top of the file that looks like this:

```
/* the common directory where wav files are put and mp3 are created */
#define WAVDIR          "/home/music"
```

You will need to edit this file and change */home/music* to the name of the directory where you wish to store the audio tracks and MP3 file that is accessible to all of the cluster nodes you plan on using.

Providing that your cluster has been built from the CD-ROM supplied with this book, all of the environment variables should be set and the PVM software installed so that *mp3pvm* can be compiled with a single command:

```
[root@master /root]# aimk
making in LINUX/ for LINUX
gcc -g -I/usr/local/pvm3/include -DSYSVSIGNAL -DNOWAIT3 -DRSHCOMMAND=\"/usr/bin/rsh\" -
DNEEDENDIAN -DFDSEINOTSTRUCT -DHASERRORVARS -DCTIMEISTIMET -DSYSERRISCONST -o mp3pvm /
root/mp3pvm/mp3pvm.c  -L/usr/local/pvm3/lib/LINUX -lpvm3 -lgpvm3
mv mp3pvm /usr/local/pvm3/bin/LINUX
```

The *aimk* program is a PVM utility that automatically builds and links a PVM application. Once the application is built, *aimk* will attempt to install the binary, called *mp3pvm,* into the PVM binaries directory. On clusters built with the Linux Clusters CD-ROM, the default location for PVM applications is */usr/local/pvm3/bin/LINUX/.* If you are not the superuser, the installation process will return an error message when an attempt is made to copy the executable into this PVM binaries directory. As with the other files, you will have to "su" to *root* or have the cluster administrator install the *mp3pvm* executable. Alternatively, you can run the *mp3pvm* application in the build directory, but you will have to ensure that all nodes in the cluster have this executable in the same place so that the parallel virtual machine can find it when it needs to start the application.

Installing the Files Cluster-wide

Before these programs can be used to make MP3 files on a cluster, each node must have copies of all three of these applications: *bladeenc, cdparanoia,* and *mp3pvm.*

Assuming that these applications are installed in the following locations:

/usr/local/bin/bladeenc
/usr/local/bin/cdparanoia
/usr/local/pvm3/LINUX/mp3pvm

the files should be copied using *rcp, ftp,* or any other method to each of the cluster nodes that you wish to use for MP3 processing. *All copies of these applications must be installed in the same place on each node.* If the applications are missing on some nodes, or installed in different places on some of the nodes, the *mp3pvm* application will fail. This is because the *mp3pvm* application will try to launch applications based on where it finds them on the master node of the parallel virtual machine.

How to Use It

The *mp3pvm* application is very easy to use. The whole system can be up and running in three easy steps:

Step 1: Starting the virtual machine

Start the parallel virtual machine software by typing the command *pvm*:

    [spector@master /home/music]# **pvm**

The PVM system will respond with a PVM prompt:

    pvm>

If your system was set up using the cluster management system from the Linux Clusters CD-ROM, then all of the nodes in your cluster should already be known to PVM, and you can list them by entering the *conf* command:

```
pvm> conf
5 hosts, 1 data format
                        HOST      DTID     ARCH   SPEED         DSIG
    master.cluster.ny.zeitgeist.com   40000   LINUX   1000    0x00408841
                       node2     80000    LINUX   1000    0x00408841
                       node3     c0000    LINUX   1000    0x00408841
                       node4    100000    LINUX   1000    0x00408841
                       node5    140000    LINUX   1000    0x00408841
pvm>
```

In this example, there are five nodes in the parallel virtual machine.

If the PVM returns with simply the name of the node you are on (presumably the master node), such as:

```
pvm> conf
1 host, 1 data format
                        HOST      DTID     ARCH   SPEED       DSIG
    master.cluster.ny.zeitgeist.com   40000   LINUX   1000 0x00408841
pvm>
```

you will need to add the nodes that you wish to use with the *mp3pvm* application by hand. To accomplish this, type the *add* command, along with the name of the node to be added to the parallel virtual machine:

```
pvm> add node2.cluster.ny.zeitgeist.com
1 successful
                        HOST      DTID
    node2.cluster.ny.zeitgeist.com    80000
pvm>
```

This will need to be done for each of the slave/compute nodes that will be used. Once all the desired nodes have been added, the *conf* listing will look very much like the first one shown above.

Once the PVM is set up, exit from the PVM shell by typing *quit*. This will place you back at the command shell.

Step 2: Setting up the CD

Place an audio CD that you wish to convert to MP3 format in the CD-ROM drive of the master node of the cluster. You do not need to mount the CD (which isn't mountable anyway—audio CDs are not a recognized filesystem under Linux).

For our example, we'll use the soundtrack to *The Rocky Horror Picture Show*, a CD that has 16 tracks totalling 54 minutes and 45 seconds.

Step 3: Starting the parallel application

Start the *mp3pvm* parallel application by typing the full pathname of the application, plus the number of tracks that should be converted. For example:

```
[spector@master /home/music]#  /usr/local/pvm3/bin/LINUX/mp3pvm 16
```

Of course, if your copy of *mp3pvm* is located someplace else, you should use the appropriate path name for your installation. The application will start up and report on its progress on a track by track basis:

```
Preparing to translate 16 tracks.
Spawning 17 tasks ... SUCCESSFUL
Broadcasting init info
Waiting for tasks to init.
Farming...
Collector finished: track1.wav
Sending WID:(track1.wav) to worker #0
Collector finished: track2.wav
    :
```

At the same time the output is going to standard output, it might be interesting to see what XPVM thinks is going on. XPVM (see Chapter 7) is an execution monitor for PVM applications. It can be started up by opening another X terminal or other command shell, and typing *xpvm* at the shell prompt.

XPVM shows a very different view of the *mp3pvm* application in action.

The XPVM window shown in Figure 9-1 shows the master node in communication with four slave nodes. The task/time graph in the bottom half of the window shows that the first task is the copy of *mp3pvm* running on the master node. The message lines on the graph show the master spawning subordinate tasks on other nodes in the parallel virtual machine and giving them work to do.

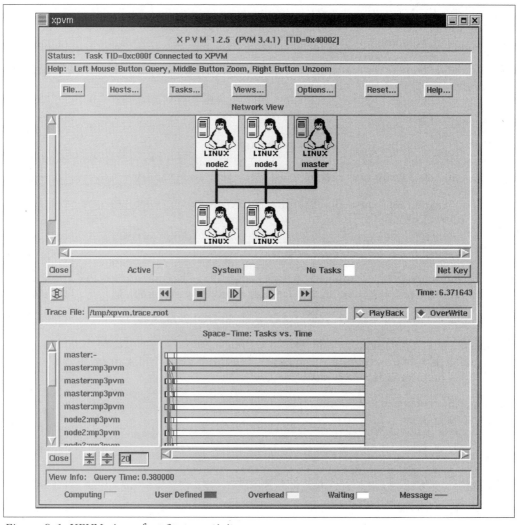

Figure 9-1. XPVM view of mp3pvm activity

You may notice that there is a flurry of activity right at the start, and then all of the activity bars for the slave nodes are white while the master node is highlighted.

A more detailed look at this may be seen in "task versus time" display by using the middle mouse button (or its equivalent if you are not using a three-button mouse) to select an area of the task graph. When you release the mouse button, the display will "zoom in" on the tasks and show greater detail of the interaction between the PVM tasks.

Figure 9-2 shows that the master node is starting up, spawning the worker tasks, and then processing the audio CD itself, pulling the tracks and putting them in the shared disk space. While the master task is processing the CD, the slaves are sleeping, waiting to be assigned a track to convert to MP3 format.

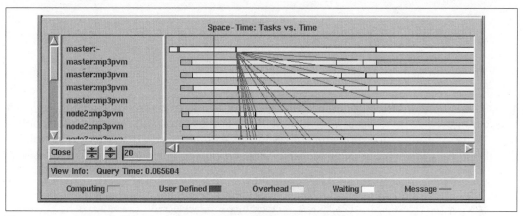

Figure 9-2. A detailed look at the mp3pvm application startup communications

The processing will continue for quite some time; the exact time depends upon the speed of the nodes in your cluster and how large the input audio files are.

It is also possible, using other display options in XPVM, to watch the output from the individual PVM worker processes, as is shown in Figure 9-3. This display is accessible from the XPVM "Views" menu.

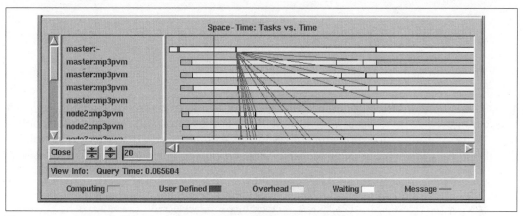

Figure 9-3. XPVM's task_output display

At the end, you will see a message from the master copy of the *mp3pvm* application indicating that the MP3 conversion process has completed:

```
        :
Collector finished: track16.wav
Sending WID:(track16.wav) to worker #15
Collector is done
Cleaning up... 18 in group
[spector@master /home/music]#
```

To check on the work, simply get a file listing of the shared directory where *mp3pvm* was configured to place the MP3 output files. For example, if *mp3pvm* was configured to use the directory */home/music* as in our examples, the first set of files will be the MP3 files, and then the original audio (known canonically as "wave" files) files:

```
[spector@master /home/music]# ls /home/music
track1.mp3    track2.mp3    track3.wav    track4.mp3    track5.mp3    track6.mp3
track7.mp3    track8.mp3    track9.mp3    track10.mp3   track11.mp3   track12.mp3
track13.mp3   track14.mp3   track15.mp3   track16.mp3   track1.wav    track2.wav
track3.wav    track4.mp3    track5.wav    track6.wav    track7.wav    track8.wav
track9.wav    track10.wav   track11.wav   track12.wav   track13.wav   track14.wav
track15.wav   track16.wav
```

All of the files have been copied from the CD and converted to MP3 format.

They are now ready to be played either via an MP3 player on a desktop-style machine or to be downloaded to a hand-held MP3 player.

Possible extensions

Obviously this is a minimalist application, there are a number of areas where it could be improved to make transforming audio files into MP3 easier. Some areas that might be easy targets for enhancement are:

Automatic track counting
> This would enable the *mp3pvm* application to figure out on its own how many tracks are present on the target CD. Right now, the number of tracks to process must be specified on the command line. Conversely, custom track selection would allow the user to select which tracks would be processed. This would be useful where you want to pull your favorite tracks from a CD and leave the ones you don't like.

Album and track name processing
> This would allow the *mp3pvm* application to make the resulting MP3 files more easily identifiable. Right now the tracks are simply numbers (e.g., "track1.mp3") and you have to rename them by hand if you want to know which track is which.

> This can be accomplished by reading a binary ID number stored on every commercially produced CD. This "disc ID" can be used to find out the title, artist, and other information about the CD and can be used to query any of several databases

on the Internet that store album names, track titles, and even lyrics of entire songs. This kind of functionality would be very useful in a "jukebox" type of application where you might want to be able to automatically process CDs in your collection or to be able to display this kind of information to the user in a MP3 player application.

Database integration

Hooks could be added to *mp3pvm* that could allow the program to automatically store the resulting MP3 files in a database, which would come in handy in the previously mentioned jukebox application. As the application stands right now, there is a lot of grunt work involved in taking the MP3 files generated by this process and doing something interesting with them.

PVMPOV

PVMPOV, or the Parallel Virtual Machine version of the Persistence of Vision ray tracing system, is a way to use clusters to generate realistic images. The PVM extensions to POV were originally written by the PVM team at Oak Ridge National Labs and extended by Harald Deischinger who is the current maintainer of the PVM patches to the POV package.

PVMPOV can be used either for static images or to generate frames for computer generated animation. The results are quite striking, as seen in Figure 9-4, which is an image generated from the demo files included with the standard POV package. Although the black and white version here doesn't do justice to the depth and complexity of the color version, it is plain to see that the image is quite detailed. The coolest thing about it is that it was generated completely inside the memory of a computer.

Figure 9-4. A ray-traced sunset from the POV samples, designed by Dan Farmer

How Does POV Work?

Ray tracing is, literally, tracing the path of a light beam as it reflects off of an object. The POV ray tracing system works by reading a set of textual instructions that describe a scene, and then applying a system of algorithms that figure out what would happen (i.e., how something would look) if a beam of light were cast on objects in the scene, and then the reflected light were captured on film.

The description file sets up a scene and the objects in it down to the last detail of their characteristics. The format of the description file is pretty straightforward; it consists of three main sections:

Includes section
> This section is where pre-defined objects, textures, and other tools are included from a defined set of library files and made available to subsequent parts of the description file.

Camera section
> This section defines where the "camera" that records the scene is placed. This is defined in terms of X, Y, and Z coordinates that represent vertical, horizontal, and depth parameters.

Objects section
> This section defines the elements of the scene itself. It is in this section where, as in the sunset example, the sun, the glowing halo around the sun, and the sea itself are defined. This section also defines where in the scene each object is, relative to the other objects in the scene.

The complete description file for the sunset image is defined by less than 93 lines of image definitions. The file itself is composed of vanilla text and looks like the fragment shown here, which is from the *sunset3.pov* file:

```
#include "colors.inc"
#include "textures.inc"
#include "skies.inc"
#include "metals.inc"

camera {
    location <0,  0.075, -0.45>
    up y
    right  <4/3, 0, 0>
    direction z
    look_at <0, 0.075, 0>
}

// Dark cloudy sky
sky_sphere {
    pigment {
        wrinkles
        turbulence 0.3
        omega 0.707
        octaves 5
        color_map {
            [0.0 color DustyRose * 2.5]
            [0.2 color Orange ]
```

```
            [0.8 color SlateBlue * 0.25]
            [1.0 color SkyBlue]
        }
        scale <0.5, 0.1, 1000>
    }
}
:
:
:
#end of file
```

This file fragment shows the three major sections of the POV scene description, starting with the include directives, the camera settings, and then the beginnings of the object descriptions, here describing the parameters of the cloudy sky shown in the final image.

Where to Get POV

Thanks to Chris Cason, the current leader of the POV efforts, we are privileged to be able to distribute both the complete sources to the POVRAY package as well as a set of binaries that will work on an Intel-based Linux cluster. Updates to the POV software is freely available from the POV Ray Tracing home page at *http://www.povray. org*.

The sources for the main package and the patches required to make POVRAY work on a Beowulf cluster under the PVM package are included on the CD-ROM in the *ExampleApps* directory in the *POVPVM* subdirectory.

How to Install POV

If you have built your cluster from the CD-ROM supplied with this book, then the PVMPOV version of the executables will be installed by default and should run exactly as described in the next section.

If you are running your cluster on a different architecture, or if you have retrieved a newer version of the POVRAY software from the POV FTP site, you will need to re-apply the patches that are used to make a parallelized version of the software for cluster use.

The PVM patches to POVRAY are very easy to install. The entire operation should take only a few minutes once you have the POV source code. Here's a step-by-step guide to applying the patches and making a parallel version of POV. It is important to point out that these patches are not part of the POV distribution, and if you were to ask the POV authors about them, they would disavow any knowledge of them—in other words, these patches are very cool, useful, and *unsupported*.

Step 1: Getting the POV sources

The POV sources are available from either the POV home page at *http://www.povray. org* or via anonymous FTP at *ftp.pov.org*. The sources for the Unix version of POV are in the directory */pub/povray/Official/Unix*; the files that are required to build the package are *povuni_d.tgz* and *povuni_s.tgz*. The first file is a collection of data files, documentation, and examples that are part of the POV sources, and the second file is the actual source code itself. You should put these files someplace easily accessible that has at least 20MB of free space; for the purposes of rest of these examples, we will presume the sources are in */tmp*.

The following script is an example of an FTP session to retrieve the entire POV package:

```
gatekeeper.zeitgeist.com % ftp ftp.povray.org
Connected to ftp.povray.org.
220 ProFTPD 1.2.0pre3 Server (ftp.povray.org) [ftp.povray.org]
Name (ftp.povray.org:spector): ftp
331 Anonymous login ok, send your complete e-mail address as password.
Password: your-email@yoursite.org
230 Anonymous access granted, restrictions apply.
Remote system type is UNIX.
Using binary mode to transfer files.
ftp> cd  pub/povray/Official/Unix
250-POVUNI_S.TGZ - Official POV-Ray 3.1e C source code for Unix systems.
               This file is not required if you have one of the complete
               POV-Ray Unix distributions such as POVLINUX.TGZ. If
               compiling POV-Ray separately, you MUST get POVUNI_D.TGZ.
   POVUNI_D.TGZ - POV-Ray 3.1e Documentation and Scene files for Unix. This
               archive is not needed if you already have another POV-Ray
               3.1e distribution such as POVLINUX.TGZ, POVMSDOS.ZIP, etc.
               They ARE needed if you only have the POVUNI_S.TGZ archive.
250 CWD command successful.
ftp> get    povuni_d.tgz
local: povuni_d.tgz remote: povuni_d.tgz
200 PORT command successful.
150 Opening BINARY mode data connection for povuni_d.tgz (911334 bytes).
226 Transfer complete.
911334 bytes received in 69.3 secs (13 Kbytes/sec)
ftp> get    povuni_s.tgz
local: povuni_s.tgz remote: povuni_s.tgz
200 PORT command successful.
150 Opening BINARY mode data connection for povuni_s.tgz (945669 bytes).
226 Transfer complete.
945669 bytes received in 71.1 secs (13 Kbytes/sec)
ftp> bye
221 Goodbye.
```

Step 2: Unpacking the sources

When using the */tmp* directory as a starting point, unpack the sources:

```
[spector@master]# tar zxvf   povuni_s.tgz
[spector@master]# tar zxvf   povuni_d.tgz
```

These commands will show you what they are doing as the files are being unpacked. Once both *tar* commands have both been executed, you will have a directory called *povray*NN where the "NN" is a version number. In the case of this example, the directory is called *povray31* because the version that was current at the time of this book was being written was POV version 3.1g; your version may be of a newer vintage.

If you change directory to the POV directory and get a directory listing, you should see that the POV distribution consists of a number of documentation files, some initialization files, and a sources directory:

```
[spector@master]# ls

CMPL_Unix.doc  compile.doc    pngflc.ini    povwhere.get  res640.ini    slow.ini
zipfli.ini
README.unix    gamma.gif      pngfli.ini    rerunpov.sh   res800.ini    source
allscene       gamma.gif.txt  povlegal.doc  res.ini       revision.doc  tgaflc.ini
allscene.ini   htm2html       povray.1      res120.ini    runpov.sh     tgafli.ini
allscene.sh    include        povray.ini    res1k.ini     scenes        xpovicon.xpm
betanews.txt   install        povuser.txt   res320.ini    shapes.pov    zipflc.ini
```

It is in this directory that you will unpack the sources to the patch files that will enable POV to work on a cluster.

Step 3: Unpacking the PVMPOV patches

The PVM patches for the POV system are available on the Linux Clusters CD-ROM. If we presume that the CD-ROM is mounted on the device */dev/cdrom* and that your current working directory is the *povray* directory unpacked in the last step, then the patches can be unpacked directly with one command:

```
[spector@master]# tar  zxvf  /mnt/cdrom/ExampleApps/POV/pvmpov-3.1.tgz
```

This will extract five files and one directory of sources into the current directory. The files are documentation, the patch file itself, and a small script that will apply the patches to the POVRAY source files.

Step 4: Patching POV

Apply the patch to the sources by running the *inst-pvm* shell script, as in:

```
[spector@tmaster povray31]# ./inst-pvm
Trying to apply the patch.

Searching for rejected files
```

If you see nothing listed between the "trying to apply..." and "searching..." lines, the patch was successfully applied to the POV sources, and you can continue to Step 5 and build the modified sources.

If there are problems with the patch (for example, some of the patches are misaligned with regard to the current version of the source), you will get error messages from the patch program, as in this next listing:

```
[spector@tmaster povray31]# ./inst-pvm
Trying to apply the patch.

2 out of 18 hunks FAILED -- saving rejects to source/povray.c.rej
2 out of 8 hunks FAILED -- saving rejects to source/render.c.rej
1 out of 2 hunks FAILED -- saving rejects to source/render.h.rej

Searching for rejected files

./source/povray.c.rej
./source/render.c.rej
./source/render.h.rej
```

If this happens, all is not lost! It's pretty easy to look at the *.rej* files and then compare them to the sources and insert the patches by hand. The patch program just makes things a little more convenient.

Step 5: Building the patched POV

Building the package is pretty easy, there are two commands that need to be executed to build the bulk of the package:

```
[spector@master]# cd source/unix
```

This will place you in the appropriate directory to build the binaries; then type:

```
[spector@master]# make newunix
[spector@master]# make newxwin
```

The build will continue for quite a while; POV is a very large package. Eventually it will complete, and you will then want to build the PVM binary that can take advantage of the cluster.

To install the main POV executables, type *make install* at the shell prompt; this will install the files *x-povray* and *povray* in the directory */usr/local/bin*. If you would like to install these programs somewhere else, you will need to modify the makefile to point to the appropriate place.

Lastly, as root, you should copy all the installed files to all the nodes of the cluster you wish to use for ray tracing. POV will need the executables and the supporting files in order to operate on each of the nodes.

Step 6: Building the PVM-specific component

To start this process, change directory to the *pvm* directory, as in:

> *[spector@master]#* **cd ../pvm**

Next, you will need to invoke the *aimk* utility, which is a PVM tool that is used to build PVM applications:

> *[spector@master]#* **aimk**

The *aimk* utility will read the makefile in this directory and build the *PVMPOV* application. If you are logged or su'd to root, *aimk* will automatically install the *PVMPOV* executable in the default location for PVM binaries on your cluster. In the case of clusters built with the Linux Clusters CD-ROM, that location will be */usr/local/pvm3/bin/LINUX/*. If you are not root, you will need to install as root in a place that is globally accessible. In either case, you should, as with the *x-povray* and *povray* binaries, ensure that copies of the *PVMPOV* are on all the nodes of your cluster that you would like to use for ray tracing.

How to Use POV

POV is a very easy program to use once you have a scene description file that you want to render. For this example, we'll use the files that generated the pretty sunset image from earlier in this chapter. These files can be found in the *pov3demo* directory in the showoff subdirectory.

In order to render this image, we'll need two files: a *.pov* file that describes the scene and an initialization or *.ini* file that can be used by the *povpvm* program to set some basic parameters. In this case the files should be *sunset3.pov* and *sunset3.ini*.

The "showoff" directory in some of the standard POV distributions may not have an initialization file for all of the demo scene descriptions. If there is not one for this file, just copy any of these files to a new file named *sunset3.ini* and edit the first line of the file so that it uses the *sunset3.pov* scene description.

Once you have the *.ini* and *.pov* files, you are ready to start rendering.

Actually running the application is quite easy and can be started with a single command line.

Before running the application, you should start up the parallel virtual machine with the number of nodes that you wish to use, then the following steps will begin the rendering process.

Step 1: Copying the scene and initialization files

The scene and initialization files will have to be available on each node where *PVMPOV* runs. If home directories are shared with NFS or the automounter, placing a copy in your home directory will suffice. Otherwise, the files will have to be copies to each node in the parallel virtual machine.

Step 2: Running PVMPOV

The *PVMPOV* application can be run quite simply with one command:

```
[spector@master]# pvmpov  -NS/usr/local/bin/pvmpov /home/spector/pov3demo/showoff/
sunset3.ini
```

The -NS directive* tells *PVMPOV* where to find itself—usually this isn't necessary, but it ensures that the *PVMPOV* application can be found on all of the compute nodes, even if there are differences in your PATH environment variables on the different compute nodes.

This will start as many slave tasks as you have compute nodes defined in your parallel virtual machine.

POV will print out a lot of information about the job as it starts up that relate to the job parameters and files that will be included to generate the ray-traced scene.

When the scene is complete, POV will print out some statistics about the scene and how the slave/compute nodes performed, and the resulting image file will be left in the same directory.

Step 3: Viewing the results

The output file is in what is known as *tga* file format. This is a high-resolution graphics file format that can be viewed with most viewers, including the *ee* ("Electric Eyes") application that comes with Linux.

To view the sunset file, start up *ee* with the filename *sunset3.tga* as its argument, as in:

```
[spector@master]# ee /home/spector/pov3demo/showoff/sunset3.tga
```

The image that is displayed should be very close to what was shown in Figure 9-4, except with much better colors.

POV as a Clustered Application

PVMPOV as a clustered application is very interesting to examine. If we were to run the XPVM execution monitor, and then rerun *PVMPOV*, we would see just how much computation is done in parallel. A small snippet of this activity can be seen in the screen shot of XPVM shown in Figure 9-5, which shows the intense back and forth

---

* POV has one of the longest lists of command-line options in the history of computing. For the sake of brevity they will not be recounted here, but you can see all of them by typing *man povray* for the generic POV options and *man pvmpov* for options specific to the parallelized version.

communications between the master *PVMPOV* process and the five slave processes that each render a portion of the final image.

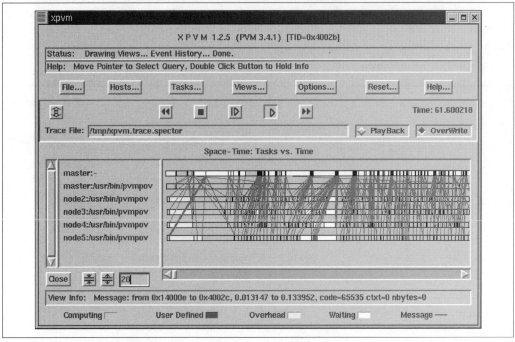

Figure 9-5. Communications activity rendering sunet3.pov

At another level, the degree of utilization of the cluster nodes can be seen in the graph shown in Figure 9-6.

Over 85 percent of the total time used in the cluster is spent actually rendering the image; the rest is used by the master in communication with the compute-bound processes getting pieces of the image back so that it can be assembled into the final image.

Another interesting comparison is to look at the output of the POV application as it renders the same scene file both on a single CPU and on a five-node parallel virtual machine.

On the five-node cluster:

```
POV-Ray statistics for 5/5 slaves:
Done Tracing
sunset3.pov Statistics, Resolution 360 x 400
------------------------------------------------------------------------
Pixels:         153288      Samples:  310536   Smpls/Pxl: 2.03
Rays:           612870      Saved:    0        Max Level: 0/5
------------------------------------------------------------------------
```

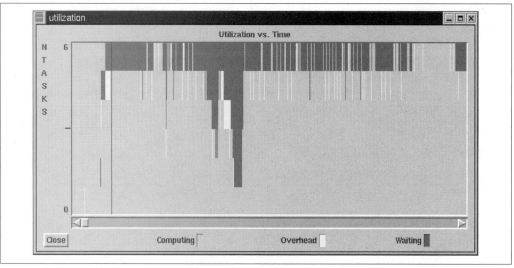

Figure 9-6. CPU utilization over time while rendering sunset3.pov

Ray->Shape Intersection	Tests	Succeeded	Percentage
Plane	1124477	251054	22.33
Sphere	132760	94792	71.40
Bounding Box	646086	164572	25.47
Light Buffer	257237	257237	100.00
Vista Buffer	754668	680972	90.23

```
Calls to Noise:        3104570   Calls to DNoise:    3810795
```

Halo Samples:	384200	Supersamples:	0
Shadow Ray Tests:	511686	Succeeded:	24361
Reflected Rays:	225846		
Transmitted Rays:	76488		

Smallest Alloc:	24 bytes	Largest:	40004
Peak memory used:	74488 bytes		

```
Time For Trace:      0 hours  0 minutes  5.0 seconds (5 seconds)
     Total Time:     0 hours  0 minutes  5.0 seconds (5 seconds)
```

On a single node:

```
sunset3.pov Statistics, Resolution 360 x 400
```

Pixels:	144360	Samples:	279096	Smpls/Pxl: 1.93
Rays:	557264	Saved:	0	Max Level: 5/5

Ray->Shape Intersection	Tests	Succeeded	Percentage
Plane	1045275	229499	21.96

```
Sphere                          126858          90738     71.53
Bounding Box                    595304         157503     26.46
Light Buffer                    234745         234745    100.00
Vista Buffer                    659743         598771     90.76
-------------------------------------------------------------------
Calls to Noise:        2790140    Calls to DNoise:       3445800
-------------------------------------------------------------------
Halo Samples:                   367250    Supersamples:  0
Shadow Ray Tests:               488093    Succeeded: 23590
Reflected Rays:                 205072
Transmitted Rays:                73096
-------------------------------------------------------------------
Smallest Alloc:               10 bytes   Largest:          12308
Peak memory used:         178437 bytes
-------------------------------------------------------------------
Time For Trace:    0 hours  0 minutes  38.0 seconds (38 seconds)
     Total Time:   0 hours  0 minutes  38.0 seconds (38 seconds)
```

Obviously ray-tracing on a cluster can save a lot of time. Of course, this is not a very valid benchmark; it's more of a feel-good test. Clusters will be better in some applications and worse in others; it all depends on the image being rendered. For example, if you are using *PVMPOV* to render cells for animation, you are probably better off dedicating a single compute node to each frame rather than trying to have the cluster intermix slices of many cells—the communications overhead will be lower and the individual frames will probably run to completion faster.

Where to Go from Here

This is just the tip of the iceberg in rendering. There are numerous tools and utilities that can be used with a ray tracer such as POV (and PVMPOV isn't the only ray tracing package in the world—it just happens to run on a cluster and is readily obtainable). I would recommend taking a look at the POV web site for some links to tools that can be used to make your own models for rendering. There are also links there to other ray tracing packages as well as lots of good information on advanced computer graphics.

PVFS

PVFS, the Parallel Virtual File System, is a way to use a Beowulf-style cluster for something other than strictly computational tasks.

PVFS is a package that allows a cluster of workstations to be used as a high-performance filesystem. PVFS can be used to implement at RAID-like Storage Area Network (SAN) that can deliver very high performance with very low computational overhead. Such a file service is very useful for parallel applications that need access to high volume data delivery such as data mining and other database-like applications.

Overview

PVFS can work on either multiple disks on a single machine, or on multiple disks spread across multiple machines on a network. It delivers its high performance by a combination of data striping (splitting up data over a number of disks *or* servers) and multiple network interfaces that are used to deliver data to applications that consume it.

Disk striping

Disk striping is a process by which a filesystem is spread out over more than one physical device. The interface to the filesystem remains the same from the operating system perspective, but the underlying software that manages a striped filesystem does the hard work of getting required bits of data as they are needed off of the various devices where the data is and recombines it so it can be presented to a calling program. This is not a new concept, it has been used in filesystems for many years in the form of RAID systems.

PVFS services

PVFS brings this concept to a new level in that it changes the dynamics of this concept in several ways. First, PVFS moves the striping out of the operating-system level and makes it a user-level process. PVFS allows these virtual files to be spread out over an arbitrary number of hosts on regular network workstations that may be doing other things (i.e., the devices do not have to be dedicated to PVFS).

Lastly, PVFS provides a set of tuning utilities that allow the performance of the filesystem to be tuned to meet the needs of applications. It also provides a programmatic interface that allows parallel programs to bypass the regular Unix filesystem calls to grab data in using a streams interface that allows for higher levels of throughput than the regular Unix filesystem would allow.

Installation

PVFS and its supporting libraries are supplied in both source and RPM format on the Linux Clusters CD-ROM. As with the mp3pvm example above, you will need to have the Linux Clusters CD-ROM mounted on your master node.

Presuming the Linux Clusters CD-ROM is mounted on */dev/cdrom*, the RPMs for PVFS should be copied to a convenient place on your master node. The usual place is */usr/src/redhat/RPMS,* and the files can be copied with the single command:

```
[spector@master /home/music]# cp /dev/cdrom/ExampleApps/PVFS/*.rpm   /usr/src/
redhap/RPMS/
```

This will copy two RPM files, *glibc-objs-libio-2.0.6-2.i386.rpm* and *pvfs-1.2.3-1.src. rpm*, into the default location for packages.

glibc-objs-libio-2.0.6-2.i386.rpm is a set of extensions to the standard GNU C libraries that support the specialized I/O capabilities that PVFS provides, while *pvfs-1.2.3-1.src.rpm* is the PVFS code itself. These RPMs have been built to install into the */usr* tree. This is because they are so closely linked to other system-level libraries that they use. Most of the packages supplied on the Linux Clusters CD-ROM are installed into */usr/local* to ensure that they aren't overwritten during any upgrades. If you wish to have PVFS installed in */usr/local* or some other part of the filesystem, you will have to compile the package from the sources, which are in the same directory that the binary RPMs are in. The PVFS package is only a few megabytes, but the supporting *glibc* sources take about 40MB and will take the better part of an hour to compile, even on a fast machine.

Configuration

PVFS, since it can be used to create a filesystem that spans multiple machines, has very stringent configuration parameters that must be followed in order for the product to work correctly. The following steps will ensure that everything is set up correctly for use.

Step 1: Selecting a home

PVFS requires two directories in which to store files and filesystem meta-data (data about the filesystem). The place that you select should have enough disk space to hold whatever information you are planning to make available via PVFS.

Since PVFS is a *virtual* filesystem, as discussed, it is implemented as a distributed filesystem whose data exists across several *actual* filesystems on several machines. If you wanted to make a 1GB filesystem in PVFS across four nodes, you would want to reserve at least 250MB of space on each machine. You will actually need to have a bit more because space is needed for the meta-data directory that will contain information about the files on the distributed filesystem.

By default, PVFS looks for the directories */pvfs* and */pvfs_data*.

Step 2: Creating the directories

The directories for the PVFS data and meta-data can be located anywhere, but it's easiest from a configuration point of view to make these directories on their own filesystems mount at the root, or as links from the root filesystem where PFVS expects to find them so you don't have to make too many modifications to the package defaults.

If you are planning on using existing partitions, for example on an extra partition called */spare,* you will want to use *mkdir* to make directories as follows:

```
[spector@master /home/music]# mkdir /spare/pvfs
[spector@master /home/music]# mkdir /spare/pvfs_data
```

You could then use links from the root filesystem such as:

```
[spector@master /home/music]# ln -s  /spare/pvfs     /pvfs
[spector@master /home/music]# ln -s  /spare/pvfs_data    /pvfs_data
```

to allow PVFS to find the directories in the default locations.

As a last step, you should set the ownership of the */pvfs* directory so that it has no explicit privilege with:

```
[spector@master /home/music]# chown nobody.nobody    /spare/pvfs
```

Step 3: Configuring PVFS

PVFS has several configuration files that need to be set up before the daemons can be started to initialize the system, both on the master node that controls the operation of PVFS and on each node that will be used as a slave node where pieces of the virtual filesystems will reside.

Fortunately, the initialization is performed with a configuration program so the configuration files don't have to be hand-edited. To start the configuration, invoke the configuration program, */usr/pvfs/bin/mkiodtab,* on the master node. This will need to be done as root:

```
[spector@master /home/music]# /usr/pvfs/bin/mkiodtab
```

The *mkiodtab* configurator will ask for a several key pieces of information, including the name of the PVFS root directory, permissions for the directory and the hostnames for the master node and the slave nodes. The process will need to be repeated for each node that will participate in the parallel virtual filesystem:

```
This is the iodtab setup for the Parallel Virtual File System.
It will also make the .pvfsdir file in the root directory.

Enter the root directory:
/pvfs
Enter the user id of directory:
root
Enter the group id of directory:
root
Enter the mode of the root directory:
777
Enter the hostname that will run the manager:
localhost
Searching for host...success
Enter the port number on the host for manager:
(Port number 3000 is the default)    return

Enter the I/O nodes: (can use form node1, node2, ... or
nodename{#-#,#,#})
localhost,node5
```

```
Searching for hosts...success
I/O nodes: localhost node5
Enter the port number for the iods:
(Port number 7000 is the default) return
```

Done!

In the example configuration session listed above, the user input is listed in **bold**. The key point that needs to be noted is the */pvfs* directory should be the place where you want to house the virtual filesystem. If you have made links from the root filesystem to someplace where the actual PVFS directory is located, you can use the */pvf* directory as indicated in the session example. It is also important when configuring the *non-manager* nodes to use the hostname of the actual manager node and not `localhost`, as in the example.

Finally, you will need to set an environment variable that forces a library to be loaded, which will allow the PVFS to be tied into the regular processing of commands:

```
[spector@master /home/music]# LD_PRELOAD=/usr/lib/libpvs.so ; eport LD_PRELOAD
```

If your shell is not a *bash* or *ksh* derivative, you will have to use whatever syntax is used in your shell to define shell variables. This shell variable will need to be defined in every process and on each node that uses the parallel virtual filesystem.

The *LD_PRELOAD* environment variable controls which libraries are loaded and available before the standards *libc* library in the chain of execution. What this means is that for every command that is linked with libc (such as *ls*, *rm*, *mkdir*, etc.) the libraries listed in the *LD_PRELOAD* variable will be searched first for any shared library code. Since commands like *ls* use standard I/O routines which are in *libc*, the program loader will look in the *libpvfs.so* file for routines needed by *ls* and will execute those routines as though they were the ones that *ls* expected to see; the *libpvfs.so* code will then execute the "real" *libc* code once it has finished doing whatever PVFS operations were required by the command. In this way PVFS adds support for a non-standard filesystem transparently.

PVS Uses in Parallel Programming

One of the most interesting uses for PVFS is as an enhanced I/O system for parallel programs on a cluster.

With most Unix systems, including Linux, the filesystem supports very primitive operations. It is possible to:

- Open a file
- Close a file
- Read or write a character

- Read or write a buffer

- Seek to an arbitrary position in the file

A full description of the capabilities of PVFS is beyond the scope of this discussion, but it's worth noting some of the advanced features of PVFS. A specialized filesystem like PVS can provide capabilities not available in Linux's *ext2* filesystem. These include I/O needs, such as changing the default block size delivered by a vendor write call, or filespace operations, such as directly stripping the filesystem to increase throughput for parallel processes.

PART III

APPENDIXES

RESOURCES

This appendix is a resource guide to other avenues for exploring and understanding parallel clusters. Wherever possible, I have included URLs for online sources of information. Keep in mind that the Web is a dynamic and changing resource, so some of these URLs may have changed by the time you are reading this book.

In case you're not inclined to type in all of the long URLs that are found throughout this appendix, an HTML version of this section has been provided on the CD-ROM that accompanies this book. The CD-ROM is in the ISO-9660 format and can be used from both the Lynx (or other Unix-like) and Windows environments. The file is stored in the *Resources* directory at the top-level of the CD-ROM; simply open the *index.html* file with any browser, and as long as you are connected to the Internet, you should be able to browse the sites referenced there.

This appendix, and the HTML pages on the CD-ROM, are organized by subject area, such as "Beowulf" for items relating to Beowulf clusters specifically, and "Motherboard Vendors" that will have links to motherboard vendors and their data sheets, and so on.

Beowulf and Linux Clusters

As clusters have become more popular, there is no shortage of references to them on the Web, but there are two main sites that are at the forefront of Linux cluster research. These sites are invaluable to cluster builders and are updated frequently with useful information:

- The Beowulf Project at NASA's CESDIS Project: *http://www.beuwulf.org*
- The Extreme Linux Project: *http://www.extremelinux.org*

Parallel Programming Libraries

Parallel program libraries are the core of what makes a Linux cluster possible.

The Message Passing Interface (MPI), http://www-unix.mcs.anl.gov/mpi

MPI is a standard specification for message-passing libraries. MPICH is a portable implementation of the full MPI specification for a wide variety of parallel computing environments, including workstation clusters and massively parallel processors (MPPs).

MPI is the basis of much of the clustering work being done today. It's the result of an industry consortium comprised of computer hardware vendors, software vendors, and users of parallel systems.

MPI is installed by default on clusters built with the CD-ROM that accompanies this book.

The Parallel Virtual Machine (PVM), http://www.epm.ornl.gov/pvm/pvm_home.html

PVM is the result of parallel programming research that started at Oak Ridge National Labs. It is a software package that permits a heterogeneous collection of Unix computers hooked together by a network to be used as a single large parallel computer.

PVM is another package that is installed by default on clusters built with the CD-ROM that accompanies this book.

AdSmith, http://archi1.ee.ntu.edu.tw/~wyliang/adsmith

Adsmith is an object-based Distributed Shared Memory (DSM), which is built completely on top of PVM. It provides a user-level library in C++. The primary goal of Adsmith is to provide a low-cost, portable, and efficient DSM for networks of workstations (NOW). Adsmith provides primitives to create and allocate shared objects, accesses to shared objects, and operations to synchronize among processes. Adsmith also incorporates many techniques to optimize its performance, including supports for release memory consistency models, different coherence protocols, load/store-style memory accesses, object-based multiple writer protocols, bulk transfers, prefetches, nonblocking stores, and other specialized accesses.

ADSM is also provided on the CD-ROM that accompanies this book.

Hardware Sources

Unless you have a favorite computer dealer through which you buy computers and get really deep discounts, you are probably going to need to find a source for parts that will fit within your budget. Tables A-1 through A-5 list some of the resources that I use when I am building clusters or looking for bits and pieces to add to my existing cluster.

Table A-1. System-board Suppliers

Intel-based System-boards	
Intel Corporation	*http://www.intel.com/design/motherbd*
Tyan Corporation	*http://www.tyan.com*
ASUS International	*http://www.asus.com*
SuperMicro	*http://www.supermicro.com*
Micron	*http://www.micron.com*
Alpha-based System-boards	
Compaq	*http://www.digital.com/alphaoem/alphamb.htm*
SPARC-based System-boards	
Sun Microsystems	*http://www.sun.com/sparc/products/sparceng.html*
Tatung Science & Technology	*http://www.tsti.com*
EIS Computers	*http://www.eis.com*
Force Computers	*http://www.forcecomputers.com*
StrongARM-based System-boards	
Intel	*http://developer.intel.com/design/strong/index.htm*
Hardware Canada a.k.a,. "Rebel"	*http://www.rebel.com*
ARM Ltd.	*http://www.arm.com*

Table A-2. Hard Disk Vendors

Hard Disk Manufacturers	
Western Digital	*http://www.westerndigital.com*
Seagate	*http://www.seagate.com*

Table A-3. Network Interface Manufacturers

Network Interface Cards	
Standard Microsystems Corp. (10/100Mbit)	*http://www.smcc.com*
3Com (10/100Mbit)	*http://www.3com.com*
Packet Engines (gigabit)	*jhttp://www.packetengines.com*
Myrinet (gigabit)	*http://www.myri.net*
Lucent (100Mbit/Gigabit)	*http://www.lucent.com*

Table A-4. Network Communications Manufacturers

Switches and Routers	
CISCO Systems	*http://www.cisco.com*
Nortel	*http://www.nortel.com*

Table A-4. Network Communications Manufacturers (continued)

Switches and Routers	
3Com	*http://www.3com/com*
Myrinet	*http://www.myri.net*
Cabletron Systems	*http://www.cabletron.com*

Table A-5. KVM Manufacturers

Console Switches	
Raritan Systems	*http://www.raritan.com*
Belkin	*http://www.belkin.com*
Network Technologies	*http://www.nti1.com*
Cybex	*http://www.cybex.com*

Aftermarket (Used/Surplus) Dealers

Aftermarket dealers are usually wholesalers that buy used, surplused, or excessed equipment and offer it for sale either as-is or after reconditioning it. These dealers are usually a great place to find a large collection of hardware for cluster building. Often it is possible to find large lots of identical systems that have been sold by large companies that usually buy identical systems in order to reduce the number of hardware configurations they have to maintain.

Some of these vendors have online auction sites where you can bid on equipment. Online auctions are a mixed blessing that can either land you an excellent deal or cost you a lot more than you bargained for (*caveat emptor*). These auction sites include:

- Rave Computer Association: *http://www.rave.com*

- Egghead Auctions: *http://www.egghead.com*

- EBay: *http://www.ebay.com*

Periodicals

There are several good publications that can aid the cluster builder. Most of these focus on software methods. However, there are two publications that are good places to look for components and pricing:

Computer Shopper, http://www.computershopper.com
> This is one of the largest monthly magazines published. It is a cross between a yellow pages and a giant ad for suppliers of commodity computer components.

From mother boards and power supplies to rack mounts, if it can be used to build a computer, it can be found in here.

Computer Shopper is mostly a place where intrepid computer junkies go to look for rock-bottom prices on hardware, but there are also reviews and articles on everything from selecting displays to finding the best deal on bulk purchases of video cards. Opening *Computer Shopper* for the first time can be intimidating, since at first glance it looks like one giant ad. However, once you have perused a couple of issues it becomes easier to sift your way through and find suppliers who have what you're looking for. But you should know what it is you are looking for and what you are willing to pay for it.

Remember, when building a cluster from parts from an unfamiliar dealer, you should always start with a small order. Assure yourself of the quality of components before ordering in bulk. *Computer Shopper* accepts advertising from an amazing array of vendors, and it is not responsible for checking all of them out or verifying their business practices.

Computer Shopper (ISSN: 0886-556) is available at large newspaper and magazine stores, via subscription, and on the Web.

Performance Computing, http://www.performance-computing.com

Performance Computing is a trade publication aimed at system administrators. Each monthly issue usually has a theme that revolves around some aspect of hardware or software that is useful in running large numbers of systems. Often they feature hardware performance reviews of items useful to the cluster builder, such as RAID systems, SMP systems, etc.

APPENDIX B

MESSAGE PASSING APIS

This appendix will give you a quick reference to the two most common interface libraries for parallel programming: MPI, the Message Passing Interface (version 1.1.x), and PVM, the Parallel Virtual Machine (version 3.x).

This quick reference will present the most important API features of each of these systems, but it is not meant to be comprehensive or complete. For complete references for each of these systems, I recommend *MPI: The Complete Reference* and *PVM: A User's Guide for Networked Parallel Computing*. More information on these and other parallel programming references may be found in the bibliography at the end of the book.

The APIs in this appendix are grouped in order of function class. This means that I have grouped like-functions together.

MPI Application Programming Interface

MPI is a standard interface library used in many parallel applications. The constants listed here may be used in both C and Fortran.

Error Return Codes

MPI_ERR_ARG	MPI_ERR_INTERN	MPI_ERR_TAG
MPI_ERR_BUFFER	MPI_ERR_LASTCODE	MPI_ERR_TOPOLOGY
MPI_ERR_COMM	MPI_ERR_OP	MPI_ERR_TRUNCATE
MPI_ERR_COUNT	MPI_ERR_OTHER	MPI_ERR_TYPE
MPI_ERR_DIMS	MPI_ERR_RANK	MPI_ERR_UNKNOWN
MPI_ERR_GROUP	MPI_ERR_REQUEST	MPI_PENDING
MPI_ERR_IN_STATUS	MPI_ERR_ROOT	MPI_SUCCESS

Assorted Constants (Both C and Fortran)

MPI_ANY_SOURCE   MPI_BSEND_OVERHEAD   MPI_PROC_NULL

MPI_ANY_TAG   MPI_KEYVAL_INVALID   MPI_UNDEFINED

MPI_BOTTOM

Status Size and Reserved Index Values (Fortran)

MPI_ERROR   MPI_SOURCE   MPI_STATUS_SIZE   MPI_TAG

Error-Handling Specifiers (C and Fortran)

MPI_ERRORS_ARE_FATAL   MPI_ERRORS_RETURN

Maximum Sizes for Strings

MPI_MAX_ERROR_STRING   MPI_MAX_PROCESSOR_NAME

Elementary Datatypes (C)

MPI_BYTE   MPI_LONG   MPI_UNSIGNED

MPI_CHAR   MPI_LONG_DOUBLE   MPI_UNSIGNED_CHAR

MPI_DOUBLE   MPI_PACKED   MPI_UNSIGNED_LONG

MPI_FLOAT   MPI_SHORT   MPI_UNSIGNED_SHORT

MPI_INT

Elementary Datatypes (Fortran)

MPI_BYTE   MPI_DOUBLE_COMPLEX   MPI_LOGICAL

MPI_CHARACTER   MPI_DOUBLE_PRECISION   MPI_PACKED

MPI_COMPLEX   MPI_INTEGER   MPI_REAL

Datatypes for Reduction Functions (C)

MPI_2INT   MPI_FLOAT_INT   MPI_LONG_INT

MPI_DOUBLE_INT   MPI_LONG_DOUBLE_INT   MPI_SHORT_INT

Datatypes for Reduction Functions (Fortran)

MPI_2DOUBLE_PRECISION   MPI_2INTEGER   MPI_2REAL

Optional Datatypes (Fortran)

MPI_INTEGER1	MPI_INTEGER4	MPI_REAL4
MPI_INTEGER2	MPI_REAL2	MPI_REAL8

Optional Datatypes (C)

MPI_LONG_LONG_INT

Special Datatypes for Constructing Derived Datatypes

MPI_LB   MPI_UB

Reserved Communicators (C and Fortran)

MPI_COMM_SELF   MPI_COMM_WORLD

Results of Communicator and Group Comparisons

MPI_CONGRUENT	MPI_SIMILAR
MPI_IDENT	MPI_UNEQUAL

Environmental Inquiry Keys (C and Fortran)

MPI_HOST	MPI_TAG_UB
MPI_IO	MPI_WTIME_IS_GLOBAL

Collective Operations (C and Fortran)

MPI_BAND	MPI_LOR	MPI_MIN
MPI_BOR	MPI_LXOR	MPI_MINLOC
MPI_BXOR	MPI_MAX	MPI_PROD
MPI_LAND	MPI_MAXLOC	MPI_SUM

Null Handles

MPI_COMM_NULL	MPI_ERRHANDLER_NULL	MPI_OP_NULL
MPI_DATATYPE_NULL	MPI_GROUP_NULL	MPI_REQUEST_NULL

Empty Group

MPI_GROUP_EMPTY

Topologies (C and Fortran)

MPI_CART	MPI_GRAPH

The following are defined C type definitions, also included in the file *mpi.h* on the CD-ROM:

Opaque Types (C)

MPI_Aint	MPI_Status

Handles to Assorted Structures (C)

MPI_Comm	MPI_Group	MPI_Request
MPI_Datatype	MPI_Op	

Prototypes for User-Defined Functions (C)

```
typedef int  MPI_Copy_function(MPI_Comm oldcomm, int keyval, void *extra_state, void\
    *attribute_val_in, void *attribute_val_out, int *flag);

typedef int  MPI_Delete_function(MPI_Comm comm, int keyval, void *attribute_val, void\
    *extra_state)

typedef void MPI_Handler_function(MPI_Comm *, int *, ...);

typedef void MPI_User_function( void *invec, void *inoutvec, int *len, MPI_Datatype\
    *datatype);
```

For Fortran, here are examples of how each of the user-defined functions should be declared.

The user-function argument to MPI_OP_CREATE should be declared like this:

```
FUNCTION USER_FUNCTION( INVEC(*), INOUTVEC(*), LEN, TYPE)
<type> INVEC(LEN), INOUTVEC(LEN)
INTEGER LEN, TYPE
```

The copy-function argument to MPI_KEYVAL_CREATE should be declared like this:

```
PROCEDURE COPY_FUNCTION(OLDCOMM, KEYVAL, EXTRA_STATE, ATTRIBUTE_VAL_IN, ATTRIBUTE_\
    VAL_OUT, FLAG, IERR)
INTEGER OLDCOMM, KEYVAL, EXTRA_STATE, ATTRIBUTE_VAL_IN, ATTRIBUTE_VAL_OUT, IERR  LOGICAL\
    FLAG
```

The delete-function argument to MPI_KEYVAL_CREATE should be declared like this:

```
PROCEDURE DELETE_FUNCTION(COMM, KEYVAL, ATTRIBUTE_VAL, EXTRA_STATE, IERR)
INTEGER COMM, KEYVAL, ATTRIBUTE_VAL, EXTRA_STATE, IERR
```

Initialization, Startup, Shutdown, and Error Functions

```
int MPI_Get_processor_name(char *name, int *resultlen)
```

```
int MPI_Errhandler_create(MPI_Handler_function *function, MPI_Errhandler *errhandler)
```

```
int MPI_Errhandler_set(MPI_Comm comm, MPI_Errhandler errhandler)
```

```
int MPI_Errhandler_get(MPI_Comm comm, MPI_Errhandler *errhandler)
```

```
int MPI_Errhandler_free(MPI_Errhandler *errhandler)
```

```
int MPI_Error_string(int errorcode, char *string, int *resultlen)
```

```
int MPI_Error_class(int errorcode, int *errorclass)
```

```
int double MPI_Wtime(void)
```

```
int double MPI_Wtick(void)
```

```
int MPI_Init(int *argc, char ***argv)
```

```
int MPI_Finalize(void)
```

```
int MPI_Initialized(int *flag)
```

```
int MPI_Abort(MPI_Comm comm, int errorcode)
```

Data Sending/Receiving Functions

```
int MPI_Send(void* buf, int count, MPI_Datatype datatype, int dest, int tag, \
    MPI_Comm comm)
```

```
int MPI_Recv(void* buf, int count, MPI_Datatype datatype, int source, int tag, \
    MPI_Comm comm, MPI_Status *status)
```

```
int MPI_Get_count(MPI_Status *status, MPI_Datatype datatype, int *count)
```

```
int MPI_Bsend(void* buf, int count, MPI_Datatype datatype, int dest, int tag, \
    MPI_Comm comm)
```

```
int MPI_Ssend(void* buf, int count, MPI_Datatype datatype, int dest, int tag, \
   MPI_Comm comm)

int MPI_Rsend(void* buf, int count,  MPI_Datatype datatype, int dest, int tag, \
   MPI_Comm comm)

int MPI_Buffer_attach( void* buffer, int size)

int MPI_Buffer_detach( void* buffer, int*size)

int MPI_Isend(void* buf, int count, MPI_Datatype datatype, int dest, int tag, \
   MPI_Comm comm, MPI_Request *request)

int MPI_Ibsend(void* buf, int count, MPI_Datatype datatype, int dest, int tag, \
   MPI_Comm comm, MPI_Request *request)

int MPI_Issend(void* buf, int count, MPI_Datatype datatype, int dest, int tag, \
   MPI_Comm comm, MPI_Request *request)

int MPI_Irsend(void* buf, int count, MPI_Datatype datatype, int dest, int tag, \
   MPI_Comm comm, MPI_Request *request)

int MPI_Irecv(void* buf, int count, MPI_Datatype datatype, int source, int tag, M\
   PI_Comm comm, MPI_Request *request)

int MPI_Wait(MPI_Request *request, MPI_Status *status)

int MPI_Test(MPI_Request *request, int *flag, MPI_Status *status)

int MPI_Request_free(MPI_Request *request)

int MPI_Waitany(int count, MPI_Request *array_of_requests, int *index, MPI_Status
*status)

int MPI_Testany(int count, MPI_Request *array_of_requests, int *index, int *flag, \
   MPI_Status *status)

int MPI_Waitall(int count, MPI_Request *array_of_requests, MPI_Status *array_of_statuses)

int MPI_Testall(int count, MPI_Request *array_of_requests, int *flag, MPI_Status \
   *array_of_statuses)

int MPI_Waitsome(int incount, MPI_Request *array_of_requests, int *outcount, int \
   *array_of_indices, MPI_Status
*array_of_statuses)

int MPI_Testsome(int incount, MPI_Request *array_of_requests, int *outcount, int \
   *array_of_indices, MPI_Status *array_of_statuses)

int MPI_Iprobe(int source, int tag, MPI_Comm comm, int *flag, MPI_Status *status)
```

```
int MPI_Probe(int source, int tag, MPI_Comm comm, MPI_Status *status)

int MPI_Cancel(MPI_Request *request)

int MPI_Test_cancelled(MPI_Status *status, int *flag)

int MPI_Send_init(void* buf, int count, MPI_Datatype datatype, int dest, int tag, \
    MPI_Comm comm, MPI_Request *request)

int MPI_Bsend_init(void* buf, int count, MPI_Datatype datatype, int dest, int tag, \
    MPI_Comm comm, MPI_Request *request)

int MPI_Ssend_init(void* buf, int count, MPI_Datatype datatype, int dest, int tag, \
    MPI_Comm comm, MPI_Request *request)

int MPI_Rsend_init(void* buf, int count, MPI_Datatype datatype, int dest, int tag, \
    MPI_Comm comm, MPI_Request *request)

int MPI_Recv_init(void* buf, int count, MPI_Datatype datatype, int source, int tag, \
    MPI_Comm comm, MPI_Request *request)

int MPI_Start(MPI_Request *request)

int MPI_Startall(int count, MPI_Request *array_of_requests)

int MPI_Sendrecv(void *sendbuf, int sendcount, MPI_Datatype sendtype, int dest, \
    int sendtag, void *recvbuf, int recvcount, MPI_Datatype recvtype, int source, \
    MPI_Datatype recvtag, MPI_Comm comm, MPI_Status *status)

int MPI_Sendrecv_replace(void* buf, int count, MPI_Datatype datatype, int dest, \
    int sendtag, int source, int recvtag, MPI_Comm comm, MPI_Status *status)

int MPI_Type_contiguous(int count, MPI_Datatype oldtype, MPI_Datatype *newtype)

int MPI_Type_vector(int count, int blocklength, int stride, MPI_Datatype oldtype, \
    MPI_Datatype *newtype)

int MPI_Type_hvector(int count, int blocklength, MPI_Aint stride, MPI_Datatype oldtype,\
    MPI_Datatype *newtype)

int MPI_Type_indexed(int count, int *array_of_blocklengths, int *array_of_displacements,\
    MPI_Datatype oldtype, MPI_Datatype *newtype)

int MPI_Type_hindexed(int count, int *array_of_blocklengths, MPI_Aint *array_of_\
    displacements, MPI_Datatype oldtype, MPI_Datatype *newtype)

int MPI_Type_struct(int count, int *array_of_blocklengths, MPI_Aint *array_of_\
    displacements, MPI_Datatype *array_of_types, MPI_Datatype *newtype)

int MPI_Address(void* location, MPI_Aint *address)
```

```
int MPI_Type_extent(MPI_Datatype datatype, MPI_Aint *extent)

int MPI_Type_size(MPI_Datatype datatype, int *size)

int MPI_Type_lb(MPI_Datatype datatype, MPI_Aint* displacement)

int MPI_Type_ub(MPI_Datatype datatype, MPI_Aint* displacement)

int MPI_Type_commit(MPI_Datatype *datatype)

int MPI_Type_free(MPI_Datatype *datatype)

int MPI_Get_elements(MPI_Status *status, MPI_Datatype datatype, int *count)

int MPI_Pack(void* inbuf, int incount, MPI_Datatype datatype, void *outbuf, int \
    outsize, int *position, MPI_Comm comm)

int MPI_Unpack(void* inbuf, int insize, int *position, void *outbuf, int outcount, \
    MPI_Datatype datatype, MPI_Comm comm)

int MPI_Pack_size(int incount, MPI_Datatype datatype, MPI_Comm comm, int *size)
```

C Bindings for Collective Communication

```
int MPI_Barrier(MPI_Comm comm )

int MPI_Bcast(void* buffer, int count, MPI_Datatype datatype, int root, MPI_Comm comm )

int MPI_Gather(void* sendbuf, int sendcount, MPI_Datatype sendtype, void* recvbuf, \
    int recvcount, MPI_Datatype recvtype, int root, MPI_Comm comm)

int MPI_Gatherv(void* sendbuf, int sendcount, MPI_Datatype sendtype, void* recvbuf, \
    int *recvcounts, int *displs, MPI_Datatype recvtype, int root, MPI_Comm comm)

int MPI_Scatter(void* sendbuf, int sendcount, MPI_Datatype sendtype, void* recvbuf, \
    int recvcount, MPI_Datatype recvtype, int root, MPI_Comm comm)

int MPI_Scatterv(void* sendbuf, int *sendcounts, int *displs, MPI_Datatype sendtype, \
    void* recvbuf, int recvcount, MPI_Datatype recvtype, int root, MPI_Comm comm)

int MPI_Allgather(void* sendbuf, int sendcount, MPI_Datatype sendtype, void* recvbuf, \
    int recvcount, MPI_Datatype recvtype, MPI_Comm comm)

int MPI_Allgatherv(void* sendbuf, int sendcount, MPI_Datatype sendtype, void*\
    recvbuf, int *recvcounts, int *displs, MPI_Datatype recvtype, MPI_Comm comm)

int MPI_Alltoall(void* sendbuf, int sendcount, MPI_Datatype sendtype, void* recvbuf, int\
    recvcount, MPI_Datatype recvtype, MPI_Comm comm)

int MPI_Alltoallv(void* sendbuf, int *sendcounts, int *sdispls, MPI_Datatype sendtype,\
    void* recvbuf, int *recvcounts,
```

```
        int *rdispls, MPI_Datatype recvtype, MPI_Comm comm)

int MPI_Reduce(void* sendbuf, void* recvbuf, int count, MPI_Datatype datatype MPI_Op op,\
        int root, MPI_Comm comm)

int MPI_Op_create(MPI_User_function *function, int commute, MPI_Op *op)

int MPI_Op_free( MPI_Op *op)

int MPI_Allreduce(void* sendbuf, void* recvbuf, int count, MPI_Datatype datatype,\
        MPI_Op op, MPI_Comm comm)

int MPI_Reduce_scatter(void* sendbuf, void* recvbuf, int *recvcounts, MPI_Datatype\
        datatype, MPI_Op op, MPI_Comm comm)

int MPI_Scan(void* sendbuf, void* recvbuf, int count, MPI_Datatype datatype, MPI_Op op,\
        MPI_Comm comm )
```

C Bindings for Groups, Contexts, and Communicators

```
int MPI_Group_size(MPI_Group group, int *size)

int MPI_Group_rank(MPI_Group group, int*rank)

int MPI_Group_translate_ranks (MPI_Group group1, int n, int *ranks1, MPI_Group group2, int\
        *ranks2)

int MPI_Group_compare(MPI_Group group1,MPI_Group group2, int *result)

int MPI_Comm_group(MPI_Comm comm, MPI_Group *group)

int MPI_Group_union(MPI_Group group1, MPI_Group group2, MPI_Group *newgroup)

int MPI_Group_intersection(MPI_Group group1, MPI_Group group2, MPI_Group *newgroup)

int MPI_Group_difference(MPI_Group group1, MPI_Group group2, MPI_Group *newgroup)

int MPI_Group_incl(MPI_Group group, int n, int *ranks, MPI_Group *newgroup)

int MPI_Group_excl(MPI_Group group, int n, int *ranks, MPI_Group *newgroup)

int MPI_Group_range_incl(MPI_Group group, int n, int ranges[][3], MPI_Group *newgroup)

int MPI_Group_range_excl(MPI_Group group, int n, int ranges[][3], MPI_Group *newgroup)

int MPI_Group_free(MPI_Group *group)

int MPI_Comm_size(MPI_Comm comm, int *size)

int MPI_Comm_rank(MPI_Comm comm, int *rank)
```

```
int MPI_Comm_compare(MPI_Comm comm1,MPI_Comm comm2, int *result)

int MPI_Comm_dup(MPI_Comm comm, MPI_Comm *newcomm)

int MPI_Comm_create(MPI_Comm comm, MPI_Group group, MPI_Comm *newcomm)

int MPI_Comm_split(MPI_Comm comm, int color, int key, MPI_Comm *newcomm)

int MPI_Comm_free(MPI_Comm *comm)

int MPI_Comm_test_inter(MPI_Comm comm, int *flag)

int MPI_Comm_remote_size(MPI_Comm comm, int *size)

int MPI_Comm_remote_group(MPI_Comm comm, MPI_Group *group)

int MPI_Intercomm_create(MPI_Comm local_comm, int local_leader, MPI_Comm\
    peer_comm, int remote_leader, int tag, MPI_Comm *newintercomm)

int MPI_Intercomm_merge(MPI_Comm intercomm, int high, MPI_Comm *newintracomm)

int MPI_Keyval_create(MPI_Copy_function *copy_fn, MPI_Delete_function *delete_fn,

int *keyval, void* extra_state)

int MPI_Keyval_free(int *keyval)

int MPI_Attr_put(MPI_Comm comm, int keyval, void* attribute_val)

int MPI_Attr_get(MPI_Comm comm, int keyval, void* attribute_val, int *flag)

int MPI_Attr_delete(MPI_Comm comm, int keyval)
```

C Bindings for Process Topologies

```
int MPI_Cart_create(MPI_Comm comm_old, int ndims, int *dims, int *periods, int reorder\
    MPI_Comm *comm_cart)

int MPI_Dims_create(int nnodes, int ndims, int *dims)

int MPI_Graph_create(MPI_Comm comm_old, int nnodes, int *index, int *edges, int reorder,\
    MPI_Comm *comm_graph)

int MPI_Topo_test(MPI_Comm comm, int *status)

int MPI_Graphdims_get(MPI_Comm comm, int *nnodes, int *nedges)

int MPI_Graph_get(MPI_Comm comm, int maxindex, int maxedges, int *index, int *edges)

int MPI_Cartdim_get(MPI_Comm comm, int *ndims)
```

```
int MPI_Cart_get(MPI_Comm comm, int maxdims, int *dims, int *periods, int *coords)

int MPI_Cart_rank(MPI_Comm comm, int *coords, int *rank)

int MPI_Cart_coords(MPI_Comm comm, int rank, int maxdims, int *coords)

int MPI_Graph_neighbors_count(MPI_Comm comm, int rank, int *nneighbors)

int MPI_Graph_neighbors(MPI_Comm comm, int rank, int maxneighbors, int *neighbors)

int MPI_Cart_shift(MPI_Comm comm, int direction, int disp, int *rank_source, int *rank_dest)

int MPI_Cart_sub(MPI_Comm comm, int *remain_dims, MPI_Comm *newcomm)

int MPI_Cart_map(MPI_Comm comm, int ndims, int *dims, int *periods, int *newrank)

int MPI_Graph_map(MPI_Comm comm, int nnodes, int *index, int *edges, int *newrank)
```

C Bindings for Profiling

```
int MPI_Pcontrol(const int level, ...)
```

PVM Commands and API

Starting PVM

```
pvmd [-nhostname] [-d<debugmask>] [hostfile]

pvm [hostfile] (starts console)
```

PVM Console Commands

```
help [command] { get information about commands

conf { lists hosts in virtual machine

add host(s) { add host(s) to virtual machine

delete host(s) { delete host(s)

spawn [opt] file { spawn process

-<count> { number of tasks to spawn
-<host> { host to spawn on
-> { redirect task output to console
->file { redirect task output to _l e
->>file { append task output to _l e
ps [-a] { lists processes on virtual machine
```

alias { de_ne/list command aliases

unalias { unde_ne command alias

setenv { set /show environment variables

echo { echo arguments

version { print libpvm version

id { print console t i d

sig num tid { send signal num to process

kill tid { terminate a process

reset { kill all processes and reset PVM

quit { exit console (PVM continues)

halt { kill all pvmds and console

Compiling PVM Applications

Make sure that you include:

> #include "pvm3.h"

with your other include files. This file defines the interface and constants for the PVM libraries. Use one of the following styles of command lines, depending upon the languange you are using to compile your application:

cc -o task myprog.c libpvm3.a

f77 -o task myprog.f libfpvm3.a libpvm3.a

For groups add libgpvm3.a before libpvm3.a

Process Control Routines

int tid = pvm_mytid(void)

int info = pvm_exit(void)

int info = pvm_kill(int tid)

int info = pvm_addhosts(char **hosts, int nhost, int *infos)

```
int info = pvm_delhosts(char **hosts, int nhost, int *infos)

int numt = pvm_spawn(char *task, char **argv, int flag, char *where, int ntask, int\
    *tids)
```

Spawn Flag Options	Options	Meaning
PvmTaskDefault	0	Don't care where
PvmTaskHost	1	*where* contains host
PvmTaskArch	2	*where* contains arch
PvmTaskDebug	4	Start tasks with debug on
PvmTaskTrace	8	Start tasks with trace on
PvmHostCompl	32	Use complement host set

Informational Routines

```
int tid = pvm_parent(void)

int dtid = pvm_tidtohost(int tid)

int info = pvm_perror(char *msg)

int info = pvm_config(int *nhost, int *narch, struct pvmhostinfo **hostp)

int info = pvm_tasks(int which, int *ntask, struct pvmtaskinfo **taskp)

int val = pvm_getopt(int what)

int oldval = pvm_setopt(int what, int val)
```

What Option SETS/GETS This

```
PvmRoute 1 routing policy : PvmRouteDirect

PvmDebugMask 2 debug level | PvmAllowDirect

PvmAutoErr 3 auto error reporting

PvmOutputTid 4 stdout device for children

PvmOutputCode 5 output msgtag

PvmTraceTid 6 trace device for children

PvmTraceCode 7 trace msgtag
```

Signaling Routines

```
int info = pvm_sendsig(int tid, int signum)

int info = pvm_notify(int about, int msgtag, int ntask, int *tids)
```

"About" Options	Value	Meaning
PvmTaskExit	1	Notify if task exit
PvmHostDelete	2	Notify if deletion
PvmHostAdd	3	Notify if addition

Message Buffer Routines

```
int bufid = pvm_mkbuf(int encoding)

int info = pvm_freebuf(int bufid)

int bufid = pvm_getsbuf(void)

int bufid = pvm_getrbuf(void)

int oldbuf = pvm_setsbuf(int bufid)

int oldbuf = pvm_setrbuf(int bufid)

int bufid = pvm_initsend(int encoding)
```

Constants Used in Message Encoding

Encoding	Options	Meaning
PvmDataDefault	0	XDR
PvmDataRaw	1	No encoding
PvmDataInPlace	2	Data left in place

Data Sending Routines

```
int info = pvm_packf( printf-like format... )

int info = pvm_pkbyte( char *cp, int cnt, int std )

int info = pvm_pkcplx( float *xp, int cnt, int std )

int info = pvm_pkdcplx( double *zp, int cnt, int std )

int info = pvm_pkdouble(double *dp, int cnt, int std )
```

```
int info = pvm_pkfloat( float *fp, int cnt, int std )

int info = pvm_pkint( int *np, int cnt, int std )

int info = pvm_pklong( long *np, int cnt, int std )

int info = pvm_pkshort( short *np, int cnt, int std )

int info = pvm_pkstr( char *cp )

int info = pvm_send( int tid, int msgtag )

int info = pvm_mcast( int *tids, int ntask, int msgtag )

int info = pvm_psend( int tid, int msgtag, void *vp, int cnt, int type )
```

Data Receiving Routines

```
int bufid = pvm_recv( int tid, int msgtag )

int bufid = pvm_probe( int tid, int msgtag )

int bufid = pvm_nrecv( int tid, int msgtag )

int bufid = pvm_precv( int tid, int msgtag, void *vp, int cnt, int type int *rtid, int\
    *rtag, int *rlen )

int bufid = pvm_trecv( int tid, int msgtag, struct timeval *tmout )

int info = pvm_bufinfo( int bufid, int *bytes, int *msgtag, int *tid)

int info = pvm_unpackf( printf-like format... )

int info = pvm_upkbyte( char *cp, int cnt, int std )

int info = pvm_upkcplx( float *xp, int cnt, int std )

int info = pvm_upkdcplx( double *zp, int cnt, int std )

int info = pvm_upkdouble(double *dp, int cnt, int std )

int info = pvm_upkfloat( float *fp, int cnt, int std )

int info = pvm_upkint( int *np, int cnt, int std )

int info = pvm_upklong( long *np, int cnt, int std )

int info = pvm_upkshort( short *np, int cnt, int std )

int info = pvm_upkstr( char *cp )
```

Group Operations

```
int inum = pvm_joingroup(char *group)

int info = pvm_lvgroup( char *group)

int size = pvm_gsize( char *group)

int tid = pvm_gettid( char *group, int inum)

int inum = pvm_getinst( char *group, int tid)

int info = pvm_barrier( char *group, int count)

int info = pvm_bcast( char *group, int msgtag)

int info = pvm_reduce( void *op, void *vp, int cnt,

int type, int msgtag, char *group, int root)
```

op Options	vp Type		Options
PvmMax	PVM_BYTE	PVM_FLOAT	PVM_STR
PvmMin	PVM_SHORT	PVM_DOUBLE	PVM_UINT
PvmSum	PVM_INT	PVM_CPLX	PVM_USHORT
PvmProduct	PVM_LONG	PVM_DCPLX	PVM_ULONG

INSTALLATION SCRIPTS

This appendix contains listings and descriptions of the installation components that can be found on the two installation disks for the Building Linux Clusters CD-ROM. This appendix also includes descriptions of how the boot process works, how the installation process locates packages to be installed, and how these setup scripts may be modified to meet other requirements in the development of Parallel Linux Clusters.

Structure of a Boot Floppy

A minimal boot disk contains just a few files:

File	Description
vmlinuz	This is the kernel. On boot floppies it's usually a stripped down version because space is at a premium.
SYSLINUX.CFG	This file contains the boot and startup parameters for the Linux kernel. On a running system, this information is kept in the *lilo.conf* file.
ks.cfg	This is the KickStart configuration file. This file is used solely for the automation of Linux installations. Standard boot floppies do have this file, and their installations are very interactive, with the user being asked for all of the information needed to configure a system.
initrd.img	This file is actually a whole disk image compressed down to fit on the boot floppy. Its name stands for "initial RAM disk," and it contains all of the device drives that might be needed to access devices connected to the system, such as SCSI controllers and Ethernet cards.

These are the minimal files needed to bootstrap a system. On a standard Linux installation floppy there are also various files with extension *.msg*. These are message files that contain various messages displayed during the boot process. They are purely informational and may be removed (as is the case with the installation disks for the Linux Clusters described in this book) to make more space available.

The installation images provided on the Linux Clusters CD-ROM use Red Hat's Kick-Start system for automating the installation process controlled by the *ks.cfg* file. If you have built a cluster using the techniques described in this book, you have probably seen the the effects of booting with one of these automatic installation disks: there is almost no input required from the user to build systems.

The Boot Process

The Linux boot process is actually very simple. Every disk, whether a floppy disk or a multi-gigabyte hard disk, has an area designated as the *boot sector*. The boot sector contains a number of bits of information, most importantly, the name of a program to run as the *bootstrap loader*. In the case of Linux, the bootstrap loader is usually called LILO (the LInux LOader). On SPARC- and ALPHA-based Linuxes there are different bootstrap loaders, SILO and MILO respectively, due to different requirements of these architectures as compared to the Intel x86 family.

LILO is just a small program that runs another program, passing it whatever arguments are necessary to start it up properly. On a fully installed Linux system, LILO gets its start-up information from a special file on the *root* partition of the boot disk called */etc/lilo.conf*. On a boot floppy, this information is stored in a file called *SYSLINX.CFG*. This file takes the place of the *lilo.conf* file and contains substantially the same information.

When the system boots from a floppy, the system's BIOS instructs the floppy to read the bootstrap loader from the disk and place it in memory. Once the bootstrap program is loaded, the system runs it. This program then tries to load the program indicated in its configuration file—a Linux kernel. If the kernel loads and runs, the system will start booting. If for some reason the bootstrap of the kernel fails, an error message is posted to the screen and the system waits for the user to do something (like try again with a different disk).

Locating the Installation Materials

After getting the system to boot from a floppy, the most critical part of a Linux installation is the location and contents of the software packages that are going to be installed.

Different Linux distributions have different conventions as to where files are stored on CD-ROM, but since the version of Linux that comes with the CD-ROM that accompanies this book is based on Red Hat Linux, we'll stick to the conventions it has used.

The structure of the Linux Clusters CD-ROM, if one were to remove all of the additional tools and packages other than the Linux distribution itself, would consist of exactly one directory: *RedHat*.

The *RedHat* directory contains all of the software needed to bring up a functional system. Inside this directory are three key subdirectories:

base

The base directory is perhaps the most important. This is the location of the configuration files that let the installer know what's on the rest of the disk.

installer

The installer directory contains the pieces of the Red Hat installation system that can't fit onto the install disk. This includes a variety of shared libraries and other components needed by Red Hat Linux installation and bootstrap programs.

RPMS

This directory contain everything else that makes up Linux, from the C compiler through window managers line GNOME though applications such the The GIMP. All of these are stored in "RPM" or RedHat Package Manager files. RPM files are specialized archvies that either contain all of the binary files (i.e., the actual executables), configuration files and manual pages for a given package, or it contains the sources needed to compile that application and make a binary package for installation. RPM is a very versatile package format and is used by a number of Linux vendors in their distribution.

Modifying the Disk Images

There are two ways to work with the boot images that are provided on the Linux Clusters CD-ROM. The first way is to make a set of boot floppies, as you did when you were getting ready to set up your master and slave nodes, and then work on the configuration files on the disks directly. Copies of the KickStart files are also provided in the BootFloppies directory so that they can be edited and copied to installation disks.

The second way is to copy the disk *images* to a work area on some Linux machine, and then using some clever sleight of hand with file systems, mount the disk images as filesystems and work on them that way. This second option allows you to make changes directly to copies of the boot images, from which an unlimited number of actual installation disks may be created (rather than making individual boot disks and then working to modify each one).

In order to mount the disk images on the CD-ROM, you will have to copy the installation materials to some convenient place on a hard disk and you will need to have a Linux kernel that has been configured to have *loopback filesystem* support and the ability to read MS-DOS filesystems.

The loopback filesystem is a facility that allows specially formatted files that are stored on disk to be mounted as filesystems—in short, a filesystem in a filesystem.

All of these examples of filesystem manipulation, and modification of these boot images, should be done as *root*.

Mounting the Linux Clusters CD-ROM

The command:

```
# mount -r -t iso9660 /dev/cdrom /mnt/cdrom
```

will mount the Linux Clusters CD-ROM as the standard mount point.

Copying the Installation Materials to Disk

You should choose a space on your filesystems that can hold several megabytes of files and data that is accessible to those users who will be working on any modifications you plan on making. In this example, we'll use */a/projects/cluster* as our target directory:

```
# cd /mnt/cdrom/BootFloppyInfo
# ls
MasterBootFloppy  SlaveBootFloppy
#cp -R MasterBootFloppy  SlaveBootFloppy  /a/projects/cluster
#cd /a/projects/cluster
#ls -lR
BootFloppyInfo/MasterBootFloppy:
total 12
-r-xr--r--    1 spector   spector      743 Apr 29 19:01 BOOT.MSG*
-r-xr--r--    1 spector   spector     5075 May 27 12:35 KS.CFG*
-r-xr--r--    1 spector   spector      130 May  2  1999 MasterFloppy2Img*
drwxr-xr-x    2 spector   spector     1024 Jun  8 10:32 RCS/
-r-xr--r--    1 spector   spector      118 May 27 11:46 SYSLINUX.CFG*
-r-xr--r--    1 spector   spector       86 Aug 14  1999 mkMasterFloppy*

BootFloppyInfo/SlaveBootFloppy:
total 11
-r-xr--r--    1 spector   spector      763 Apr 29 19:01 BOOT.MSG*
-r-xr--r--    1 spector   spector     4780 May 26 08:09 KS.CFG*
drwxr-xr-x    2 spector   spector     1024 Jun  8 10:32 RCS/
-r-xr--r--    1 spector   spector      112 May  2  1999 SYSLINUX.CFG*
-r-xr--r--    1 spector   spector      136 May  2  1999 SlaveFloppy2Img*
-r-xr--r--    1 spector   spector       85 Aug 14  1999 mkSlaveFloppy*
```

You will now have copies of all of the installation materials from the CD-ROM in a form that can be customized. The nice thing about having the source materials on CD-ROM of course is that if you make a mistake, and accidentally delete or modify a file in a way that you wish you could undo, you can always copy the affected file off the CD-ROM again and start over.

Mounting the Installation Images

The Red Hat Linux installation disks are in MS-DOS format. With the loopback filesystem it is possible to actually mount the *.img* file for a given installation disk and edit its contents as though you put the information on a floppy disk.

Before we attempt to mount these disk images, we have to make mount points for them to be attached to. This is done, as *root*, as follows:

```
# mkdir -p /mnt/masterimg /mnt/slaveimg
```

The *mkdir* command makes the directories, and the *-p* flag tells *mkdir* to make any parent directories necessary.

Once we have mount points, the commands to actually mount the disk are simple. Simply change directory (*cd*) to the directory where you copied the contents of the *BootFloppies* directory from the CD-ROM:

```
# cd /a/projects/cluster
```

Then execute the following command:

```
# mount -o loop -t msdos MasterBootFloppy/MasterNode.img /mnt/masterimg
# mount -o loop -t msdos SlaveBootFloppy/SlaveNode.img /mnt/slaveimg
```

The results will be visible from the output of *df*:

```
#df
:
/dev/loop0          1423    1408      15     99%    /mnt/masterimg
/dev/loop1          1423    1407      16     99%    /mnt/slaveimg
```

Superfluous output from *df* has been deleted, but you can see that the images that are stored on a real filesystem on your system are now accessible as filesystems in their own right.

One important caveat to be aware of here is the these are images in memory of floppy disks. Make sure that you do not try to put more than 1.4Mb of data into these images! Overloading the image will corrupt it and render unusable the actual floppies made from the image.

When you are done modifying these images to suit your needs, make sure you execute a *sync* command to flush any modified data back to the image, and then unmount the image by using the *umount* command. These images may then be used to create installation floppies as described in Chapter 5, *Software Installation and Configuration*.

The Master Node Installation Disk

The master node installation disk that is created with the images on the Linux Clusters CD-ROM is completely generic except for three files: *ks.cfg*, *syslinux.cfg* and *boot.msg*. These files turn an otherwise ordinary Linux installation disk into a cluster building tool. If you need to customize the installation of a cluster, all you need to do is edit copies of these files, which can be done even on a Windows machine, and copy them back onto an installation floppy.

Master Node Kickstart Script

```
### Building Linux Clusters master-node KS.CFG file
### by David HM Spector
###
### Language Specification
lang en_US

### Network Configuration
###
### For this configuration, we'll us a static address
network --bootproto static --ip 10.0.2.1 --netmask 255.255.255.0 --gateway 10.0.2.1 --
nameserver 10.0.2.1

### Source File Location
cdrom


### Ethernet Device Configuration
#device ethernet wd --opts "io=0x280, irq=3"

### Keyboard Configuration
### Will get set to 'us' by default
### if nothing specified in /etc/sysconfig/keyboard
keyboard us

### Partitioning Information
### Whether to clear out the Master Boot Record (yes/no)
### Which partitions to format (--linux/--all)
###      --linux - only format existing linux partitions
###      --all   - format all existing partitions
### Which partitions to set up on new system as well
### as size of those partitions
###
### Before RedHat6.2, the /boot partition could be a subdirectory of the root filesystem;
### as of the 6.2 release the /boot partition must be the first partition on the boot
### device.  For some reason Redhat doesn't document this fact very well, and, if you
### attempt to build a node, especially with KickStart, and this partition doesn't exist
### you will have what appears to be a successful installation, but the resulting system
### will panic when the kernel tries to launch init.
```

```
zerombr yes
clearpart --all
part /boot --size 16
part swap --size 127
part / --size 128
part /usr --size 1024
part /tmp --size 512
part /var --size 750
part /home --size 1000 --grow

### Here's where we'd set up RAID devices if any.  You might use this if you have a lot
of disks
### and wanted to set up disk mirroring, striping or a full RAID-5 setup for your
cluster.
###
#part raid.0 --size 80
#part raid.1 --size 80
#raid swap raid.0 raid.1 --level 1 --device md0

### Since we're installing the master node from scratch here, this is an "install" as
opposed
### to an "upgrade"
install

### Mouse Configuration
### Will only setup 3 types of mice
###     generic        - 2-button serial
###     genericps/2    - 2-button ps/2
###     msintellips/2  - MS Intellimouse
### All three can be setup with or without 3-button
### emulation
### Run 'mouseconfig --help' in order to see other
### supported mouse type and make appropriate change
### NOTE: You will need to run 'mouseconfig' manually
### after installation if you have a non-ps/2 mouse
### and are installing X, as a ps/2 mouse is setup
### by default
#mouse generic --device ttyS0
mouse generic3ps/2

### Time Zone Configuration
### Will get set to 'US/Eastern' if ZONE is missing
### from /etc/sysconfig/clock or if file is missing entirely
timezone --utc US/Eastern

### X Configuration
### Will set up system for minimal resolution and color depth;
### may wish to run Xconfigurator manually after system installation
#xconfig --server "SVGA" --monitor "viewsonic g773"
```

```
### Root Password Designation
### '--iscrypted' does not work properly with release 6.1 as shipped;
### will need to get updates from http://support.redhat.com/errata
### in order for this to work correctly; can also just specify
### root password in plain text and change it after system installation;
### e.g. 'rootpw ThisIsThePassword' will get root's password to
### "ThisIsThePassword"
rootpw mr.linux

### Authorization Configuration
auth --enablemd5

### Lilo Configuration
### Does not support pulling kernel 'append' arguments, but those
### can be added into config file using '--append' argument;
### e.g. 'lilo --append "mem=128M" --location mbr' will put the
### memory argument in the /etc/lilo.conf file at install


lilo --location mbr



### Package Designation
### The package names, as well as the groups they are a part of can be
### found in the /RedHat/base/comps file; individual packages can be
### specified by entering their names one per line;
### groups (e.g. 'X Window System') can be specified
### by appending a "@" in front of the group name;
### e.g. '@ X Window System'
%packages
python
xntp3
dhcp
dhcpcd
@ X Window System
@ Networked Workstation
@ NFS Server
@ Web Server
@ Development
@ Clustering
@ GNOME
@ Emacs

### Commands To Be Run Post-Installation
###
### These commands activate some of the more esoteric packages. For some wierd reason
### (the way these RPMs were packaged) they are not turned on by default on installation.
### This can cause a lot of confusion if you were just expecting the packages to work
### without having to fiddle around with them too much.
##
%post
```

```
### This ensures that we can have consistent time across the cluster
chkconfig --level 35  xntpd on

### This ensures that the slave nodes will be able to talk to the master-node in order to
boot
chkconfig --level 35  dhcpd on

### This enables the Network Information Service, or "NIS" which will allow easy
automounting
### of the cluster's user filesystems and allow users to have a single login credential
### across the cluster.
chkconfig --level 35  ypserv on
chkconfig --level 35  ypbind on
```

Master Node SYSLINUX.CFG

```
default ks
prompt 0
timeout 600
display boot.msg
label ks
  kernel vmlinuz
  append ks=floppy initrd=initrd.img
```

Utility Scripts

Included in the *MasterBootFloppy* directory are two utilities scripts that will allow you to either make a boot floppy from an image you have on a hard disk, or to create a master image from a boot floppy. These are tiny little utilities but can save you from those annoying little typos that can waste your time.

mkMasterFloppy

This script will create a master boot floppy from an image file, specified as the first arguemnt to the command:

```
#!/bin/sh
echo "Creating master floppy from \"$1\" "
dd of=/dev/fd0 if=${1}
```

MasterImage2Floppy

This script will read the floppy disk in drive A and make it into a disk image (which could then be turned back into a floppy disk by the *mkMasterFloppy* script above).

```
#!/bin/sh
echo "Creating disk image of Master node boot floppy..."
dd if=/dev/fd0 of=MasterNode-'/bin/date '+%d%b%Y-%H%M'' bs=72k
```

The Slave Node Installation Disk

The slave node installation disk is exactly the same as the master node disk, except for changes in the *ks.cfg* file that build the node as a slave/compute node, and install the software via NFS rather than via a CD-ROM.

Slave Node Kickstart Script

```
### Building Linux Clusters slave-node KS.CFG file
### by David HM Spector
###### Language Specification
lang en_US

### Network Configuration
### This is a slave node, we'll bootstrap ourselves off of the master node
network --bootproto dhcp

### Source File Location
###
### The installation materials are located on the Master node on the installation
### CD-ROM
nfs --server 10.0.2.1 --dir /mnt/cdrom

### Ethernet Device Configuration
#device ethernet wd --opts "io=0x280, irq=3"

### Keyboard Configuration
### Will get set to 'us' by default
### if nothing specified in /etc/sysconfig/keyboard
keyboard us

### Partitioning Information
### Whether to clear out the Master Boot Record (yes/no)
### Which partitions to format (--linux/--all)
###      --linux - only format existing linux partitions
###      --all   - format all existing partitions
### Which partitions to set up on new system as well
### as size of those partitions
zerombr yes
clearpart --all
part /boot --size 16
part / --size 128
part swap --size 127
part /usr --size 1024
part /tmp --size 512
part /var --size 750
### this partition is created just in case you want to have a local filespace for your
cluster users
### but this is actually not needed if the home directories are automounted over the
network
```

```
part /spare --size 1000 --grow

### Again, like the master-node, we're doing a complete installation
install

### Mouse Configuration
### Will only setup 3 types of mice
###     generic        - 2-button serial
###     genericps/2    - 2-button ps/2
###     msintellips/2  - MS Intellimouse
### All three can be setup with or without 3-button
### emulation
### Run 'mouseconfig --help' in order to see other
### supported mouse type and make appropriate change
### NOTE: You will need to run 'mouseconfig' manually
### after installation if you have a non-ps/2 mouse
### and are installing X, as a ps/2 mouse is setup
### by default
###
### Technically, since this is a slave node which will not be running the XWindow
### system, we don't care about the mouse... However, KickStart DOES care about
### mice and will fail if we don't specify a mouse here.
###
#mouse generic --device ttyS0
mouse generic3ps/2

### Time Zone Configuration
### Will get set to 'US/Eastern' if ZONE is missing
### from /etc/sysconfig/clock or if file is missing entirely
timezone --utc US/Eastern

### X Configuration
### Will set up system for minimal resolution and color depth;
### may wish to run Xconfigurator manually after system installation
###
### Again, we're not running the XWindow system on slave/compute nodes, so this
### section is commented out.  See also, the Packages section -- we won't specify
### any XWindow packages there either.
###
#xconfig --server "SVGA" --monitor "viewsonic g773"


### Root Password Designation
### '--iscrypted' does not work properly with release 6.1 as shipped;
### will need to get updates from http://support.redhat.com/errata
### in order for this to work correctly; can also just specify
### root password in plain text and change it after system installation;
### e.g. 'rootpw ThisIsThePassword' will get root's password to
### "ThisIsThePassword"
rootpw mr.linux
```

```
### Authorization Configuration
auth --enablemd5

### Lilo Configuration
### Does not support pulling kernel 'append' arguments, but those
### can be added into config file using '--append' argument;
### e.g. 'lilo --append "mem=128M" --location mbr' will put the
### memory argument in the /etc/lilo.conf file at install
lilo --location mbr
#lilo --location none

### Package Designation
### The package names, as well as the groups they are a part of can be
### found in the /RedHat/base/comps file; individual packages can be
### specified by entering their names one per line;
### groups (e.g. 'X Window System') can be specified
### by appending a "@" in front of the group name;
### e.g. '@ X Window System'
%packages
python
xntp3
@ Networked Workstation
@ Development
@ Clustering

### Commands To Be Run Post-Installation
%post

### This ensures that we can have consistent time across the cluster
chkconfig --level 35  xntpd on
### This enables the Network Information Service, or "NIS" which will allow easy
automounting
### of the cluster's user filesystems and allow users to have a single login credential
### across the cluster.  In the case of this slave/compute node we'll be an NIS client.
chkconfig --level 35  ypbind on
```

Slave Node SYSLINUX.CFG File

This file is identical to the *SYSLINUX.CFG* file on the master node installation:

```
default ks
prompt 0
timeout 600
display boot.msg
label ks
  kernel vmlinuz
  append ks=floppy initrd=initrd.img
```

Utility Scripts

Paired with those included in the *MasterBootFloppy* directory are two utilites scripts in the *SlaveBootFloppy* direcory that will allow you to either make a boot floppy from an image you have on a hard disk, or to create a slave image from a boot floppy. These are tiny little utilities but can save you from those annoying little typos that can waste your time.

mkSlaveFloppy

This script will create a master boot floppy from an image file, specified as the first argument to the command:

```
#!/bin/sh
echo "Creating slave floppy from \"$1\" "
dd of=/dev/fd0 if=${1}
```

SlaveImage2Floppy

This script will read the floppy disk in drive A and make it into a disk image (which could then be turned back into a floppy disk by the *mkSlaveFloppy* script above).

```
#!/bin/sh
echo "Creating disk image of slave/compute node boot floppy..."
dd if=/dev/fd0 of=SlaveNode-'/bin/date '+%d%b%Y-%H%M'' bs=72k
```

THE CLUSTER ADMINISTRATION DATABASE

The Cluster Administration Database is a complete user, node, and cluster management system that allows you to keep track of all aspects of the operations of your clusters.

This appendix presents a compete description of the schema that makes up the database and provides advice on how the system might be used and extended.

The database as presented here was developed and tested under the PostgreSQL database version 6.4.2. To the best of my knowledge, the schema does not depend on non-standard SQL statements, so porting it to a different relational database should not be too difficult. However, it has not been tested under any other database.

Goals

The goal when designing this database was the ability to keep track of all aspects of a cluster from a single point of contact that could be used to provide a uniform, web-based interface to the cluster administrator.

The information that needs to be tracked in a cluster can be boiled down to the following areas:

Nodes

Nodes are the primary element of a cluster. They are, simply, computers. The information about a node that is relevant to the cluster builder is the node's Ethernet address (or addresses) and basic information about the node's characteristics, such as number of CPUs, CPU speed, available main memory, OS version, and amount of disk space. Other information that should be recorded for a given node are the serial numbers of key components that may need to be serviced, replaced, or upgraded.

Packages

The packages that are installed on a node are relevant in the context of systems maintenance. It is usually the case that a cluster owner/administrator will want to keep every node in the cluster at the same revision level for each and every node in the cluster. However, there are instances when it might be useful to have different software on one or more nodes; for example, when testing a new package or cluster tool.

Clusters

Clusters are the entities created by grouping a collection of nodes together. In the context of the Cluster Administration Database, a cluster is a collection of nodes, with one of the nodes designated as the *master node*. The master node is the point from which jobs that run on the cluster originate and where users log in and work on their files.

Groups

Groups are administrative entities that represent a collection of users who are working on similar or related projects. All users are members of a minimum of one group, called their *primary group*. They may also be members of other groups.

Groups have resources and costs assigned to them that define how much of a given resource may be used by the group as a whole. For example, if we have a group called "physics," that group could have a budget of $50,000 in terms of CPU, disk, and connect time that may be used by all of the sub-entities that belong to the group.

Projects

Projects are subgroupings of users that are working on a particular problem in a specific group. In the Cluster Administration Database projects are directly tied to groups (i.e., all projects exist as part of an explicit group). All users must be part of at least one project in any group of which they are a member. When a new group is created, a default project, called "general," is created along with it. The general group is used to contain any users that may be assigned to that group that have not been assigned to a specific project.

Users

Users are the final element in the chain of information in the cluster administration hierarchy. Users are members of projects, which in turn are part of groups, which have privileges and resource allocations on a given cluster, which is a collection of nodes.

Users can use the quota grants that have been assigned to the projects in which they work, or a project administrator may allocate a subset of the project resources to a specific user.

Entity–Relationship Diagram

There are several points of interest in the entity-relationship diagram pictured in Figure D-1.

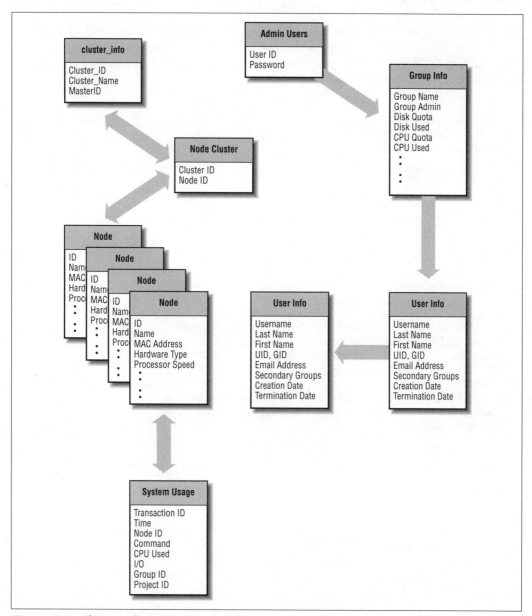

Figure D-1. Cluster Administration Database entity-relationship diagram

In the diagram, the system usage table shows no links to any other data. These links are left out of the diagram because they would make the diagram too complex.

The Schema

The schema of a given database is the collection of SQL commands used to create its tables. The Cluster Administration Database is a fairly complex schema that is comprised of eight different tables, which are used to create a variety of relations. Here is the code for the Cluster Administration Database schema:

```
/*
  Table Creation Scripts
  Last Modified August 3, 1999
  Michelle D. Smith
*/


/*
  8/3/99 -- modified after creation of ER diagram.  Removed
  some tables and fields which were superfluous.


/*
Table node contains information specific to an individual
node.  The field master will contain the node_id of this
node's master.  Currently, master nodes will be identifiable
by a null value in the field master.  (Is this accurate?)
It should also be possible to achieve this type of relationship
by creating a type, and using a reference, but I'm not sure
of the performance ramifications for Postgres, and it
certainly would not be supported by other relational databases.



I have not put in constraints for things like uniqueness
(node_id) and allowable values (hardware type).  We can
add these later.

I have not implemented any referential integrity checks.

No indices have been created.

*/


/*********************************************/
/** Tables describing the cluster         **/
/*********************************************/


create table node
(node_id int,
```

```
     cluster_id int,
     name      char(32),
     mac_addresss char(32),
     ip_address char(30),
     hardware_type  char(15),
     cpu_count      int,    /* how many CPUs */
     serial_number  char(20),
     other_info     char(128),   /* can be used to hold other serial numbers, etc. */
     processor_speed int,
     memory int,
     total_disk_space int
     );

create table node_packages
( node_id int,
  package char(64)
);

/***************************************/
/*The cluster table stores the name of the cluster
 and the id of the master of that cluster.*/

/*cluster is a reserved word in Postgres, so I've named this table
cluster_info*/

create table cluster_info
(cluster_id int,
 cluster_name char(32),
 master int); /*master is the node_id of a node*/



/*********************************************/
/**  Tables describing users            **/
/*********************************************/
/*
Table user_info contains information about an individual
user.

user is a reserved word in Postgres, so I've named the table
user_info.

*/

create table user_info
(user_id int,
 last_name char(20),
 first_name char(20),
 username char(20),
 uid     int,
 gid     int, /*user's primary group membership*/
```

```
email_address char(45),
phone1 char(20),
phone2 char(20),
pager   char(40),
pager_pin char(20),
fax     char(20),
notify_method char,/* '1' indicates that phone 1 is the prefered contact method;
    2 for  phone 2, 3 for pager, 4 for fax.*/
status char,
creation_date timestamp,
termination_date timestamp,
deletion_date timestamp
);


/****************************************/
/* We define the cost for various resources at the project
   level.  If the value is set to NULL for a particular project,
   use the group price.  (hmmm -- this might be complicated from
   an SQL point of view.  If it is, then implement something to
   cause the group values to be copied into the project fields,
   if they are null.)
*/

create table project
(project_id     int,
 project_name   char(20),
 project_admin  int,
 gid            int,
 disk_quota     int,
 disk_used      int,
 disk_costfloat4,
 io_quota       int,
 io_used        int,
 io_costfloat4,
 cpu_quota      int,
 cpu_used       int,
 cpu_costfloat4,
 connect_quota  int,
 connect_used   int,
 connect_costfloat4,
 last_update    timestamp);

/*admin is a user id*/

/*Table project contains information about
which users belong to which groups.  Primary
group of membership is given here, but is
not identified as such.  For this information,
query the user table.*/
```

```
/******************************************/

create table group_info
(gid             int,
 group_namechar(20),
 group_admin     int,
 group_description char(100),
 disk_quota      int,
 disk_used       int,
 disk_costfloat4,
 io_quota        int,
 io_used         int,
 io_costfloat4,
 cpu_quota       int,
 cpu_used        int,
 cpu_costfloat4,
 connect_quota   int,
 connect_used    int,
 connect_costfloat4,
 last_update     timestamp
);
```

```
/**********************************************/
/* Note that no prices are given, since user does not
   have his/her own price for resources.*/

create table user_project_relationship
(user_id         int,
 project_id      int,
 disk_quota      int,
 disk_used       int,
 io_quota        int,
 io_used         int,
 cpu_quota       int,
 cpu_used        int,
 connect_quota   int,
 connect_used    int,
 last_update     timestamp)
;
```

```
create table admin_users
(user_id         char(20),
 password        char(20));
```

```
/********************************************/
/** Tables for system accounting       **/
/********************************************/
create table sys_usage
(transaction_id int,
 time_of_command timestamp,
 node_id        int,
 uid            int,
 command        char(40),
 cpu_usage      int,
 num_io_calls int,
 group_id       int,
 project_id     int
);
```

Creating the Database

The Cluster Administration Database is created using the PostgreSQL *createdb* command, which has the form:

>   createdb *dbname*

where *dbname* is the name you wish to give to the database.

In order to create this database, the account (user) that executes this command must already be registered with PostgreSQL and have create-database privileges.

For the purposes of these examples, we will assume that the database name is *clusteradmin*.

Unless otherwise specified, all of the examples in the rest of this appendix will be executed via the interactive transaction monitor *psql*. Queries can be entered in free form via the SQL monitor; queries are terminated by ending them with a semi-colon (;) or "\g" at the end of a line.

All SQL statements shown here can be executed either at the monitor or via any of the dozens of different PostgreSQL interface libraries available for C, C++, Perl, Python, or dozens of other languages.

Database Entities

The database consists of several entities that comprise the objects managed by the Cluster Administration Database:

Nodes
> Nodes are the primary entities that exist in a cluster. They have certain data that is useful for systems administration purposes to a cluster administrator, most notably the system Ethernet and TCP/IP address(es).

The node table is a comprehensive list of all computer resources available and may be used to create clusters and clusters of clusters by adding the nodes to the *cluster_info* table to create these kinds of aggregations.

Packages

The packages table lists the association between an installed software package and the node onto which it is installed. This table is useful not so much in the case where every node on a cluster is identical, but rather when an administrator wishes to create a set of nodes that have different software for testing or other purposes.

Clusters

Clusters are entities that represent collections of nodes via the *cluster_info* table. The *cluster_info* table has a reference to a master node, and then a list of computer nodes that make up the cluster.

Note that a cluster may be configured to contain subclusters. This can be useful for breaking up a cluster into "production" and "test" configurations, where the test configuration may be running different software than the production version.

Groups

Groups are administrative entities that serve as containers for projects and users via the *group_info* table. A group contains information that links it to the group administrator (a user who has privileges to administer the information in the group table, which includes the creation and maintenance of projects belonging to the group). Group entries also have fields to keep track of funds and quotas dedicated to the group. These resources can be suballocated to projects that are part of the group's work. Users may also belong to more than one group; however, only one group can be the user's primary or default group.

Projects

Projects are administrative containers for users. Every user is a member of at least one project, even if it is the "general" project that is created when every group is created. Projects also have resource allocations in terms of various quotas that are suballocated from the group that is the parent of the project.

Users

Users are, from the administrative perspective, the bottom of the food chain. All users must belong to a project, which must be part of a group, which is part of a cluster.

A user may be part of multiple projects and multiple groups, but only one of the groups and projects may be the default or primary group.

Resources used by a user are charged against their project quotas (which in turn come out of the group quota from the group in which the project belongs).

Administrative users

Administrative users are captured in the *admin_users* table. This is a list of privileged users who have permission to modify rows in the group and project tables.

Limitations

As delivered in this implementation, the Cluster Administration Database has several limitations. Since Linux (and most other Unix systems) doesn't support fine-grained resource controls, there is no way to connect the database in real time to activities on the system. It is possible, and even likely, that users may overrun their quota allocations until the system accounting is run at night and the accounting is reconciled with the limits set down on a group and project basis in the Cluster Administration Database.

Future Directions

There are a number of improvements to the Cluster Administration Database that would be helpful to the cluster administrator, such as:

- Real-time user information displays
- Real-time accounting generation
- Commands that act upon multiple groups/projects/users simultaneously

It would also be immensely helpful if Linux supported kernel-level resource monitoring so that user resource allocations could be more easily controlled.

BIBLIOGRAPHY

This bibliography is broken down by subject area and lists some of the most common and, in the author's opinion, most useful books on the topic of clustered/parallel computing as well as the peripheral topics needed to build and understand clusters.

Entries beginning with an asterisk (*) indicate introductory texts that you might want to look at first if you are new to the particular subject area.

General Programming

Koelbel, Charles H., David B. Loveman, Robert S. Schreiber, Guy L. Steele Jr., and Mary E. Zosel. *The High Performance FORTRAN Handbook*. Cambridge, MA: MIT Press, 1994. ISBN:0-262-61094-9

* Lippman, Stanley, and Josee Lajoie. *The C++ Primer*. New York, NY: Addison Welsley, 1998 (3rd Ed.). ISBN: 0-201-82470-1

Stroustrup, Bjarne. *The C++ Programming Language*. New York, NY: Addison Welsley, 1986 (3rd Ed.). ISBN: 0-201-88954-4

General Electronics

Danzer, Paul, Ed. *The ARRL Handbook for Radio Amateurs, 76th Edition*. Newington, CT: ARRL, 1999. ISBN: 0-872-59181-6

Hardware

Hennessy, John, and David Patterson. *Computer Architecture: A Quantitative Approach*. San Francisco, CA: Morgan Kauffman Publishing, 1996. ISBN: 1-558-60329-9

Rosch, Winn L. *The Hardware Bible*. Indianapolis, Indiana: Sams Publishing, 1997. ISBN: 0-672-30954-8

MUDs

Dibbell, Julian. *My Tiny Life*. New York: Henry Holt/Owl Books, 1998. ISBN: 0-8050-3626-1

Haynes, Cynthia, and Jan Rune Holmevik, Eds. *High Wired—On the Design, Use, and Theory of Educational MOOs*. Ann Arbor: University of Michigan Press, 1998. ISBN: 0-472-09665-6

Networking

Albitz, Paul, and Cricket Liu. *DNS and BIND*. Sebastopol, CA: O'Reilly & Associates, 1998 (3rd Ed.). ISBN: 1-56592-512-2

Parallel Programming

Barak, Amnon, Shai Guday, and Richard G. Wheeler. *The MOSIX Distributed Operating System*. (Lecture Notes in Computer Science, #572). Berlin, Germany: Springer-Verlag, 1993. ISBN: 3-540-56663-5

* Dowd, Kevin, and Charles Severance. *High Performance Computing*. Sebastopol, CA: O'Reilly & Associates, 1998 (2nd Ed.). ISBN: 1-56592-312-X

* Foster, Ian T. *Designing and Building Parallel Programs: Concepts and Tools for Parallel Software*. New York: Addison-Wesley Publishing Co., 1995. ISBN: 0-201-57594-9

Geist, Al, Adam Beguelin, Jack Dongarra, Weicheng Jiang, Robert Mancheck, and Vaidy Sunderam. *PVM: A User's Guide and Tutorial for Networked Parallel Computing*. Cambridge, MA: MIT Press, 1994. ISBN:0-262-57108-0

Gropp, William, Ewing Lusk, and Anthony Skjellum. *Using MPI: Portable Programming with Message Passing Interface*. Cambridge, MA: MIT Press, 1996. ISBN: 0-262-57104-8

Gropp, William, Steven Huss-Ledermann, Andrew Lumsdaine, Ewing Lusk, Bill Nitzberg, William Saphir, and Marc Snir. *MPI: The Complete Reference, 2nd Ed. Volume 2, The MPI Extensions*. Cambridge, MA: MIT Press, 1998. ISBN:0-262-69216-3

Lynch, Nancy A. *Distributed Algorithms*. San Francisco, CA: Morgan Kaufman Publishers, 1996. ISBN: 1-55869-384-4

* Nichols, Bradford, Dick Buttlar, and Jacqueline Proulx Farrell. *Pthreads Programming*. Sebastopol, CA: O'Reilly & Associates, 1996. ISBN: 1-56592-115-1

* Pancheco, Peter S. *Parallel Programming with MPI*. San Francisco, CA: Morgan Kaufman Publishers, 1997. ISBN: 1-55860-339-5

* Pfister, Gregory F. *In Search of Clusters*. Upper Saddle River, NJ: Prentice Hall PTR, 1998. ISBN: 0-13-899709-8

Snir, Marc, Steve W. Otto, Steven Huss-Ledermann, David W. Walker, and Jack Dongarra. *MPI: The Complete Reference, 2nd Ed. Volume 1, The MPI Core*. Cambridge, MA: MIT Press, 1998. ISBN:0-262-69215-5

Van de Geijn, Robert A. *Using PLAPACK*. Cambridge, MA: MIT Press, 1997. ISBN 0-262-72026-4

System Administration and Management

* The Enterprise Linux web pages: *http://linas.org/linux*

* Frisch, AEleen. *Essential System Administration, 2nd Edition*. Sebastopol, CA: O'Reilly & Associates, 1998. ISBN: 1-56592-127-5

Red Hat Software. *The Official Red Hat 6.0 Operating System Installation Guide*. Durham, NC: Red Hat Software, 1998. ISBN: 1-888172-28-2

Traugott, Steve, and Joel Huddleston. The Enterpise Infrastructures web page: *http://www.infrastructures.org*

Systems Programming

Rubini, Alessandro. *Linux Device Drivers*. Sebastopol, CA: O'Reilly & Associates, 1998. ISBN: 1-56592-292-1

Magazines and Periodicals

The Microprocessor Report

The Microprocessor Report is sort of the insider's guide to what's news in the field of microprocessor design. All new hardware that is worth looking at shows up here along with detailed analyses of how it works and how it compares to any previous generations of hardware from the same manufacturer (e.g., PII versus PIII from Intel).

The Microprocessor Report is not cheap at approximately $700 per year, but worth it if you're going to be building serious clusters, since it can give you insights to the new systems that come out and how you might take advantage of them in your work. *The Microprocessor Report* is published by MicroDesign Resources of Sebastopol, CA. ISSN: 0899-9341

SIGARCH Bulletin

The ACM's Special Interest Group on Computer Architecture (SIGARCH) is a very valuable resource for cluster builders. The quarterly issues and the larger annual issue contain a wealth of cutting-edge research into parallel systems and advanced computer architectures. The *SIGARCH Bulletin* is available only as part of an ACM membership. For more information on ACM membership, see *http://www.acm.org*.

SIGSUPER Proceedings

As mentioned later under *Conferences*, ACM's annual supercomputing confab is a meeting of the cutting/bleeding edge folk in supercomputer development and research. The output of the conference is a collection of both invited and submitted papers on various areas of supercomputer R&D. Topics range from new message passing paradigms to new designs for hardware I/O systems and caches. A lot of the subject matter is very theoretical, but it is a good way to get the pulse of the supercomputing community. The SIGSUPER proceedings are available through the ACM at *http://www.acm.org*.

Conferences

Linux World

Linux World is a place to meet and greet the digerati that make up the cutting edge of Linux development. There are BOF ("Birds of a Feather") sessions here for all sorts of sub-interests in Linux development, including clustered computing. The Linux Expo is usually held in Atlanta or in North Carolina and is announced months in advance in all major Linux newsgroups and Linux web sites.

Supercomputing Conference

The annual ACM supercomputing conference is the oldest such gathering around. It is where supercomputer vendors and users meet to show off their latest triumphs in the field. This is not a conference for wimps—there is a *lot* of very advanced math and theoretical computer science thrown around with abandon. So, if this kind of really deep talk and even deeper thinking isn't your bag, then you might just want to buy a copy of the conference proceedings instead from the ACM. Registration for the conference can be accessed at the ACM's web site at *http://www.acm.org*.

Hot Chips

The Hot Chips conference is another annual event sponsored by the ACM, usually in conjunction with the IEEE. This conference is focused on showcasing developments in the semiconductor arena, especially CPUs. Every semiconductor maker who has something new to show off will introduce it formally here. Information on the scheduling of the Hot Chips conference may be found at either the ACM web site at *http://www.acm.org* or the Hot Chips web site at *http://www.hotchips. org*. The Hot Chips site may only be up/available near conference times.

GLOSSARY

1U case

A 1.75 inch high computer case that is typically installed in a 19 inch rack. See also *Rack Unit*.

2U case

A 3.5-inch high computer case that is typically installed in a 19-inch rack. See also *Rack Unit*.

Alpha

A high-performance RISC microprocessor designed by Digital Equipment Corporation (DEC) and now owned by Compaq Computer Corporation. The Alpha is known for its exceptional performance, large number of on-chip execution units, and high system clock rate.

AXP

See *Alpha*.

Beowulf

The name given by Dan Becker at NASA's CESDIS project to the cluster of computers they built to solve complex problems in the domain of space data sets.

BPROC

Beowulf-distributed process space. A set of patches for a Linux Beowulf cluster that allows the cluster to have a global process space where processes can elect to be migrated from one CPU to another.

British thermal unit (BTU)

The amount of heat required to raise the temperature of one pound of water (about one pint) by one degree Fahrenheit.

Cache

Cache (also called "cache memory") is a form of secondary memory storage that is usually built into a CPU chip that is used to keep program code "closer" to the CPU logic (and therefore more readily accessible) than main system memory. Cache memory is often an order of magnitude faster to access than main system memory. Modern CPUs are designed to keep program code in cache so that data is available to the main CPU logic rather than having to retrieve the same data from main memory. Efficiently written programs take advantage of cache memory by accessing their data and instructions in such a way as to ensure that references are for data or instructions already in the cache, rather than forcing data to be fetched from main memory or from another device such as a hard disk.

Cache hit

A cache hit occurs when a CPU accesses needed data (or program instructions) from information already stored in the cache rather than forcing a read from another level of storage.

Cache miss

A cache miss occurs when a CPU accesses data but finds that the needed piece of data is not in the cache. A read from another level of storage, such as main memory or an external device, is then scheduled.

Cluster

A collection of computers configured in such a way that they can be used to solve a problem by means of parallel processing.

Ethernet hub

A network device that allows a number of devices to be connected to and share a common network segment.

Ethernet switch

A network device similar to an Ethernet hub that allows a number of devices to be connected on a common network segment. However, the Ethernet switch is capable of routing packets on the hub so that each connected device appears to have a clear channel of communication equal to the stated throughput of the device.

Extreme Linux

The name given by Redhat software to their distribution of the NASA Beowulf software that is shipped with a version of Redhat's distribution of Linux.

Hypercube

An interconnection topology where nodes are connected in the form of a cube.

ISA Bus

The Industry Standard Architecture Bus was the 8-bit and 16-bit standard for peripheral cards in the IBM PC, the IBM PC/AT, and the XT. It was superseded by the PCI bus.

LAM

The Local Area Multicomputer is an MPI-based parallel computing environment developed originally at the Ohio Supercomputer Center and now maintained at Notre Dame University.

Linux

An Open Source operating system originally developed by Finnish college student Linus Torvald. Linux is a Unix-compatible operating system that is collaboratively developed by Linus and a cast of thousands of talented programmers around the world who contribute their expertise and time to the development of this software.

Metadata

Metadata is information about information. For example, if you have a database that contains sports scores, the data in the database is "the data." Metadata is information about that data, such as the fact that the database contains 150,000 records, the database occupies 200MB of disk space, each record is composed of twelve fields, and so on. In databases and distributed file systems, metadata may also contain information about the distribution of the data, such as how many values are in a given index or block. Such information can help optimize the performance of such systems.

MIMD

Multiple Instruction Multiple Data. This is a parallel computing architecture where multiple programs execute on multiple CPUs, each operating on different data to solve a problem.

MOSIX

A set of file kernel patches for Linux systems that allow these systems to participate in a cluster where processes can migrate around the cluster to make more efficient use of the processing resources.

MPI

The Message Passing Interface is an industry standard interface for communication between processors that is designed to facilitate parallel processing.

Multiple Execution Units

Multiple Execution Units are a feature of many newer architectures. Such systems have multiple logic units on chips that allow them to process several instructions in the pipeline simultaneously. The CPU keeps track of instructions to ensure that the results of one execution unit do not cause a failure in a later instruction. This could happen, for example, at a branch point where execution of code immediately after a branch would be inappropriate if the branch were taken.

PADE

(Parallel Applications Development Environment) A parallel development tool developed at the U.S. National Institutes of Standards and Technology that provides utilities to speed the development of PVM applications.

Parallel virtual machine
See *PVM*.

PCI Bus
The Peripheral Component Interconnect Bus is a 32-bit peripheral connector and hardware protocol standard used in Intel-based PCs. PCI was the replacement for the ISA bus introduced with the first IBM PC in 1981.

PCL
The Performance Counter Library is a tool designed by the Central Institute for Applied Mathematics in Jeulich, Germany that reports very detailed information about the internal performance of a CPU. This package is exceptionally useful for precise profiling of parallel applications.

PROM
Programmable Read-Only Memory is a special form of Read-Only Memory chip that can be programmed by use of a device called a PROM programmer. PROM chips are used in all areas of computer construction, but are of interest to cluster builders who want to make network add-in cards that have the capability to boot a system over the network without a floppy or for unattended system installation.

PVFS
The Parallel Virtual File System is a software system developed at the Parallel Architecture Lab at Clemson University that allows a cluster to be used as a high-performance file system that can be used to deliver data to parallel applications more efficiently than standard Linux or Unix file systems.

PVM
The Parallel Virtual Machine is a message-passing parallel processing environment developed at Oak Ridge National Labs. PVM is notable in that out of the box it creates a parallel environment that can be run in a heterogeneous environment.

Rack unit
A unit of measurement that defines the standard component height in 19-inch rack equipment. One rack unit is equal to *1.75 inches* of vertical space.

Riser card
A hardware device that allows a full-height PCI card to be installed at a 90 degree angle in a 1U or 2U rack-mount case that would normally be too small for such a card.

SIMD
Single Instruction Multiple Data. This is a parallel architecture where multiple copies of the same program operate on different data to solve a problem

SPARC
A series of high-performance microprocessor designs manufactured by Sun Microsystems. The SPARC architecture features very fast clock speeds. SPARC-based machines are extremely popular in corporate data centers and can be good for cluster builders since aftermarket machines can be acquired at very low cost.

Speculative execution
This is the process used in machines with multiple execution units to speed the processing of instructions.

Stride
A stride is a logical step through data that generates the least number of cache misses. Data can be arranged so that a program can access it in such a way that processing is done as "close" to the CPU as possible. In other words, properly arranged data can cause a program to process all data in the CPU's cache before causing the program to force data to be loaded in from a slower storage level (such as main memory).

TAU
Tuning and Analysis Utilities. A package written at the University of Oregon that provinces very precise execution profiling capabilities.

XPVM
An X-Window program that functions as an execution monitor for PVM programs. XPVM has a number of options that allow a parallel developer to view a number of performance-related statistics and charts that aid in the analysis of running parallel programs.

INDEX

Numbers

100Mbit Ethernet cards, 60
10Mbit Ethernet cards, 59
2U rack mount cases, 102, 104

A

Absoft FORTRAN compilers, 85
academic management packages, 188
accounting module, 143
accounting system and cluster
       management, 183
accounts
    clusteradmin (see clusteradmin account)
    root (see root account)
    superuser, 125, 143
ACM supercomputing conference, 318
addresses
    Class A network, 37, 128
    Class B network, 35
    Class C network, 35
    Ethernet, 94
    hardware, 94–95
    IP, 34–39, 127
    Media Access Control (MAC), 94
    Net 10, 128
addressing, TCP/IP, 34–39
Adsmith (ADSM), resources, 272
advanced clusters, 76
Advanced Computing Lab (ACL)
    libraries, 204
Advanced RISC Machines (ARM), 48
aftermarket dealers, 274
agglomeration (design methodology), 227
air conditioning issues, building
    clusters, 88–92
algorithmic parallelism, 22–25
allocation, resource, 167–169
Alpha (AXP)
    architecture, 46
    motherboards, 47
    SMP systems and, 73

Andrew Project (CMU), 189
APIs (application programming interfaces)
    MPI, 276–286
    PVM, 286–291
application examples
    mp3pvm, 241–253
    PVFS, 263–268
    PVMPOV, 253–263
architecture
    Alpha (AXP), 46
    ARM, 48
    SPARC, 45
artificial intelligence (AI), 12
Artificial Life (ALife), 12
ASICs (application-specific integrated
    circuits), 59
AT form factor motherboards, 96
Athena Project, 188
ATM (Asynchronous Transfer Mode), 70
ATX form factor motherboards, 97

B

backplanes and performance, 55
bandwidth, 30
Barak, Professor Amnon, 214
base queues, 176
batch processing systems, 83
batch queues, 171
    creating, 175–177
    editing, 178
    GNQS, 173–174
    qmgr command, 182
    qstat command, 181
    qsub command, 180
    showing activity, 177
Becker, Donald, x, 8, 14
Beowulf, x, 9
    resources, 271
Beowulf Underground, 85
Beowulf Watch (Tcl/Tk tool), 189
Berrendorf, Rudolf, 208
bibliography, 315–318

About the Author

David HM Spector is an independent software developer and computer-networking specialist. He has been in the information service and delivery business for more than 13 years, specializing in network design, electronic mail, and firewall/network security systems. He has been profiled in numerous publications for his work, including *Fortune Magazine*, *Information Week*, *Communications Week*, and *Business Week*.

Colophon

Our look is the result of reader comments, our own experimentation, and feedback from distribution channels. Distinctive covers complement our distinctive approach to technical topics, breathing personality and life into potentially dry subjects.

The cover image of a bison and its calf is adapted from a 19th-century engraving from the Dover Pictorial Archive. Hanna Dyer designed the cover layout based on a series design by Edie Freedman. Emma Colby produced the cover with Quark-XPress 4.1 and Adobe Photoshop 5.5 software, using the ITC Garamond Condensed font. Alicia Cech and David Futato designed the interior layouts, based on a series design created by Edie Freedman and Jennifer Niederst and modified by Nancy Priest. Mike Sierra implemented the design in Framemaker 5.5.6. Interior fonts are ITC Garamond and Constant Willison. Chapter opening graphics are from the Dover Pictorial Archive and *Marvels of the New West*. Lar Kaufman suggested the western theme for O'Reilly's Linux series. Emma Colby designed the CD label.

Nicole Arigo and Sarah Jane Shangraw copyedited *Building Linux Clusters*; Paulette A. Miley proofread the text. Claire Cloutier, Jane Ellin, and Sarah Jane Shangraw provided quality control. Robert Romano and Rhon Porter created the illustrations using Adobe Photoshop 5 and Macromedia FreeHand 8. Judy Hoer wrote the index. Interior composition was done by Darren Kelly, Emily Quill, Molly Shangraw, and Sarah Jane Shangraw.

Whenever possible, our books use a durable and flexible lay-flat binding. If the page count exceeds that binding's limit, perfect binding is used.